Programming
with
dBASE III

Programming
with
dBASE III

Cary N. Prague & James E. Hammitt

TAB BOOKS Inc.
Blue Ridge Summit, PA 17214

FIRST EDITION

SEVENTH PRINTING

Printed in the United States of America

Reproduction or publication of the content in any manner, without express permission of the publisher, is prohibited. No liability is assumed with respect to the use of the information herein.

Library of Congress Cataloging in Publication Data

Prague, Cary N.
Programming with dBASE III.

Includes index.
1. Data base management.   2. dBASE III (Computer program) 3. Microcomputers—Programming. I. Hammitt, James E.   II. Title.
QA76.9.D3P728 1985   001.64′2   84-23979
ISBN 0-8306-0976-8
ISBN 0-8306-1976-3 (pbk.)

Contents

Introduction

dBASE III is a very powerful database language. It features user-friendly commands that can be used to create database structures and to add, change, and delete data items. dBASE III also allows the searching, selecting, and displaying of records in the database. Reports can easily be designed and printed. For many users, these commands are sufficient to provide them with simple database queries and reports. Other users, however, would like to unlock the power of dBASE III as a programming language.

In the ever expanding world of microcomputers, dBASE III is quickly gaining popularity as a programming language. For many people it has replaced BASIC or PASCAL. In big business it is even used as a replacement for COBOL, FORTRAN, and PL /1. dBASE III has a "full" programming language that is capable of solving almost any data processing problem. Because of its use of database techniques, dBASE III makes programming easier than with traditional languages.

All normal programming techniques can be used with dBASE III, including decision making, looping, sorting, searching, selecting, displaying, data manipulation, and custom reporting. Full screen selection and data entry menus are simple to design and implement. Many database programming commands can also be integrated into dBASE II programs. These include the setting of the programming environment or housekeeping with very simple commands. If a record description needs to be changed after the program is substantially complete, it is a simple task to change the program. It is not a complicated task as it is with nondatabase languages. Database query commands used to sort, search, and select records are also used as programming commands to replace many programming statements found in traditional languages. dBASE III is truly the fourth generation programming generator for the eighties.

This book is written for the computer novice as well as the experienced programmer wishing to add a new language to their toolbox. The book will help both the weekend hacker and the businessman. It is expected that the reader is somewhat familiar with dBASE III and has at least created a database and produced simple reports. The novice will find this book a good introduction to programming concepts and database techniques. The use of dBASE III is explained in depth with each of these topics. The experienced programmer will find the book a complete guide to making the transition from whatever languages they already know to dBASE III.

The book is organized into three main sections: Programming Fundamentals, Database Fundamentals, and Programming with dBASE III. In each section, you will meet Fred. Fred owns a fish market and will help teach you to program.

Programming Fundamentals covers a complete introduction to programming, along with comparisons of how dBASE III differs from traditional programming languages. Database Fundamentals explains what a database is and how to efficiently and effectively design and use the databases. The final section, Programming with dBASE III, is subdivided into several chapters. Each shows how to use the appropriate dBASE III command to perform a specific task. Each chapter presents the topic as a stand-alone subject and also integrates it with the previously discussed topics. This allows the reader to break down the programming topics into individual subjects and understand how they come together to form the complete program.

After reading this book, both novice and expert will be prepared to design, code, and implement the solution to any problem using the dBASE III solution.

Section I
PROGRAMMING FUNDAMENTALS

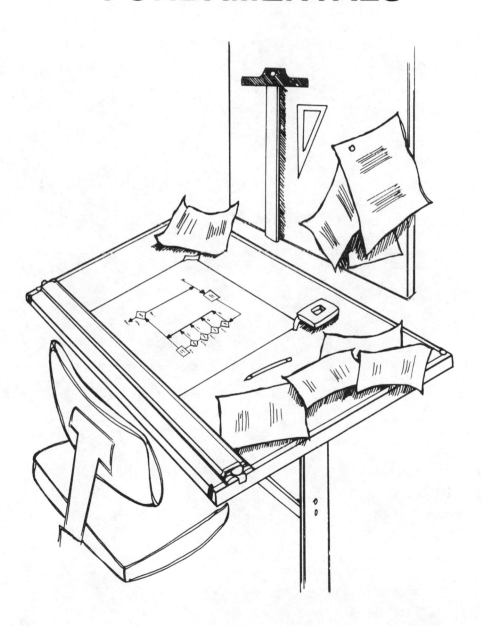

Chapter 1

The Basics of Programming

Database programming is the use of specialized language statements to manipulate items of information. The purpose of this manipulation is to produce a desired result that is presented in the form of reports, graphs, or tables of information. The name that programmers give to unprocessed information is *data*.

DATA VERSUS INFORMATION

Simply stated, data is the raw form of information; that is, facts and figures that alone have very little or no meaning. The purpose of computer programs is to arrange data into more meaningful and /or useful forms.

For example, if you saw a list of numbers 199462482010454, the numbers appear totally meaningless. The list could be anything. However, when it is broken up slightly, the result is 199462482-010454. The list is still data; that is, no new information has resulted from that division. If the number is broken into its smallest components, 199-46-2482-01-04-54, it appears, and I mean *ap-*

pears, to be a social security number and a date. If the data is now labeled

SSN   DATE
199-46-2482/01-04-54

you know something that was not known before; the meaningless *data* as become *information*. This example explains the difference between data and information.

DATA TYPES

Computer programming is the manipulation of data to form information. The data items that are manipulated can take two basic forms: *character* and *numeric*.

Character data includes things like names, addresses, telephone numbers, and any other items that are later reported in the same form that they are stored in. Character data items can be manipulated in some ways but cannot be used in mathematical calculations. For example, names can be stored in a last, first, middle order, but appear on a report in a "first middle last" format. The manipulation in this case involved the rearrangement of the characters that make up the data item. Any attempt to add, subtract, multiply, divide, or perform any other type of mathematical calculation using the name information would not only be meaningless, but would quite probably cause an error.

Numeric data is stored in a slightly different manner. This type of data can be reported as-is, or can be used in mathematical calculations. Numeric data items include dollar amounts, dates, counts of anything, or any other data item that is to be used in a calculation. Numeric information can be added to totals, averaged, or used in calculations to obtain another data item.

When character or numeric data items appear in computer programs they are called *expressions*, whether they are used alone or in combination with other data items. Expressions contain only one type of data. Using character data in a numeric expression is called *mixing modes* and is illegal in a program.

VARIABLES

Variables are "areas of storage" used in a program to hold data items. The use of variables is what gives the computer program its basic flexibility. Because of variables, computer programs can be written to work for any value that the variable can contain.

Variables can be thought of as buckets that hold the values that the program will use. In this manner, a program might refer to a variable called NAME, which can hold any value. Without knowing the exact contents, the NAME variable can be positioned on an output report, displayed as a title of section, or used for whatever function is needed. If the maximum length of the NAME variable is 25 characters, the program must allow for 25 characters in the *output* (the printed report or screen display in most cases).

As an example a *record* may contain a NAME (25 characters) and a PHONE number (10 characters). The first record on the file may read

CARY PRAGUE   2035557685

The second record may read

JIM HAMMITT   2035556281

Now, if the first record is requested, the value of NAME will be CARY PRAGUE and the value of PHONE will be 2035557685. If the purpose of the program is to print a name and phone number list, the program would first read a record, print the values of the variables NAME and (possibly with some modifications) PHONE, and then loop back to read the next record. By referring to NAME and PHONE, the program becomes general; that is, it works for any record that is set up in the same format with the same variable names (NAME and PHONE).

The ability to work with variables is the most useful feature of computers in general. Computers work with the values, but you, in your programming, do not.

The manipulation of variables is the most important function of computer programs, and the concept of variables is important to understanding the way programs work. When a variable is assigned a certain value, the value stays in that variable until it is either replaced with a new value or the program ends, which ever comes first. The only way to change the value of a variable is to place a new value into it. So, if you create a variable called TITLE to use as the title of your output report and never change it, you may use it throughout your program, and it will retain its value.

LITERALS

Another way a value can be used in a program is by the value itself appearing in the program. This type of value is called a *literal,* and cannot be manipulated by the program. A literal is inserted directly into the expression in which it is to be used.

Let's look at an example of an expression. The calculation that is necessary to convert Fahrenheit temperatures into Celcius temperatures is

$$C = (F - 32)*5/9$$

In this expression, the F and the C are variables;

that is, they can have varying values. The 32, 5, and 9 are literals, because their values never change. In a mathematical expression like the one just used, the equal sign (=) is used to show equality between the left and right halves of the equation. In a computer language, such an equation is called an assignment statement and does not express equality. It tells the computer to take the value expressed on the right side of the statement and *place* it into the variable on the left side.

STATEMENTS

Computer languages are comprised of *statements* like the one mentioned in the previous paragraph. That statement is an assignment statement, because it assigns a new value to the variable C. No matter what value F has when that particular statement is executed, the calculation is performed using that value and the literal values. The result, the Celcius temperature, is placed into the variable C. This procedure does not change the value of F, nor are the literals changed. Only the variable that is on the left side of the equals sign is changed. Most of the statements in a computer program are assignment statements.

The assignment statement in dBASE III is

variable name = expression

or

STORE [expression] TO variablename

The computation of Celcius temperature would then appear as:

$$CELCIUS = (F-32(*(5/9)$$

or

STORE (F-32)*(5/9) TO CELCIUS

This form of the assignment is probably more readable than the traditional format shown in the previous paragraphs. It shows action occurring left-to-right: STORE value TO variable.

STATEMENT TYPES

There are generally four types of statements in a computer language. Apart from the assignment statement, there are decision statements, loop control statements, and input/output statements.

Computer language statements are used to cause action. Assignment statements cause new values to be assigned to variables: those new values can be the result of calculations. *Decision statements* can cause a section of statements to be executed or skipped over depending on the value of variables. *Loop statements* can cause a series of statements to be executed over and over until some condition occurs, such as a count exceeding a target value. *Input/output statements* cause the computer to copy information to or from some external device. Computer language statements always cause action of some type.

Chapter 2

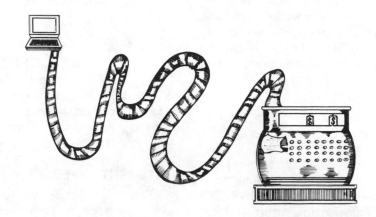

Developing Programs

The result of all the actions taken in a computer program is the output. It was the need for the output that caused the program to be written in the first place. To assure that a computer program is written properly, every item of information that is required from that program must be defined before the program can be written. As with all problem solving methods, including the scientific method, the first step in finding the solution is to have an accurate definition of the problem. This is the first step in the seven-step problem solving method that will be used in creating a computer program. The seven steps are:

1. Define the problem.
2. Define the output.
3. Define the input.
4. Determine the process.
5. Code the program.
6. Test the program.
7. Evaluate the program.

THE BUSINESS PROBLEM

A business problem occurs when the current way of performing some business-oriented activity can no longer produce acceptable results. This can happen for a variety of reasons: a reduction in staff, an increase in the workload, a need for instantaneous retrieval of information, or a need for a change in the way of doing things. In a company where the entire payroll is four persons, including the president, there is probably no need for a computer program to handle the payroll. If, however, that company expands to four hundred people, whatever method is used to process the payroll for the smaller group would probably be a seven-day-a-week job when performed for the larger group.

Another example of a problem that would make a small company need a computer: what if that company with four people on the payroll handles sales to two hundred companies with an inventory that runs into hundreds of thousands of dollars? Unless all four people are doing nothing but inventory control seven days a week, nothing could be shipped! Now, this example might be a little exaggerated, but it illustrates the point at which an automated method of handling the business could be necessary. Then, once the computer was installed and set up for inventory control, the payroll could be computerized if time and resources permit.

DEFINING THE PROBLEM

Whatever the business need, the correct first step in finding a solution to it is defining just what has to be done, when it has to be done, how much is to be done, etc. This overall statement of objective is necessary to keep the process of finding the solution on course, without troublesome wrong turns and side issues.

A problem definition should state why action is necessary, and just what is expected from any solution. A problem definition should also avoid precluding a solution by placing restrictions on how it is to be achieved. This means you should not include any mention of what tools are to be used to construct the final solution, whether computer-based or not.

It is also important to include a description of the expected results in the problem definition. The description should not be vague and should be as complete as possible. This description will help determine just what information is needed to produce the desired results. If a computer solution is to be implemented, extensive data entry work may be necessary to make the required information available to the computer system. Data entry time must also be taken into account when creating cost estimates of the new system.

A well-written problem definition will reduce the time spent on speculation; this will make the solution available faster.

DEFINING THE OUTPUT

The next step after completing the problem definition is to define the exact content of what the solution is to produce, in short, "define the output." Output is any product that is essential to solving the business problem. The output in a payroll system is the checks, reports to management about the hours worked, vacation and sick time reports, reports to the IRS, and the pay stubs. These are varied in form, and some, at least from an employee's point of view, seem irrelevant. However, each output form helps to solve a part of the total business problem. There might also be files to be kept for year-end reporting; these are also output.

A complete output definition would include a description of each data item to appear in the output. A proper description should include the data type (character or numeric), a name for each variable to be used, the length of the item, and its source, whether from an already existing file or through calculation. The necessity of this step should be apparent: without knowing the exact output specifications, it would be impossible to determine what input is needed. It is unlikely that all the input that a new computer system must use would be available in usable form. Problems of data entry must therefore also be considered. If existing files are to be used, are they available for use, and what format are they in? Consideration of these key points at this time can save time and sweat later.

DOCUMENTATION AND DESIGN

Once there is a complete, clearly-written definition of the problem, coupled with a complete, clearly-written set of specifications for the output, these two documents will be used as the basis for the rest of the problem solution. Any such important documents should be finished prior to coding any computer programs, the textbook writers will tell you. So why do most companies spend less time at these activities than at program coding?

The answer is obvious. The time spent upfront in designing a program is inversely proportional to the time that will be spent coding. In simpler terms, when the design of a program is complete and well-documented, the programs almost code themselves! When the necessary designing is skipped over in the name of "productivity," coding takes many times longer, because mistakes that should have been eliminated in the design phase did not surface until program coding phase.

DEFINING THE INPUT

The next step in the design phase is defining the input necessary to produce the output that was

7

just defined. Since, in the output definition, care was taken to note the source of all items, the input definition should be the process describing these data items and in what form they are available. They may need to be entered by hand, in which case this is probably a good time to find out who will do the work. In new systems, probably all the input data items needed will be entered by hand. Fortunately, with dBASE III, this is a task that is performed more easily than with most other languages. With dBASE III, when you define what your data files/databases will look like, dBASE will allow you to start entering data immediately. dBASE III generates input screens that allow easy entry of the items to be stored. This may be an answer to management's productivity obsession, because the data entry can start while the next step of the design process is going on. If management wants to see production, you can show them the data entry effort and give yourself some additional design time.

DEFINING THE PROCESS

Now the problem has been defined, the output specifications have been written, and the input has been determined. With these documents firmly in hand, you are ready to define the actual process of turning the input data items into the output information.

The overall functions of the system, as set out in the problem definition, must each be divided into their component functions. This is when the actual process of programming takes place. The problem, output, and input definitions were the beginning of this process, but only now is the actual process defined. This can be done using many different methods.

Chapter 3

Mapping the Process

The methods used by professional programmers to define processes most often are flowcharting and pseudocoding. These are representative of the two categories of process mapping: *charting* a process involves drawing a pictorial representation of the flow of control using symbols that depict the functions; *pseudocoding* means to define the process in terms of its functions using a structured style that mirrors the workings of computer programs.

Breaking down a process into its component functions makes the program coding phase go faster. This is because each piece of the solution is easier to master than the entire solution all at once. By dividing the functions during the design state coding becomes faster and more controlled.

FLOWCHARTING

Flowcharting has been used since the inception of computers in the business environment. There are some advantages and disadvantages that you should be aware of before choosing the use of flowcharts as the standard for your business.

First, the pictorial representation of the logic of a program is very readable; that is, it can be understood easily and by anyone. Unfortunately, they are hard to draw. They are difficult to envision and cumbersome to change, and because of this, they are usually not finished before coding starts. A system design should be living and evolving as new, efficient paths are discovered. Flowcharts have to be redrawn each time a change is made.

Flowchart Examples

By using the flowchart symbols shown in Fig. 3-1, a programmer or process designer can show the flow of paperwork through a department. Think of the rectangles as desks. The paperwork moves from desk to desk along the lines of control (Fig. 3-2). If there is a decision, a choice between desks, the decision point is denoted by a diamond.

Any process, whether a computer process or not, can be depicted with a flowchart. For example, Fig. 3-3 shows a flowchart of boiling water for tea.

In many programming classes, this type of

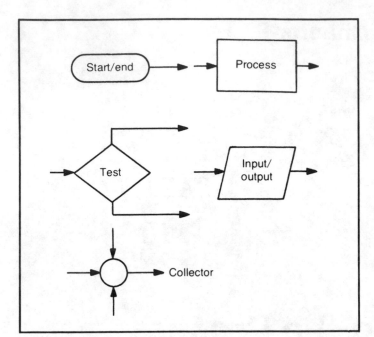

Fig. 3-1. The flowcharting symbols.

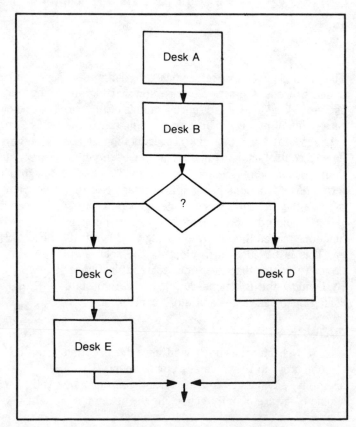

Fig. 3-2. An example of a flowchart.

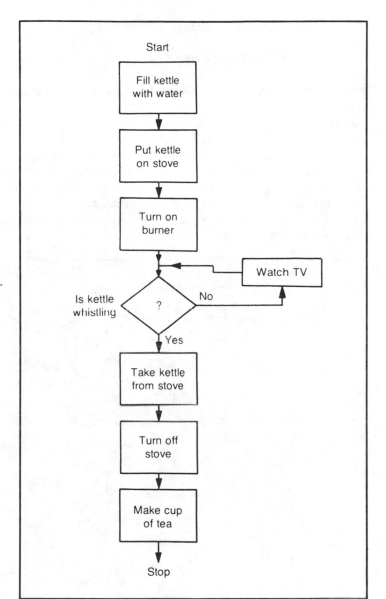

Fig. 3-3. A flowchart for making a cup of tea.

flowchart is used to drill future programmers in breaking a process down into its simplest components. If you want to practice flowcharting, try making flowcharts of answering the phone, or choosing a television show. As you find simpler and simpler steps to break the process into, you will find yourself drawing and redrawing your flowchart.

Note that the following examples use *logical constructs* which demonstrate how both flowcharts

and pseudocodes are developed. These constructs are explained in detail in Chapter 5 and are used here only to help clarify the initial mapping process.

Let's look at another example of a flowchart. In this process, a company is looking through its employee records, and they are choosing records that meet certain criteria. The employees that meet the qualifications are going to be asked if they would like to transfer to a foreign branch office. The process could be defined (flowcharted) as shown in Fig. 3-4.

The flowchart in Fig. 3-4 actually works; that is to say, it will perform the requested process. However, it is not very consistent or readable. Notice that all of the diamond blocks have NO legs on the left, except the last one, which has a YES. This flowchart falls short on readability and consistency.

A better way of depicting the process can be accomplished by using the logical construct flowchart shown in Fig. 3-5. Notice that every diamond block has the YES leg out to the right side. The entire process is contained in a *READ LOOP*, in which the records are read. After each read opera-

tion, a question is asked; "are there any more records to read?" This determines whether or not the last record has been processed.

Another thing you might notice is that the flowchart could define the logical structure of a program or could show the flow of paperwork in the office! If the records were sheets of paper in a file cabinet and all the questions were answered by human examination of the document, this flowchart would still be valid. A process definition does not have to be computer-based.

On first sight, the second flowchart seems to be larger and more complicated than the first. However, each logical construct is apparent, and the

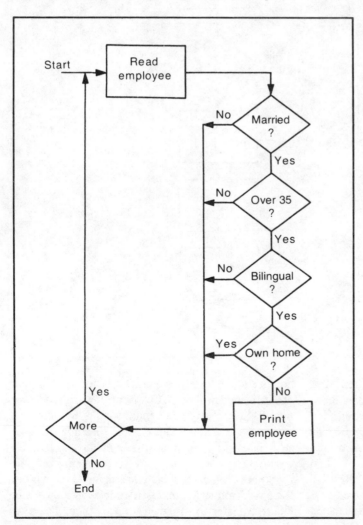

Fig. 3-4. A flowchart for an employee search.

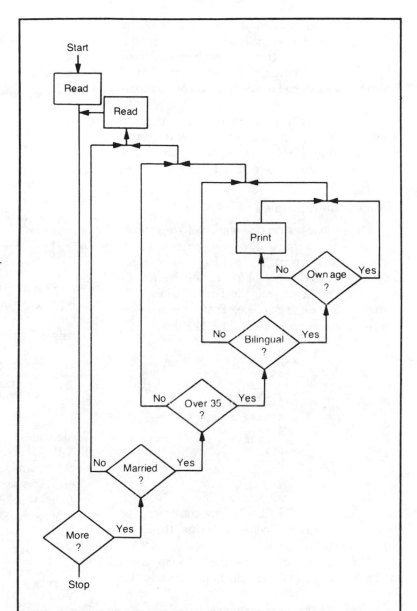

Fig. 3-5. A logical construct flowchart.

resulting chart is much more readable.

You can see the problems with trying to modify flowcharts. Usually the whole chart must be re-drawn. In a growing, evolving system design this can be a drawback.

PSEUDOCODING

In recent years, pseudocoding has become the

backbone of the programmer's tool chest. It reduces programming into the coding of the simplest re-lationships. Pseudocoding uses *logical constructs* that appear in some form in most computer lan-guages.

With logical constructs, processes may be mapped out in very general terms, and slowly be made more detailed, until the final solution has evolved. Each subfunction may be concentrated on until it is solved and eventually becomes a part of the system. This divide and conquer method of problem solving is the answer to the problem of complexity. Functions are reduced to subfunctions of less complexity until a detailed, accurate map of the process has been obtained. Coding is now just a matter of translating the *pseudo* code into a real computer language. Coding takes less time, and testing can be started at the same time coding commences.

Pseudocode Examples

Pseudocode is a representation of a logic flow, but unlike the pictorial flowchart, pseudocode is written in plain language. This fact makes pseudocode easier to change and /or rewrite than a flowchart. Figure 3-2 showed the flow of paperwork from desk to desk in an office. That same process, shown as pseudocode, would look like this:

```
DESK A
DESK B
IF  X
   THEN
      DESK C
      DESK E
   ELSE
      DESK D
ENDIF
...
```

The diamond block, with its YES and NO legs, becomes an IF-THEN-ELSE logical construct. The THEN part is done if condition X is true; the ELSE part if condition X is false.

The "waiting for the teakettle" process shown in Fig. 3-3 would look like this in pseudocode:

```
PLACE KETTLE ON BURNER
TURN ON BURNER KETTLE IS ON
DO WHILE KETTLE NOT WHISTLING
      WATCH TV
ENDDO
REMOVE KETTLE FROM HEAT
TURN OFF BURNER
MAKE TEA!
```

The DO WHILE construct is a loop that is performed over and over again while the condition "kettle not whistling" is true.

For a final example of pseudocode, let's look at the process flowchart in Fig. 3-5.

```
READ EMPLOYEE
DO WHILE MORE RECORDS
   IF MARRIED
      THEN
         IF OVER 35
            THEN
               IF BILINGUAL
                  THEN
                     IF OWNS HOME
                        THEN NOTHING
                        ELSE PRINT EMPLOYEE
                     ENDIF
               ENDIF
         ENDIF
   ENDIF
   READ NEXT EMPLOYEE
ENDDO
```

First, notice the IF OWNS HOME construct. The THEN leg of the flow has no process associated with it. That construct could be changed to a negative comparison by the addition of NOT:

```
...
IF DOES NOT OWN HOME
   THEN PRINT EMPLOYEE
ENDIF
...
```

Also notice that there is a series of IF-THEN-IF-THEN... . These constructs could be replaced by a single IF if you make the condition complex. This is accomplished by connecting the conditions with AND. The final version of the pseudocode would look like this:

```
READ EMPLOYEE
DO WHILE MORE EMPLOYEES
   IF MARRIED AND OVER 35 AND BILINGUAL
      THEN
         IF DOES NOT OWN HOME
            THEN
               PRINT EMPLOYEE
         ENDIF
   ENDIF
   READ MORE RECORDS
ENDDO
```

The pseudocode has become simpler than the flowchart by use of a complex condition. It is much easier to combine expressions in pseudocode than to type all those conditions in a little diamond block! Since pseudocode is so easily changed, it is much more desirable than a flowchart for a *design* tool. Flowcharts are excellent *documentation* tools; they should be drawn after the design is complete.

SUMMARY

In the first pages of this book you have seen the initial stages of the development of a computer software system. This is the design phase, when the whole shape of the system is determined. After the design is completed, the actual process must be constructed. In the cases that are addressed by this book, that means that it is time to code the programs in a computer language—dBASE III. The steps taken so far have been

1. Defining the problem.
2. Define the output.
3. Define the input.
4. Define the process.

Chapter 4

Designing Processes

The design phase of a project should be completed prior to program coding. To make use of the design techniques advocated by this book, the completion of the design should be a hard-and-fast rule: be alert to and suspicious of any other course of action. An incomplete design will guarantee a late and unproductive solution.

Another obstacle that faces the programmer is alteration of the design during the coding phase. By changing the system requirements during coding, more time must be spent adding "bells and whistles" and not enough time can be given to the construction of the required solution.

The new business computer programmer and those others who find programming tedious, time consuming, and frustrating should consider these rules:

Always complete the design phase prior to program coding.

Freeze the design until coding and testing are complete.

Once coding and testing are done in a structured manner, enhancing the system or program is merely a problem of adding or changing already existing functions. A *plug-in* sort of structure can be changed with very little trouble.

DESIGNING THE PROCESS

Up to this point, you have been introduced to the system (or program) development process. The next step is to design the process. This step depends on understanding the three fundamental concepts involved in a good program (or system). They are generality, modularity, and hierarchy. Also, it is important to keep in mind the "EZ2s" of development: easy to write, easy to read, easy to test.

FUNCTION CHARTING

The first step in system/program development is to chart the major functions of the system. These should be listed in the program definition that was developed earlier. Each of the major functions should be written in a box on a blank sheet of paper, one function to a sheet. These sheets of paper will become the function hierarchy charts for the system. Figure 4-1 shows a sample function hierarchy chart.

FUNDAMENTALS OF A GOOD PROGRAM

The first fundamental of a good program, generality, means that the system will work for all input received by the system. In effect, this means that a program should check each input variable for validity and show error messages for any invalid data. This is done by making sure that numeric fields have numeric data in them, and checking numeric data items for a proper range of values. Character data may have to be checked for specific values or formats. When one of the criteria is not met, an error message must be displayed (somehow).

Modularity describes the result of breaking individual functions into separate programming problems. This approach means easier programming, because only one function need be addressed at one time. With large systems, this is particularly necessary, because quite often, one person could not conceive and design the entire system. By making the system modular, this problem is eliminated.

This method of system design also results in a hierarchy of functions. The top-level boxes that you have drawn on the otherwise blank sheets of paper become the top of the functional hierarchy of the system. Then, as each major function is divided into still smaller functions, you can add interconnecting boxes that describe the hierarchical relationship between the functions. In programming terms, each function becomes a *module* or *subroutine*, each of which calls still other modules until the lowest level of function is reached. By using this top-down hierarchical approach, lowest level functions that are not unique can be seen readily. They can then be shared between modules as needed, without repeating the work.

THE EZ2s OF PROGRAMMING

If you follow this type of approach to program design, the EZ2s take care of themselves. Once the functional hierarchy is determined, the first step is designing the logic for the top-level functions / modules. When the design of the major functions is complete, they can be coded and, using a program-

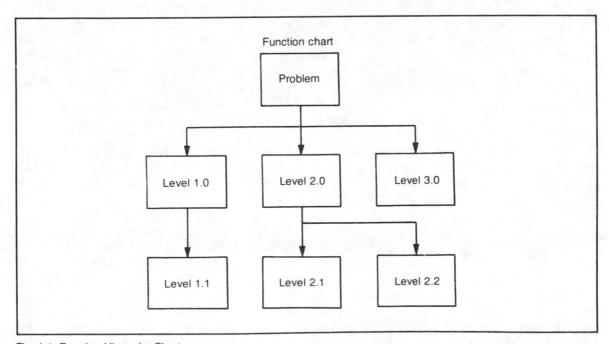

Fig. 4-1. Function Hierarchy Chart.

ming trick called *program stubs*, can be tested for logical correctness. Since the major functions will become the most-used code in the program, they can also be the most-tested. As each lower level function is designed and coded, it can be inserted into its stub and tested. When the lowest-level functions have been tested and the output approved, the system will be ready for implementation, with the program logic completely tested out.

Keep the fundamentals of a good program in mind as you step into the world of process design. They are (once again):

GENERALITY
MODULARITY
HIERARCHY

STYLES OF PROGRAMMING

There are two major styles of programming, interactive and passive. Passive programs are processes that can run from start to finish with no interruption by the operator. Sometimes misnamed *batch* programs by professional programmers, passive programs make up most of the work cycle at large installations. Huge number of transactions are accumulated during normal business hours and then processed during the second and third shifts. The series of passive programs process these transactions, update files, create reports, print bills, and so forth. All this happens with little or no direct input from the computer operators; the operations staff has enough to do! They place the media containing transactions records, cards, tapes, or disks, into the proper units, put paper in the printers, align the bill forms, and determine the order that the programs are to be run in.

Interactive programming, on the other hand, requires extensive communication with the operator. This type of program would not be welcome in a batch environment, since in big shops there are large numbers of programs running at any given time; the operations staff cannot (and will not!) devote a lot of attention to an individual program. Microcomputers, however are ideal for interactive programming. They are usually run as dedicated

systems, which means that only one program can be running at a time.

Interactive programs usually handle just one transaction at a time. The operator requests a function, enters the data, and a file is updated. He then requests another function, and a report is produced. The interactive quality of the program lets the operator control which functions are performed and in what order. Interactive programming also helps alleviate operator boredom by showing the operator that the system is working and by allowing him control over the outcome.

SELECTION MENUS

One method of creating an interactive program is to design use of selection menu as shown in Fig. 4-2. The program displays a list of the functions available on the computer monitor. The operator then chooses an option and enters data, and the file is updated. He can choose another function, and a report is produced. In this manner, the operator can choose the functions and the order the functions are to be performed in.

Usually, the function selections are displayed with an option number for the operator to select. In some limited instances, the operator may have to type the first letter of the function name or the entire function name. Since the design and creation of the menus is up to you (the programmer), you may design your menus in a manner comfortable to you and /or your operator (probably you, also). There are, however, two guidelines you should observe:

Don't make the operator enter too many characters, because it's easy to make typing errors. Make the option choice easy to read and understand.

When considering interactive programming, remember that people make mistakes, and people will be interacting with your programs. Just as it is important for you to design the screens and menus for human understanding, it is important for the program to double-check input typed by a human. People make mistakes because of fatigue or misunderstanding, a trait that computers (fortunately)

```
+---------------------------------------+
:                                       :
:        MAIN MENU SCREEN               :
:                                       :
:    ENTER SELECTION ==>  __            :
:                                       :
:                                       :
:                                       :
:      1  -    ADD RECORD               :
:      2  -    CHANGE RECORD            :       Fig. 4-2. An example of a Menu Screen.
:      3  -    REMOVE RECORD            :
:      4  -    DISPLAY RECORD           :
:                                       :
:      P  -  PRINT RECORD               :
:                                       :
:      X  -  EXIT SYSTEM                :
:                                       :
:                                       :
:                                       :
+---------------------------------------+
```

lack. Even a simple mistake such as typing with the shift-lock key engaged can cause endless havoc with your data.

So is that the computer program must judge the input data for itself. Each piece of input, including a menu selection, must be examined for validity before a function can be performed. If there is a list of functions and selection codes on the menu screen, the program must match the input from the operator against a list of the valid selections. If the code is typed wrong, an error message should be displayed. An error message of this type should be readable, and list the valid choices for the operator.

DATA ENTRY SCREENS

Interactive programs can use screens for the entry of data. A sample screen is shown in Fig. 4-3.

Fig. 4-3. An example of a Data Entry Screen.

```
+---------------------------------------+
:                                       :
:        DATA ENTRY SCREEN              :
:                                       :
:                                       :
:                                       :
:   Name:      :                  :     :
:                                       :
:   Address:  :                  :      :
:   City:     :                  :      :
:   State:    :  :   Zip: :    :        :
:                                       :
:   Date of Birth: :  /  /  :           :
:                                       :
:   Credit Limit: :          :          :
:                                       :
:                                       :
+---------------------------------------+
```

These screens are forms for the data, just like any paper form that you fill out with a pencil. The data entry screen is filled out by using the keyboard to enter information into each area on the screen. This information is then stored into variables by the program. The program can then examine each entry for validity.

Data entry screens should be designed for ease of use. The operator must be able to read the screen and understand the placement of data on the form. Sometimes, when a shop is first automating, the input screens are designed directly from the paper form being replaced. This helps to add a sense of continuity to the system, but a better practice is to ask the people who fill out and /or read those forms for their suggestions. They can tell you what they would like to see changed and how to best design the screens for ease of data entry. This is most important in companies where large number of transactions are entered daily, but it can help to cut down needless work and increase productivity even in small shops.

EDITING DATA

Once the operator has entered the data on the screen, the program must examine it for validity. This means that the input data should meet certain predetermined criteria.

First, the data must conform to the required data type. If the input data is numeric, that is, to be used in calculations, the program must be sure that the input contains only numbers. This is called a *class* edit. Database managers like dBASE III do not allow characters in a field defined as numeric data. The keyboard locks-up or an audible alarm is sounded when the attempt is made. Most character data items are not checked, since any character is valid. In some cases, however, you might want to check for improper data, such as numbers in a name field.

Second, if the input is numeric, the contents of the field may have to fall within a certain range of values. If, for instance, a field called month is created, the value probably has to be between 1 and 12 inclusive. This is called a *range* edit.

Third, the data should conform to data already

in the file. This is called a *correctness* edit. For example, in a payroll system, a transaction can be entered to pay an employee for overtime hours worked. If the employee is not eligible to receive overtime pay, the transaction is in error (or someone is trying to put one over on you).

Programs should check data for all possible violations. Any input presented to the program, even if *you* plan to be doing the data entry, should be edited for class, range, and correctness. Remember that anyone can make mistakes, and you want your data to be as error-free as humanly possible.

ERROR MESSAGES

When errors are detected in input data, it is necessary to notify the operator. In passive-style programming, this usually means producing an error report for the data entry staff to use the next day in correcting the input transactions. In interactive programming, it means telling the operator immediately that there is something wrong.

One means of accomplishing this is the use of an audible alarm signal. Most microcomputers have a beep or bell character that sounds an alarm. Usually, the sound is used in conjunction with a message describing the error. When the alarm is used alone, the operator might not easily see the problem.

Error messages are displayed on the monitor screen. When used with the audible alarm, they alert the operator to the fact that a problem has occurred. The message should explain the problem and offer suggestions for correction. These are messages to be read by people; they should be easily understandable.

An example of a good error message from a menu selection screen would be

```
        *** INVALID SELECTION ***
    VALID OPTIONS ARE 1,2,3,4 AND X
             RE-ENTER SELECTION
```

The error is described in the first line, the correct choices are listed in the second line, and the next course of action is indicated in the third line. These are the three elements of a good error message. This is not to say that you must use three lines;

there are also good one liners, and there are other enhancements to make the message stand out more. Error messages should always appear on the same part of the screen, preferably near the top, so that the operator will know where to focus his attention. When the alarm sounds, the operator will be trained to look at that certain place for the error message. Displaying the message in color or in high intensity characters will also draw attention to it. You should not use blinking text, however, as it can be quite annoying. Another method is called *flowerboxing*. Using this technique, the message is surrounded by astericks to make it very apparent, as shown below.

```
**************************************
*          INVALID SELECTION         *
* VALID OPTIONS ARE 1,2,3,4 AND X *
*          RE-ENTER SELECTION        *
**************************************
```

SOME TYPICAL PROCESSES

One type of typical process has been discussed in detail: the edit or *data validation* process. This unit will show you some other frequently-used data processes you will need in your programs.

The first process that will be discussed is the data search. Usually, a file of records is searched for individual records that meet certain conditions, called the *search critieria*. In the simplest cases, this means comparing a field in each record to a value, and listing the records in which the field contains the value. For example, you may be searching an employee file for a particular social security number. When the record with that number is found, you may want to perform some process using it; you may change or delete the record or just display its contents. This kind of search is called a *unique* search, because only one record will be retrieved.

A search could be used as a correctness edit for input data. If you are adding a new employee to the payroll file, you could first search the file for the social security number of the new employee. If a match is found it may mean that (1) something strange is going on, (2) you entered the wrong social security number (possibly), or (3) the employee has already been added to the file (most likely). In any case, if unique data is found in the file when it should not be there, something is wrong; the transaction should fail with an appropriate error message. Pseudocode for a unique search could look like this:

```
DISPLAY "SSN TO BE SEARCHED FOR"
GET ANSWER
READ A RECORD
DO WHILE MORE RECORDS AND SSN NOT FOUND
  READ NEXT RECORD
ENDDO
DISPLAY RECORD IF FOUND
```

A *generic* search occurs when there are more than one record meeting the search criteria. For example, you may want to list all employees with the last name of Smith. This could result in several records being listed or processed in some other way.

One way of using a generic search is to use it to display fields for use in another process. In the payroll system example, you may need the social security number to change an employee record. However, if all you know is the employee's name, you could use a generic search to display all the employees with that particular last name, along with their social security numbers. You could then choose the proper social security number to use for the change transaction. Pseudocode for a generic search could look like this:

```
DISPLAY "NAME TO BE SEARCHED FOR"
GET ANSWER
READ A RECORD
DO WHILE MORE RECORDS
  IF NAME FOUND
    THEN PRINT NAME AND SSN
  ENDIF
  READ NEXT RECORD
ENDDO
```

Another frequently-used process is totalling. When billing a customer, the total of the bill is printed somewhere on the form that is sent to the customer. Administrative reports have totals of dollar amounts, employees, quantities etc.

Totals are said to be accumulated in computer programs. That is, each required total is defined as a field in the program. Each time a record is read or an amount is calculated, that amount is added to the accumulated total. Using the payroll system example, an employee record might include regular hours worked and overtime hours worked. An administrative report generated by this system would include a total for regular hours, a total for overtime hours, and a total for the total of all hours worked. Each time a record is read, the "regular hours" and "overtime hours" are added to their respective totals. Then, after calculating the total hours worked for that employee (regular + overtime), that sum is added to the "total hours" total field. When the report is examined, the "total hours" should match the sum of the total regular hours plus the total overtime hours. This is called *cross footing* in the business vernacular and is another method of checking the correctness of the process.

SUMMARY

This chapter has discussed the basis for de-signing computer processes. Keep in mind the fundamentals of a good program: generality, modularity, and hierarchy. These should be used in conjunction with the EZ2s of programming: easy to read, easy to write, and easy to change.

This chapter also discussed the styles of interactive, and passive programming, including the use of screens and menus as tools for data entry and process control. You also saw some typical processes found in computer programs: checking input data, searching files, and totalling amounts. These are not all of the possible processes—just a sample of those most frequently used.

In later chapters, you will see how the logical constructs work and how to examine your design for errors. You will also see some systems designed from start to finish.

Chapter 5

The Workings of Language

The design of a process is hierarchical in nature, proceeding from the major functions at the top of the function chart through the lowest functions at the bottom. The problem most new or nonprogrammers have is "how low to go?" To understand this, it is important to understand how a computer language is put together.

TYPES OF STATEMENTS

The concept of statements in computer programs was discussed earlier. Each statement accomplishes some purpose within the program. The general types of statements are:

```
            Assignment Statements
            Decision Statements
          Input-Output Statements
     Control Statements (Loops and Branches)
```

Assignment Statements

The assignment statement is used to assign a value to a variable. It is the most common program statement at the lowest levels of the function hierarchy. They become scarcer as you rise through the chart. However, you will be traversing the chart top-down. The first modules to be designed will be the major functions and will have few if any assignment statements.

Here are some examples of assignment statements in various languages. Each statement assigns the value of 3 + 4 to the variable A:

```
Language     Statement

BASIC        LET A = 3 + 4
dBase II     STORE 3 + 4 TO A
dBase III    STORE 3 + 4 TO A   or   A = 3 + 4
COBOL        MOVE 3 + 4 TO A
PL/1         A = 3 + 4;
Pascal       COMPUTE A = 3 + 4
```

In pseudocode, you can make up your own version of the assignment. Be sure that it can be easily understood by others. Most programmers tend to use the syntax (computer grammar) of the language that they are familiar with.

Calling Subroutines

The second-most common statement, and the most common at the top level, is the *subroutine call*. It is a control statement that causes a subroutine or subfunction to be performed. When the function is complete, control returns to the statement following the call. Subroutine calls are used to establish the hierarchy of functions. Each major function module calls the functions listed in the second level in the function chart, and they in turn, call the next level. A chart illustrating the flow of control that occurs when subroutines are used is shown in Fig. 5-1.

The program stubs that were mentioned earlier are empty lower-level modules that have not been coded yet. Since, the function chart will tell you what subfunctions there will be, it is possible to set up stubs for them. As each subfunction is coded, it can be placed in the stub, and lower level stubs added. This way, the most used program logic will be the most tested.

USING LOGICAL CONSTRUCTS IN PROCESS DESIGN

Keeping this idea of modularity in mind, let's discuss the actual form of the process design. As described before, process logic can be depicted in two ways: charting and pseudocoding. They can both be accomplished using a few logical constructs, which will be discussed next. Charting methods are good ways of documenting a complete design, because they are pictorial in nature. However, they are difficult to change as the process evolves, so the recommended procedure is to design with pseudocode and document afterwards with a chart.

As you remember, pseudocode is a language-based way of designing processes. You can design your system by using the simple logical constructs combined with plainly written "human-language" statements that describe the logic that the process will follow.

The logical constructs are

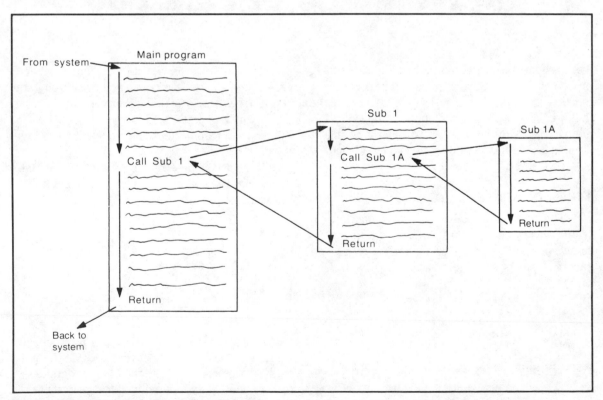

Fig. 5-1. The flow of control when calling subroutines.

```
SEQUENCE
IF-THEN-ELSE
DO WHILE
CASE
```

The SEQUENCE logical construct is just that—one statement following another. This is the simplest form of construct, and simply depicts one action following another. A SEQUENCE flowchart and an example of SEQUENCE pseudocode are shown in Fig. 5-2.

The others, IF-THEN-ELSE, DO WHILE, and CASE are decision statements, and most languages have them in one form or another. It may be necessary in some languages to use the statements available to create the construct. In dBase III they exist in these forms.

Notice that there are no input /output type statements used in pseudocode. That is because the design process should not be tied down to the exact form to be used. This type of design allows flexibility, so that a change of computers or software does not affect the design. The only necessary references to input and output might be statements such as:

GET A RECORD
GET NEXT RECORD
WRITE A LINE

IF-THEN-ELSE

The IF-THEN-ELSE logical construct is the simplest form of decision statement. It asks a question in the form of a comparison. For example, IF PAYROLL CODE IS 2. There are two possible results from a comparison of this type: true or false. If the comparison in the IF is true, then whatever processing is invoked in the THEN part of the statement is performed, and when completed, the next statement following the IF construct is performed. If the result is FALSE, the ELSE section is performed.

Some IF statements have only a THEN following them: if the comparison is false, the THEN unit is not performed, and control falls to the next statement. A flowchart and pseudocode for an IF-THEN-ELSE construct is shown in Fig. 5-3.

IF-THEN-ELSE statements, and for that matter all the logical constructs, are or can be considered individual statements. Therefore, the THEN unit of an IF-THEN-ELSE construct can also have an IF statement in it. This is called *nesting* by programmers and is quite valid. Care should be taken, however, that IFs and THENs match up with the proper ELSEs. This can be done through the use of indentation to indicate which statements

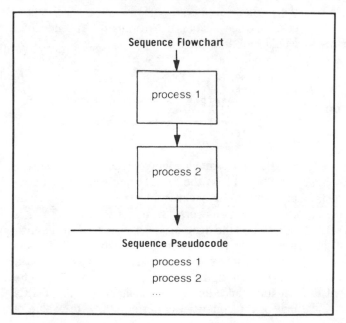

Fig. 5-2. A sequence flowchart and pseudocode.

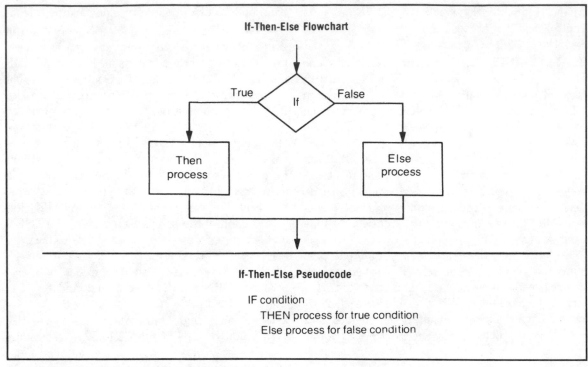

If-Then-Else Flowchart

True | If | False

Then process

Else process

If-Then-Else Pseudocode

IF condition
THEN process for true condition
Else process for false condition

Fig. 5-3. An If-Then-Else flowchart and pseudocode.

are on the same nesting level. It is not wise to nest too deeply, as this can become unwieldy and un-readable. If necessary, another function should be created.

In dBASE III, the IF statement looks like this:

```
IF conditional expression
    statements to be performed if TRUE
ELSE
    statements to be performed if FALSE
ENDIF
```

Notice that there is no word THEN in the statement. dBASE III takes the statements after the IF as the THEN part of the construct. If the expression is FALSE, dBASE III looks for an ELSE in the code and if ELSE is present, performs the statements following it. If there is no ELSE, the ENDIF is reached, and the next statement is executed. Indentation is important if IF-THEN-ELSE constructs to make the code easier to read and understand. In dBASE III the end of an IF statement is marked by an ENDIF.

Let's look at some examples of conditions in the IF-THEN-ELSE construct format. For example, if the program needs to perform some special processing when a date is in November the pseudocode would look like this:

```
IF MONTH = 11
  THEN
    perform "November processing"
  ELSE
    perform "normal processing"
ENDIF
```

In this example, the conditional expression is month = 11 on the line starting with IF. The expression asks a question to which there can be only two possible answers. "Is month equal to 11? Yes or no?" When the system sees an expression like this, it examines the value of the variable MONTH and compares it to the literal value 11. If they are equal, the system signals a true or yes answer for the question, and the process contained in the THEN unit of the construct is performed. If the value of

MONTH is not equal to "11", the ELSE unit gets control, and that processing is performed.

Here are other examples:

```
IF STATE = "CT"
   THEN ...

IF ZIP = 06040
   THEN ...

IF DATE = EXPIRE:DATE
   THEN ...
```

In the third example above, the contents of the variable DATE are compared against the contents of the variable EXPIRE:DATE. Again there are only two possibilities: the contents are either equal or not equal, so the expression is either true or false. There is no other answer to a conditional expression.

COMPARISONS

The comparisons that can be made in a decision statement such as IF-THEN-ELSE can be simple or complex. The simplest form involves testing one variable against another or against a literal value.

The comparisons that can be made are:

```
EQUALS (=)
NOT EQUALS (#)
GREATER THAN (>)
LESS THAN (<)
GREATER THAN OR EQUAL TO (>=)
LESS THAN OR EQUAL TO (<=)
```

Some languages have two more, NOT GREATER THAN and NOT LESS THAN. These should be used with caution and replaced with GREATER THAN OR EQUAL TO and LESS THAN OR EQUAL TO when possible.

Complex Comparisons

Simple comparison expressions have two possible results true or false. Comparison expressions can be combined to form complex expressions when they are connected with the *Boolean* operators AND and OR. A complex expression is evaluated by the AND and OR rules.

The AND rule. For an AND expression to be true, both sides of the expression must be true. If one of the expressions is false, the AND expression is false.

The OR rule. For an OR expression to be true, ONE side of the expression must be true. If both sides are false, the OR expression is false.

ANDs and ORs can be used within complex expressions; for instance, two OR expressions could be connected by an AND, or the expression could be even more complex. The best rule to follow is the KISS rule: Keep It Simple, Stupid! Use complex expressions only where necessary.

Let's look at some examples of complex conditional expressions. In complex expressions, each conditional expression is evaluated separately, and then the results of the ANDs and ORs are evaluated according to the AND and OR rules. For example:

```
IF STATE = "CT" AND ZIP = 06040
   THEN ....
```

In this example, the value of the variable "STATE" is compared against the literal CT. Likewise, the value of the variable ZIP is compared to 06040. Only if both of these conditions are true is the entire expression true. If either is false, the entire condition is false.

In the following example, the two simple conditions are made into a complex expression by joining them with an OR:

```
IF STATE = "CT" OR STATE = "MA"
   THEN ...
```

It is obvious that at least one of these conditions must be false; STATE cannot have two different values! However, the OR rule states that only one of the joined expressions need be true for the entire condition to be true. In this case, if the value of STATE is CT, the condition is true. The condition is also true if the value is MA. If anything other than these two values is in STATE, the condition is false.

In more complicated conditional expressions, two expressions connected with an AND can be connected to still other expressions:

```
IF (STATE="CT" OR STATE="MA")
   AND NAME="SMITH" THEN ...
```

In this example, the condition inside the parentheses is evaluated first and then ANDed with the evaluation of the third expression. If the variable STATE contains either CT or MA, the condition in the parentheses is evaluated as true using the OR rule. Then the value of the variable NAME is compared with the literal value SMITH. Therefore, this complex condition is true if NAME is equal to SMITH, and if the STATE is either CT or MA.

When evaluating complex conditional expressions, it is important to evaluate the expressions inside parentheses first and to remember the AND and OR rules. Also, don't make conditions too complex, for readability's sake; the KISS ("Keep It Simple, Stupid") method is the best compromise.

In dBASE III the symbols for AND and OR are .AND. and .OR., respectively. The above example would look like this:

```
IF (STATE="CT" .OR. STATE="MA") .
   AND. NAME="SMITH
   THEN ...
ENDIF
```

USING THE DO WHILE STATEMENT

DO WHILE is another type of conditional statement. A DO WHILE is a series of statements that is performed over and over WHILE the condition remains true. Each time the loop of statements is performed, the condition is reevaluated and if it is still true, the process in the loop is performed again. A flowchart and pseudocode for a DO WHILE process is shown in Fig. 5-4.

Programmers us DO WHILE loops to perform a series of statements as long as some condition is true. This condition can be internal to the program; for example:

```
SET COUNTER TO 1
DOWHILE COUNTER <= 15
    ...
    statements
    ...
    add 1 to counter
ENDDO
```

The DO WHILE loop will be performed 15 times; each time through the loop, the counter is incremented by one. The condition in the DO WHILE statement (COUNTER<=15) is tested immediately after each time the counter is incremented. When the value of COUNTER exceeds 15, the loop is ended, and control passes to the

Fig. 5-4. A DO WHILE flowchart and pseudocode.

Do While Pseudocode

```
DO WHILE (condition)
  process to be performed
    while condition is true
ENDDO
```

statement following the ENDDO.

Another way that DO WHILE is used is to test for a condition external to the program. One such condition is end-of-file, which answers the question "Are there any more records to read?". Using a DO WHILE loop will be performed once for each record in the file, regardless of the number of records. Most major function routines are based on this type of loop:

```
read a record
DOWHILE more records
  ...
  statements
  ...
  read next record
ENDDO
```

The condition is external to the program; the loop will be performed once for each record in the file. If records are added to the file in the future, the program will still work because the condition determines when the end-of-file is reached regardless of the number of records in the file.

Notice also that the condition is tested after both READ statements. The condition is tested at the start of the loop, as well as after each subsequent READ. While the condition remains true, the loop is executed. When the condition becomes false, the statement after the ENDDO is executed, and the program continues from there.

The DO WHILE logical construct takes the following form in dBASE III:

```
DO WHILE conditional expression
  statements to be performed
  as long as condition is true
ENDDO
```

The loop continues to be executed as long as the conditional expression tests true; it is tested each time the ENDDO is encountered. The end of the DO WHILE loop is always marked by an ENDDO in dBASE III.

THE CASE FIGURE

The last logical construct to learn is the CASE figure. A CASE is a decision point that allows more than two processes to be performed for various values of a variable. For instance, the variable SEX appears to have only two possible values. However, there are three: male, female, and invalid (not valid). Here the CASE condition has three possible processes to perform; one for MALE, one for FEMALE, and one for invalid data. The CASE figure would look like this:

```
CASE SEX
  WHEN MALE
    male processing
  WHEN FEMALE
    female processing
  OTHERWISE invalid sex code processing
ENDCASE
```

In dBASE III, there can be any number of WHEN conditions in a CASE figure, and each of them can had a process that can contain any nested logical constructs except other CASE figures. Some other languages do permit nested CASE statements. Figure 5-5 shows a flowchart and pseudo code for a case figure.

The CASE figure in dBASE III is a form of the DO command. The format looks like this:

```
DO CASE
  CASE expression 1
    commands to be performed if
    condition 1 is TRUE
  CASE expression 2
    commands to be performed if
    condition 2 is TRUE
  CASE expression 3
    commands to be performed if
    condition 3 is TRUE
  ...
  OTHERWISE
    commands to be  performed if
    all  previous conditions
    are FALSE
ENDCASE
```

Each condition is evaluated and if true, the commands are performed until the next CASE, the OTHERWISE, or the ENDCASE is reached. Then the next statement following the ENDCASE is performed, and the program continues from there. If no condition in a CASE is true, the OTHERWISE unit, if present, is executed until the ENDCASE is reached.

CHECKING OUT YOUR PSEUDOCODE

When you have finished your pseudocode for a

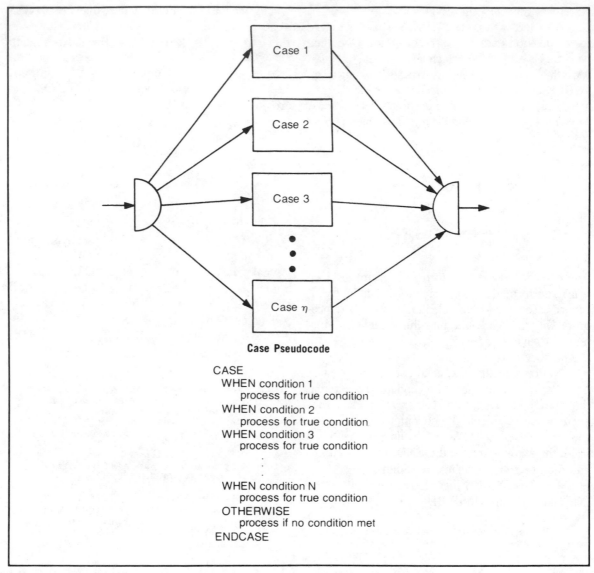

Case Pseudocode

```
CASE
   WHEN condition 1
        process for true condition
   WHEN condition 2
        process for true condition
   WHEN condition 3
        process for true condition
        .
        .
        .
   WHEN condition N
        process for true condition
   OTHERWISE
        process if no condition met
ENDCASE
```

Fig. 5-5. A case flowchart and pseudocode.

function, it is necessary to test it out, that is, to examine it for logical correctness and to make sure it does what you want it to!

To check out your pseudocode, read each statement one at a time. This is the way the computer will execute your statements when you translate your pseudocode into dBASE III code. Point a pencil to each line as you read it.

When you execute conditional statements, examine the flow of control for both true and false conditions. In CASE figures, test the flow for every WHEN condition.

Tracing the Flow in IF-THEN-ELSE Constructs

In an IF-THEN-ELSE logical construct, when the IF condition is true, the statements in the THEN unit are executed, and control passes to the statement following the ENDIF. For example:

1.   IF MONTH = 2
2.   THEN MONTH NAME is "February"
3.   ENDIF
4.   ...

If MONTH does equal 2, the flow of control, in terms of the line numbers, would be 1,2,3,4. On the other hand, if MONTH was anything other than 2, the flow would be "1,3,4". With no ELSE unit for a false condition, control passes out of the IF-THEN construct to the next statement (line 4).

If the IF construct includes an ELSE unit, slightly different processing occurs:

1.   IF STATE = "CT"
2.   THEN perform in-state process
3.   ELSE perform out-of-state process
4.   ENDIF
5.   ...

A true condition in the example above (STATE equal to CT) would result in the execution of statements 1,2,4,5. The ELSE unit is skipped over when the condition is true. A false condition in the above example would result in the execution of statements 1,3,4,5; the THEN unit is skipped over.

Tracing the Flow in CASE Constructs

In a CASE construct, control is passed to the statements in the WHEN unit when the condition tests true and then jumps to the statement following the ENDCASE. If no WHEN condition tests true, control jumps to the OTHERWISE unit, if it exists. For example:

```
 1. CASE
 2.   WHEN state="CT"
 3.       perform "in Connecticut"
 4.   WHEN state="MA"
 5.       perform "in Massachusetts"
 6.   WHEN state="NY"
 7.       perform "in New York"
 8.   OTHERWISE
 9.       perform "other state"
10. ENDCASE
11. ...
```

When this construct is executed, and the value of state is CT, the statements will be performed 1,2,3,10,11. If state is MA, the flow of processing would be 1,4,5,10,11; for state of NY, the flow would be 1,6,7,10,11. If the state was anything other than CT, MA, or NY, the flow would be 1,8,9,10,11.

Tracing the Flow in DO WHILE Constructs

In a DO WHILE construct, a loop of statements is performed as long as a condition is true. In the following example, a counter is incremented and then tested by the DO WHILE statement.

```
1. set counter to 1
2. DOWHILE counter <= 3
3.    add counter to total
4.    add 1 to counter
5. ENDDO
6. ...
```

First, the variable COUNTER is set to one. The DO WHILE then tests the variable COUNTER against a literal (3). While COUNTER remains at three or below, this loop is executed. The flow of processing would be 1,2,3,4 (COUNTER now 2),5,2,3,4 (COUNTER now 3), 5,2,3,4 (COUNTER now 4), 5,2 (condition now false), 5,6.

The variable TOTAL would now contain 6 (1+2+3), while COUNTER would be set to 4. Notice that the loop was performed three times; while COUNTER was 1, 2, and finally 3. The incrementation to 4 made the condition false and the statements inside the loop were not performed after counter became 4.

Tracing the Values of Variables

Another aid in testing your pseudocode is to write any variable names down on a separate sheet of paper and write in the values you wish to test. As the values change, cross out the old values and write in the new ones. This will show the exact values of the variables at each statement in the code.

This type of careful examination of the process design is called a *walk-thru* and is invaluable as a testing tool. By getting the design right before the actual computer program is written, you can save yourself a lot of aggravation caused by having missed problems in your design. Your program may even work the first time, if you take the time to design it properly and test the design.

31

Chapter 6

Coding, Testing, and Debugging

Now for the second phase of the project, the coding phase. In the design phase you defined the problem, the output, the input, and the process. Now it is time to code and test the new system.

DOCUMENTATION

The reference materials you will need during your coding phase are the manuals for whatever software you are using, the problem definition, the output definition, the input definition, and the process definition. These materials, aside from the reference manual, are the documentation for your system. Along with the program code, the design definition will become a package that is necessary for future changes.

When a system is to be changed or enhanced, the programmer will refer to the documentation package for a clearer understanding of the system. This will enable the programmer to find the easiest way to make the enhancement. A poorly assembled documentation package can make changes difficult,

if not impossible, to implement.

Some companies keep outdated computer equipment, some dating back to the early 1960s. Why? Because the programs were written then, and the documentation has become scattered, scrambled, and lost during the interim. In some cases, the source language for the program itself has been lost, rendering all change impossible. The executives' attitude toward this is "The programs still work well, and we don't have the time to rewrite and redocument the system." Usually, the cost of keeping the old equipment is much greater than the cost of developing a new, rewritten, and documented system.

The point of this is that the documentation package is important to you and to your business. Write it well, and keep two copies of everything!

Readability

Since the source code of the program is to become part of the documentation package, it is important to write it in a readable manner. Even the pseudocode or flowchart should be painstakingly written, so that when you come back to it later, you can understand how the process works. Many professional programmers find themselves working on systems they designed and wrote years in the past and scratch their heads in wonder at how they could have forgotten what they did. With readable, understandable documentation, reworking is a much easier task.

One way of making programs (and pseudocode) more readable is to indent subordinate code. Any code that is inside a loop should be indented to differentiate it from the main code. This one act alone makes the program much easier to read.

Another method of making a program easier to read is to start each function at the top of a new page. In some languages, it is necessary to put comments in the code, showing the break between the end of one subfunction, and the start of the next.

Finally, comment statements are available in virtually all computer languages. Use them to your advantage. By commenting effectively and changing those comments when necessary, you can put some documentation directly into the code. This is especially helpful when a complicated process is present; you can explain the process in plain language to programmers who might change the program in the future. Remember, it could be you!

MAKING SURE THE PROGRAM WILL WORK

There are two types of errors associated with program coding. They are *syntax errors* and *logic errors*. The logic errors should be obvious in the process design. Process designs (pseudocode) should be carefully examined not only by the creator, but by other, even disinterested, parties. This can be done in an informal or formal walkthrough of the pseudocode. Each decision point can be evaluated, and errors can be worked out before coding begins.

Syntax errors are usually discovered when the program is run on the computer. They can also be avoided or minimized by careful examination of the coded program. It is also good to have the language manual handy (and open) while coding a program.

Testing During Coding

When the coding of a major function is complete, testing can begin, and from then on, testing can progress simultaneously with coding. Higher level functions can be tested with stubs at the lower levels. When the high-level function works, the stubs may be filled in. Every decision path in the function should be tested before the next module is included for testing. Testing in this fashion means that any errors that appear are usually the fault of the last subroutine that was added, making error detection and correction much easier.

Using Test Data

At this point, some form of test input data is necessary. This should be, whenever possible, actual live data, gleaned from already existing files. In the case of a new system, all of the test data may have to be generated by the tester. For each item of test input, there should be a written document stating the expected results when the program is presented with that item. Test data should include erroneous and invalid information.

The test data can also become part of the documentation package. The test data can be listed, along with the expected results. If, when testing a program, unexpected results occur, either the expected results are incorrect or there is a problem in the program (most likely). Unexpected results should not be blamed on the weather, cosmic rays striking the computer, or the computer itself. The problem lies with the program in most cases, and sometimes with the interpretation of the expected results.

Most of the time, the responsibility for creating test data falls to the programmer. This may not be a good idea. Usually, the programmer is the person most closely involved with the system, and therefore he could, either consciously or unconsciously, test the program with slanted data that will produce the desired results while not testing every possible program path. One company had a system that worked well for six years. One day, a transaction was entered and the system failed. Why? That particular type of transaction was never tested, not once, during the testing phase of the project; in fact, it was never entered until that fateful day when the system came crashing down at 2:00 A.M. Poor testing practices can let errors slip in when you least expect them as the poor on-call programmer found out that morning.

One solution to this is to have some other party create the test data. This may not be possible in small shops, where one person is responsible for everything. Once the test data is created, the programmer can evaluate the transactions and write expected results for them. This will help maintain integrity in the system, while possibly testing for conditions not envisioned by the programmer.

Test It Again

When coding is complete for the entire major function, test it again. Any final errors encountered should be small and easy to fix. The expected results should be compared to the actual results and then compared against the results required by the problem definition. When all this has been satisfied, the system is ready for use and can be implemented as a new office procedure.

DESIGNING DATA

Just as important as developing the process is designing the database. Since systems are restricted by the data they have access to, deciding what data is necessary is an important step in development. This is why the output specifications are written before the input is defined. When a new system is being developed, care must be taken to include all information necessary for the system, as well as for any forseen future uses.

Identifying Records

The first data items in a record should be those data items that provide a unique identification for the record. In a personnel system, the name of the employee is not a good primary identification item, but could be used as a secondary identification item. A better primary identification item would be a social security number, because it is unique to each employee. In a payroll or personnel system, the social security number would probably be the first

data item in the record and would be the major *key* that identifies the record. A social security number is a good example of a data item that is all numbers, but is defined as character data because it is not used or manipulated in any calculations.

Arrangement of Data

An important guideline in deciding on the arrangement of data items in a record is that you should keep related fields together. The name information would be immediately followed by the address information if these are commonly used together in the output.

A third guideline is that you should describe the data in terms of *entities*. An entity is composed of all fields necessary to producing the output. This concept is most useful when more than one file is involved. In a personnel system, the major entity would be described as *employee*, even if name and address information was in one file, the rate of pay in another, and hours worked in still another. This happens often in systems that use data that was intended for other purposes and would be costly to reenter. By using the entity approach, the system can be designed as if all data resided in the same place.

Let the Computer Do the Work

One final guideline: do not include fields in the record that can be calculated from other fields already available. The computer should do any calculations—that is its purpose. Data entry people should not have to do any calculations, and their decisions should be kept to a minimum. The computer can do these things faster and more accurately, and the data entry process can be shortened accordingly.

SUMMARY

In Chapters 5 and 6 you have seen the seven step method of program design:

1. Define the Problem.
2. Define the output.
3. Define the input.
4. Define the process.
5. Code.

6. Test.
7. Evaluate.

Also discussed were the three fundamentals of a good program:

Generality
Modularity
Hierarchy

You also learned the basic types of statements found in a computer language:

Assignment Statements
Input /Output statements
Decision Statements
Loop Control Statements

You also saw the workings of decision statements, and you were introduced to the last phase in program development, the coding phase. Finally, Chapter 6 discussed documentating and testing the program, and designing and arranging data fields. In the last two sections of this book, using data with dBASE III will be discussed in more detail.

Chapter 7

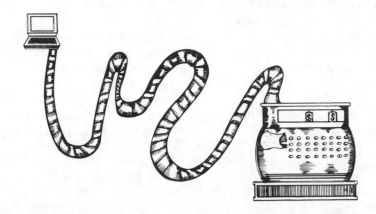

Business Considerations

This book so far has tried to generally describe some suggestions that apply to all sizes of business—from megabuck corporations to mom-and-pop operations. However, the method by which individual steps are accomplished changes with the size of the business.

LARGE VERSUS SMALL

Large corporations have large staffs of programming specialists and data entry personnel. Projects that these staffs perform can take years to complete and can cost the company a lot of person-power. The cost of the project is carefully measured against the benefits and savings that the company will realize.

On the other end of the business spectrum, even a small retail outlet can benefit from the use of a computer. The projects that would be undertaken would be shorter in duration, however; and all data entry and programming probably would be performed by the same person. Possibly the owners would have to do everything by themselves. This could mean that programming will be done during off hours and weekends, and even be forgotten for long periods of time as the problems of running the business intervene.

In large businesses, a given department can go to the programming staff with a business problem, and the staff is expected to develop the answer. Small businesses do not have this advantage. Small business managers must decide the uses of automation themselves. They should ask themselves some questions such as "What takes the most time away from customer services? What part of my job is boring, repetitious? What information must be saved for long periods of time, and would take a lot of space to store?" Once these questions have been answered, the small business manager should have some idea of what aspects of the business to automate.

ADMINISTRATIVE AUTOMATION

By using the guidelines presented in this book, even the business manager who has to program on weekends can be involved in the development of an automated system. Commonly, the first type of system that a small business would create is a payroll /personnel system. This area is often the most significant function of a company that is not directly related to increasing sales or profits. By automating administrative functions, the small business releases resources to concentrate on the profit-making areas of the business, which usually include customer relations. Automation can help you with your business, not run your business for you; data processing is notoriously a service function.

As the small business programmer becomes familiar with the equipment and language of automation, more and more uses will occur to him. It is important to adhere to the system development method described in this book while working on the second and third automation projects. This will prevent something that professional programmers know as "second system syndrome;" that is, adding too many functions to a simple system. A system that has too many bells and whistles hanging off it will be unwieldy to use and manage effectively. Remembering the KISS maxim (Keep It Simple, Stupid) will make development more manageable.

INTERACTIVE PROGRAMMING

As mentioned earlier, the advent of terminals and microcomputers has made possible the use of a programming style known as interactive programming. In the past, programs were written to run without interruption from the operator. The process used files, and sometimes "parameter" cards, to communicate changing information such as report date (usually different from the real date), start / cutoff dates, and the like. This type of information is specific to the time and this date that the program is to be run and would have to be entered at run time. This idea of batch processing meant that once the program had started, the user had to wait while the program ran all its coded instructions without interruption.

Interactive programming is just that—having a conversation with the program. The program prints certain questions on the screen, and the user must answer them to allow the program to continue running. In the cases mentioned above, the program might print ENTER REPORT DATE:, and the user would enter the date that should appear at the top of the report.

The problem with doing this in the past was that terminals were not widely used to perform program execution. They were used to enter and modify programs. The computer operations staff, the trained professionals that actually run the computer in large installations, were too busy doing their job to answer questions from the program. Now, terminal operators, who may or may not be programmers, are running their own jobs at the terminal. Since each one is the operator for his little piece of the system and would probably just sit and watch the program run anyway, he has time to respond to questions from the program. This not only gets needed data to the program, but also eliminates some boredom on the part of the operator. It is a way of letting him know that the program is working for him.

Microcomputing

Microcomputers have brought the idea of interactive programming to its peak usage. Game programs are the most obvious and notorious type of interactive program. They translate the input of the game controller (joystick) into motions of graphic characters on the display screen and dole out rewards and punishments (for the improper use of the controller). Interactive business programs do much the same thing—if the data is entered incorrectly, the program will send an error message to the user who will immediately reenter the data.

The microcomputer has another advantage: the system is not being used by anyone other than the operator. This means that all resources available to the system are available to you with no waiting. Since you are the operator, the questions and answers that you use to interact with your program can be individualized to you. This can make the programming process more fun, and the dry data entry jobs less boring and more accurate.

Menus

One way of interacting with programs is with

full screen menus. Menus are lists of functions that you may want to perform using the system and that you have programmed previously. For instance, let's say that you have created some dBASE III programs that you can use to do all your home budgeting functions. You might have a checkbook balancing program, a loan calculation program, a bill register, and a check-writing program. To produce a menu system from this, you would add the top level of the hierarchy, a new module called BUDGET perhaps. This module would display the choices available and ask you to enter an option number that is listed beside the name of the option. As an option is selected, BUDGET would then call the program that performs the chosen function. As the number of uses for the microcomputer grow, they may be added to the menu, or a new, higher-level menu could be implemented. Now when you choose BUDGET from that higher menu, the menu that was just discussed would appear on the screen. You could then choose a function from that menu.

Another hierarchy has developed: a hierarchy of menus that should mirror the hierarchy of functions discussed earlier. Note that in the example above, functions were added from lower to higher. This is a minor deviation from the top-down approach, and would not have happened at all if the future uses for the computer had been forseen. If you are using the machine to do budget work and suddenly decide to put a name and address list on the computer as well, you now have two functions that are unrelated. By adding a higher level to the hierarchy, you can bring the functions together in a bigger package, possibly called HOME MANAGEMENT. Nothing detrimental, such as developing something "bottom-up" was done, but functions were merged into a new hierarchy whole. This change will make use of the system easier because the list of functions is clear to any operator. The programmer has not undermined his control of the system.

Chapter 8

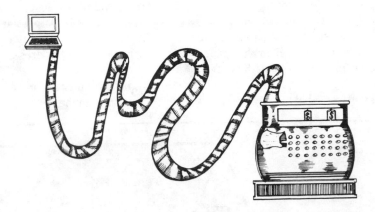

Fred's Friendly Fish Market

Now that you have seen some of the activities involved in creating and using an automated system, let's develop a system that could be used for either business or personal purposes. For the purpose of this example, let's introduce a small businessperson named Fred. Fred's business is small, that is, not him!

Fred owns a wholesale fish market. Fred is growing larger each month. Not Fred, his business! He sells all types of fish and seafood to area restaurants, supermarkets, and other smaller fish markets. Fred has decided that, in order to grow larger, he must be able to operate his business more efficiently. He is spending too much time running the business and not enough time with the lobsters and crabs. Fred's fish are ready to enter the computer age!

Fred sends circulars to his regular customers every month. This means that Fred himself needs to address every circular by hand each month, and this is excruciatingly boring work to Fred. He'd much rather be spending time with his family or improving the business, not typing out a hundred envelopes or so every month. So, after careful research, Fred has decided to purchase a personal computer that can use dBASE III software. Fred did this because he knows that, although this is the first use he has thought of for automating his business, there will be more uses in the future.

Before Fred purchased that personal computer, he defined his business problem in general terms: "I want to print labels, store an address / phone list, and produce a directory of these people."

Fred's purchase-decision was based on his immediate needs (a computer, a disk drive for storage, and a printer). Looking ahead to the future, Fred decided that buying a good all-purpose machine with a reliable service contract and useful, generalized software now and expanding his uses later was his best bet in automating his business.

PROBLEM DEFINITION

Now that he has decided on his resources, even if he hasn't made the purchase yet, he can start designing the program he will use. As shown in Fig. 8-1, the definitions of the problem is the basis upon which the whole system is built. Fred now adds more detail to his problem definition:

I need to enter and store information to be printed on mailing labels and on plain paper for a directory for use in mailing those darn circulars.

The dBASE III software that I have chosen can automatically handle data entry, storage, and editing when I supply disks to store the information on.

Also, I will need backup copies of these disks, as well as backup copies of the software.

On the mailing labels I need to have customer name, street address, city, state, and zip code.

On the directory I also need to have the telephone number.

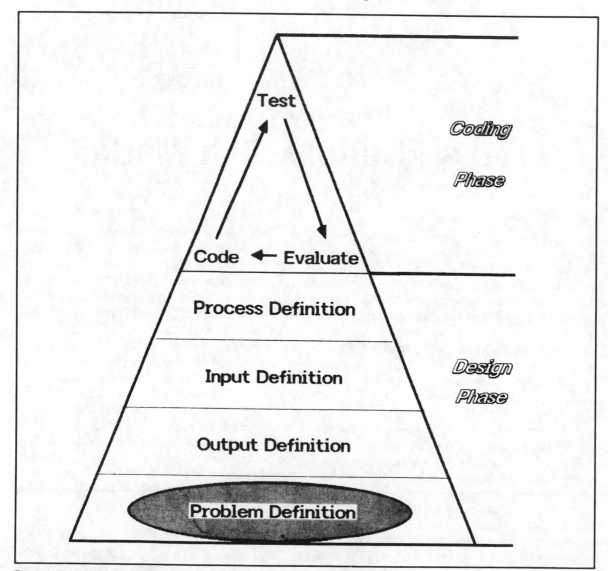

Fig. 8-1. The problem definition.

Now that Fred has written the definition in this form, breaking functions onto separate lines, he can see that the program will not be too difficult to write, and there is no calculation to be performed on the data. dBASE III will supply an entry and update facility for the information, so the thing to do now is to design the data.

DEFINING THE OUTPUT DATA

Since Fred decided to computerize his customer list, he must define precisely what he will need on that list. Fred knows that the customer directory and mailing labels are of utmost importance. Fred starts by thinking about what fields are needed in order to prepare those darn mailing labels and produce a customer directory.

The first field is "name." Fred decides that, since he wants all output to be in alphabetical order by last name, he will put last name first in his data-base. He could put all names in one field called NAME, in last—first order. However, Fred is still thinking of the future; someday, he might want to send personalized letters to his customers, and he would need to print the name in first—last order. Fred defines his first piece of output data as two fields: FNAME, and LNAME. They are character data items, and each will be twenty characters long.

The next data item is "address." Fred creates ADDRESS as a character field, up to 25 characters long. This field will hold the street address.

The "city name" field, Fred decided, would be fifteen characters long, with the name CITY. Fred is being very careful not to use meaningless names in identifying his data items, so that future enhancements will be easier. Good old Fred, always thinking about the future.

The "state" field is easy, says Fred, "Just two characters identify every state in the USA, and I only have customers in three!" So the field becomes STATE, character data, two positions long.

Now comes a toughy, Fred thought. Zip code used to be five digits long, but isn't it supposed to be changed to nine digits in the near future? Fred decides to make zip code nine digits long to be sure; although, he could have easily changed this at a later time with dBASE III. A zip code is an excellent example of a number that is not used in calculations. It could be defined as a character field. However, Fred wants dBASE III to edit the input data for him, and if he defines it as character data, the system would allow any character in the field. By defining it as a numeric field, it will accept only numbers nine positions long.

The last step is taking care of the phone number, so Fred uses the same reasoning as for ZIPCODE and comes up with PHONE, which will be ten digits long and numeric.

Fred's output description looks like this:

Field	Data Type	Length
FNAME	character	20
LNAME	character	20
ADDRESS	character	25
CITY	character	15
STATE	character	2
ZIP	numeric	9
PHONE	numeric	10

The output definition is part of the evolving system design. Since it is still a design, the definition can be changed to reflect new requirements and developments. This definition is not "cast in stone!"

The Format of the Output

Part of the output definition is also defining exactly what the output reports will look like. In a name /address file this is usually easy because there are few fields to contend with, and because the format of mailing labels is defined by the post office and is rarely changed. (Look how long it will take American businesses to implement the nine digit zip code—7 years!)

Format of the Mailing Labels

Fred has decided to buy blank labels that are three across a page, or *3-up* as they are referred to. That means that three labels must be printed at one time, or the labels on the right side of the page will go to waste. The format that would be used if there are eight names on the mailing list is shown in Fig. 8-2.

The layout of the labels does not provide enough details to be useful as an output definition.

The field names are really not enough. The length of each field should be part of the label definition to ensure the proper fit and alignment. Producing this type of format for the label will show the smallest possible size the label should be. The following shows a single label. Note that the space from one X to the next is the field length as defined previously.

```
X------FNAME-------X X------LNAME-------X
X--------ADDRESS--------X
X----CITY-----X, ST
X--ZIP--X
```

These field definitions reflect the largest possible variable that each field can hold.

Format of the Directory

The only real document Fred has to design is the directory he wants printed. This should lead to more questioning on Fred's part—does he want a hand-held, book size directory, or does he want it printed on 3 × 5 cards. Some printers can only handle forms with sprocket feed holes on the sides; some work with regular typing paper. Fred has to take these details into consideration as well.

So Fred, for the time being, has decided on 8½ × 11 inch paper because he has pin feed paper for his new printer. If at a later time he wishes to convert to ROLIDEX, he can do so without too many problems. And, if he ever runs out of the special forms, he can always convert to plain paper.

Fred decided to make his directory one column wide, with as many names as fit on each page. This is the most efficient form that he can think of, and it will probably not be used that often anyway. He just needs it to look up a name or phone number when he is not near the computer.

Fred now defines the format for an entry in the directory:

```
X------LNAME-------X, X------FNAME-------X
                      X------ADDRESS------
                      ----X
                      X----CITY-----X  ST
                      X--ZIP--X

                      Phone: X-PHONE--X
```

```
+---------------------+ +---------------------+ +---------------------+
| FNAME1 LNAME1       | | FNAME2 LNAME2       | | FNAME3 LNAME3       |
| ADDRESS1            | | ADDRESS2            | | ADDRESS3            |
| CITY1, ST1          | | CITY2, ST2          | | CITY3, ST3          |
| ZIP1                | | ZIP2                | | ZIP3                |
+---------------------+ +---------------------+ +---------------------+

+---------------------+ +---------------------+ +---------------------+
| FNAME1 LNAME1       | | FNAME2 LNAME2       | | FNAME3 LNAME3       |
| ADDRESS1            | | ADDRESS2            | | ADDRESS3            |
| CITY1, ST1          | | CITY2, ST2          | | CITY3, ST3          |
| ZIP1                | | ZIP2                | | ZIP3                |
+---------------------+ +---------------------+ +---------------------+

+---------------------+ +---------------------+ +---------------------+
| FNAME1 LNAME1       | | FNAME2 LNAME2       | |                     |
| ADDRESS1            | | ADDRESS2            | |       WASTE         |
| CITY1, ST1          | | CITY2, ST2          | |                     |
| ZIP1                | | ZIP2                | |                     |
+---------------------+ +---------------------+ +---------------------+
```

Fig. 8-2. Mailing labels.

The format shows the maximum length of each field. This is because the maximum length of the fields must be allowed for on the output forms. Otherwise, the fields may get chopped off, or *truncated*, if other fields on the form compete for the same space. Also the fields could print past the edge of a narrow form, which wastes ink and time, and doesn't do your printer much good either.

Now Fred can figure out how many of these entries will fit on a page. He already decided that he would use regular paper with a length of 11 inches for this listing. Fred's printer prints 6 lines per inch, so this means that there will be 66 lines available per page. Each individual entry takes 5 lines, and Fred wants 2 lines between entries; thus each entry will require 7 lines in all. Also, Fred decided that he didn't want the first and last entries on each page to print too near the top or bottom. He decides to leave 5 blank lines at the top and bottom of each page or a total of 10 blank lines. With a little math, Fred figures:

66 total lines − 10 margin lines = 56 effective lines

56 lines / 7 lines per entry = 8 entries per page.

Fred decides that he will print eight entries per page. Each entry will be formatted as shown previously.

TWO THINGS AT ONCE

Fred has defined his output pretty well. His next discovery is that he has also defined the input. This is because it's Fred's first stab at automation: he has no existing files, and all data that is needed will have to be present in the input or calculated from the input. Since there is no calculation involved in the solution to Fred's business problem, he has done the remarkable feat of defining his input and output in one step. Up-front planning has already paid off in this admittedly simple system.

Fred's input description looks just like his output description because there are no calculations:

Field	Data Type	Length
FNAME	character	20

Field	Data Type	Length
LNAME	character	20
ADDRESS	character	25
CITY	character	15
STATE	character	2
ZIP	numeric	9
PHONE	numeric	10

REEXAMINING THE DESIGN

Now the problem has been defined and the output specified, and Fred is ready to tear into his process definition. As he looks carefully at the documents he has created, he notices that there is not much processing to do at all. The information has only to be retrieved from wherever it is now and placed on the output form. Fred takes the sensible approach and decides to look over his requirements one more time.

On closer inspection, he notices two things. First, the nine digit zip code is broken into two parts: the five digit zip code and the new four digit part are separated by a hyphen. He decides not to create a ZIP1 and ZIP2 field for the two parts.

Second, the telephone number, when entered as a single number, is awkward to look at and needs to be divided into three parts: area code, exchange, and number. Instead of breaking up the phone number into its component parts, Fred decides that he will make the field a character field and enter all punctuation manually. Now the numeric edit will not work, so Fred will have to edit the contents of the phone number field by himself. He is prepared to do that to save processing time. So, both the zip code and the phone number fields will be character fields. The zip code will be ten characters long and have the form NNNNN-NNNN. The phone number will have the form (AAA)NNN-NNNN and will be thirteen characters long.

FRED DIVIDES TO CONQUER

Now that Fred has defined his output and input, he is ready to chart the hierarchy of the functions in the system. He first draws a square on the empty sheet of paper and labels it CUSTOMER SYSTEM. This is the overall name of the major function. He then draws six more boxes in a line an inch or two under the first box. He labels these boxes, from left

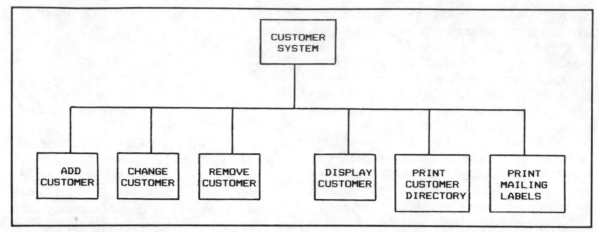

Fig. 8-3. The main function hierarchy chart.

to right, ADD CUSTOMER, CHANGE CUS-TOMER, REMOVE CUSTOMER, PRINT MAILING LABELS, PRINT MAILING LIST. These are the overall kinds of actions that Fred will need his system to perform. He then connects the boxes with lines, denoting the hierarchy of the func-

tions. The result is shown in Fig. 8-3.

Fred now adds a third level of boxes about an inch under the second row. He puts two boxes underneath PRINT MAILING LABELS box. He connects them to the box using the hierarchy lines and labels them as in Fig. 8-4. Since the function

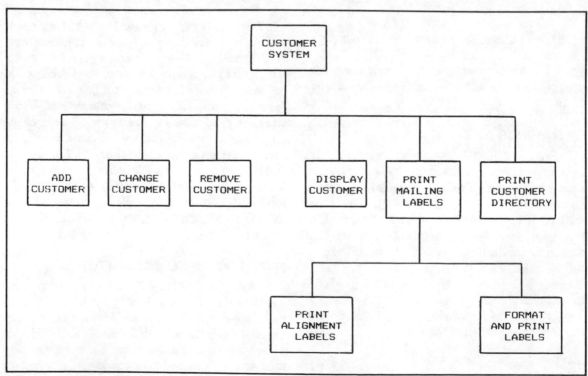

Fig. 8-4. The second level of the hierarchy chart.

```
--------------------------------------------------------
|                                                      |
|              FRED'S FRIENDLY FISH MARKET             |
|                 CUSTOMER ADDITIONS                   |
|                                                      |
|                                                      |
|        LAST NAME:   LNAME--------------X             |
|        FIRST NAME:  FNAME--------------X             |
|                                                      |
|        ADDRESS:  ADDRESS-----------------X           |
|        CITY:     CITY----------X                     |
|                                                      |
|        STATE: ST     ZIP: ZIP-----X                  |
|                                                      |
|        PHONE NUMBER: PHONE-------X                   |
|                                                      |
--------------------------------------------------------
```

Fig. 8-5. The screen design for adding customers.

PRINT MAILING LABELS will automatically print the labels each time a row of three labels are formatted, it is shown as a part of the second hierarchy rather than as a separate third level.

Fred feels that his hierarchy is now complete, and he is ready to start his screen design.

DESIGNING SCREENS

At this point in the design, Fred (or you) can take a look at how the data is to be entered. When a new customer is to be added to the file, all of the input fields must be entered; the record concerning the customer does not exist in computer-usable form. So, in order to "capture" this information, Fred designs the data input screen for customer additions to look like the screen shown in Fig. 8-5.

With this screen, Fred can enter all the information needed for each customer. Notice that he allowed for the full length of each field; he also included a heading for the screen and a label for each field. You may notice a large space between the heading and the first field. Later you will learn how error messages and informational messages can also be programmed to appear in this space.

For the CHANGE CUSTOMER function, Fred needs approximately the same screen as was defined for the ADD CUSTOMER function, except that when it appears, it should have all the informa-

tion already displayed. Then it can be changed and the record updated. With this type of process, however, Fred will have to tell his program which customer to change. He will need the screen shown in Fig. 8-6.

The name information will give the program a clue that indicates which record is to be retrieved for changes. If the record is not found the computer can be programmed to display an error message as shown in Fig. 8-7. The user will be requested to reenter the name. When the record is retrieved, it will be displayed on the screen as shown in Fig. 8-8, with all the information filled in. Fred then has the ability to change any field on the screen. After changes have been made, he can tell the system to put the record with the changes back into its place in the file.

The screens for DISPLAY CUSTOMER, shown in Figs. 8-9 and 8-10, will look almost the same as those for CHANGE CUSTOMER shown, except that no data can be changed.

For the DELETE CUSTOMER function, Fred will need a screen to enter the name of the customer to be deleted, and some way of confirming the delete. If, by chance, the name was entered incorrectly, or the wrong name was entered, he wants the ability to abort the deletion. The program should ask if the retrieve record is the correct one to remove from the file. Notice how Fred is using

```
---------------------------------------------------------
|                                                         |
|      FRED'S FRIENDLY FISH MARKET                        |
|          CUSTOMER CHANGES                               |
|                                                         |
|   *** ENTER CUSTOMER TO BE CHANGED ***                  |
|                                                         |
|      LAST NAME:    LNAME---------------X                |
|      FIRST NAME:   FNAME---------------X                |
|                                                         |
|                                                         |
|                                                         |
|                                                         |
|                                                         |
---------------------------------------------------------
```

Fig. 8-6. The screen design for customer search.

informational messages in the message area of the confirmation screen shown in Fig. 8-11.

After creating the screens for the customer data entry and the maintenance functions (called *file maintenance* in programmer talk), Fred turns to the actual application screen. The add, change, delete, and display functions are also applications, but they are support functions; that is to say, they exist only to facilitate the operation of the functions PRINT MAILING LABELS, and PRINT DIRECTORY. These last two are the output generators, the functions for which the system was written in the first place.

The input screen for the PRINT MAILING LABELS function is designed as shown in Fig. 8-12.

This screen asks if alignment labels are to be printed. When a Y is entered, the test labels will be printed. The alignment routine will print a series of Xs across the labels so the operator can properly adjust the printer. The <cr> symbol means *carriage return* and means that the operator should press the enter or return key. After the alignment labels are printed, this screen is displayed again. When Fred has aligned the printer to his satisfaction, he presses the enter key, and the customer labels are printed.

Fig. 8-7. An example of a screen error message.

```
---------------------------------------------------------
|                                                         |
|      FRED'S FRIENDLY FISH MARKET                        |
|          CUSTOMER CHANGES                               |
|                                                         |
|   *** NAME NOT FOUND - TRY AGAIN ***                    |
|                                                         |
|      LAST NAME:    LNAME---------------X                |
|      FIRST NAME:   FNAME---------------X                |
|                                                         |
|                                                         |
|                                                         |
---------------------------------------------------------
```

```
     ------------------------------------------------------
    |                                                        |
    |            FRED'S FRIENDLY FISH MARKET                 |
    |                 CUSTOMER CHANGES                       |
    |                                                        |
    |                                                        |
    |      LAST NAME:    LNAME----------------X              |
    |      FIRST NAME:   FNAME--------------X                |
    |                                                        |
    |      ADDRESS:  ADDRESS------------------X              |
    |      CITY:     CITY----------X                         |
    |                                                        |
    |      STATE: ST     ZIP: ZIP-----X                      |
    |                                                        |
    |      PHONE  NUMBER: PHONE-------X                      |
    |                                                        |
     ------------------------------------------------------
```

Fig. 8-8. The Customer change data screen.

The PRINT DIRECTORY function really does not need a screen, since the plain paper forms can be aligned without using the method described for the PRINT MAILING LABELS function. Fred decides to display a screen anyway, to confirm that the PRINT DIRECTORY function is the one that the operator wanted. So he designs the screen shown in Fig. 8-13.

When this screen is displayed, Fred will have to tell the program to start printing the directory. If he chose the option by mistake, he could abort it.

On closer examination of his screens, Fred decides that this screen could also be used in the PRINT MAILING LABELS function in the same way. Since this project is still in the design phase, writing another piece of paper is an easy task. This sort of change should be noted in the design, rather than changed when the full system is implemented. Fred now changes the Mailing Label screen to look like the one shown in Fig. 8-14.

Fred has one more screen to design—the menu screen for the entire customer system. This screen (and program) is the top level on the hierarchy chart, and will allow Fred to initiate any of his

```
  ----------------------------------------------------
 |                                                    |
 |      FRED'S  FRIENDLY  FISH  MARKET                |
 |            CUSTOMER  DISPLAY                        |
 |                                                    |
 |   *** ENTER NAME TO BE DISPLAYED ***               |
 |                                                    |
 |     LAST  NAME:   LNAME---------------X            |
 |     FIRST NAME:   FNAME--------------X             |
 |                                                    |
 |                                                    |
 |                                                    |
 |                                                    |
 |                                                    |
  ----------------------------------------------------
```

Fig. 8-9. The screen for a customer search.

47

```
FRED'S FRIENDLY FISH MARKET
       CUSTOMER DISPLAY



    LAST NAME:    LNAME---------------X
    FIRST NAME:   FNAME---------------X

    ADDRESS:  ADDRESS-----------------X
    CITY:     CITY----------X

    STATE: ST    ZIP: ZIP-----X

    PHONE NUMBER: PHONE--------X
```

Fig. 8-10. The customer display screen.

functions by entering a number or letter. Fred's menu screen is shown in Fig. 8-15.

The ENTER SELECTION line is where the selection is entered. This is called a *prompt* because you are prompted for the right answer. If you enter anything besides 1-6 or X, the system will prompt you for a correct answer by printing IN-VALID SELECTION—TRY AGAIN on the mes-sage area of the screen.

Now, Fred is ready to tackle the design of the processes his system will perform.

A MENU SYSTEM

Fred envisions the top level of the hierarchy as a menu that will invoke the next lower level of functions. This means that when he runs the pro-

```
FRED'S FRIENDLY FISH MARKET
        CUSTOMER DELETION

ENTER "D" TO CONFIRM DELETE ===> __

    LAST NAME:    LNAME--------------X
    FIRST NAME:   FNAME--------------X

    ADDRESS:  ADDRESS----------------X
    CITY:     CITY----------X

    STATE: ST    ZIP: ZIP-----X

    PHONE NUMBER: PHONE----X
```

Fig. 8-11. The deletion confirmation message.

```
 _____
|                                                 |
|           FRED'S FRIENDLY FISH MARKET           |
|             MAILING LABEL PRINT                 |
|                                                 |
|                                                 |
|        ENTER "Y" FOR ALIGNMENT PRINT            |
|           OR <cr> TO BEGIN PRINT                |
|                                                 |
|              ====>  ___                         |
|                                                 |
|                                                 |
|                                                 |
|_____|
```

Fig. 8-12. The mailing label print screen.

gram, a list of choices will appear on the screen, with an option number beside each one. The operator (probably Fred) will enter the number of his choice, and that function will be performed. It's just like ordering food in a restaurant, thought Fred. No wonder they are called menus.

Fred then writes the pseudocode shown in Fig. 8-16 for his menu program:

Inside the DO WHILE loop, Fred placed a CASE construct to test for the options he listed on his menu screen. He includes an OTHERWISE unit in case the number entered was not one listed on the screen. Fred then ends the DO WHILE loop with an ENDDO and notes that this will be the end of the program, because it has fulfilled all the functions.

Fred uses a switch, which is called EXIT, to determine if the operator has chosen the exit option. The first statement sets the switch for exiting the system to no exit. As long as this code is N, the

```
 _____
|                                               |
|                                               |
|        FRED'S FRIENDLY FISH MARKET            |
|          CUSTOMER DIRECTORY PRINT             |
|                                               |
|                                               |
|                                               |
|        ENTER <cr> TO BEGIN PRINT              |
|          OR "N" TO ABORT PRINT                |
|                                               |
|             ====>  ___                        |
|                                               |
|                                               |
|                                               |
|                                               |
|_____|
```

Fig. 8-13. Customer directory and screen.

```
 ---------------------------------------------
 :                                           :
 :      FRED'S FRIENDLY FISH MARKET          :
 :         MAILING LABEL PRINT               :
 :                                           :
 :                                           :
 :                                           :
 :    ENTER "Y" FOR ALIGNMENT PRINT,         :
 :        "A" TO ABORT PRINT,                :
 :     OR <cr> TO BEGIN PRINT                :
 :                                           :
 :                                           :
 :           ====>  ___                      :
 :                                           :
 :                                           :
 :                                           :
 :                                           :
 :                                           :
 ---------------------------------------------
```

Fig. 8-14. The revised mailing label print screen.

menu is to be displayed so that another option can be chosen. Fred wrote the statement DISPLAY MENU and then used a DO WHILE to see if the exit option (he called it option X) had been chosen.

Walking Through the Menu Program

Fred now "walks-thru" his pseudocode to determine if it is correct and performs the processes he wants when he wants. He writes EXIT on a separate sheet of paper and writes below it. After EXIT he adds OPTION and writes an X below it, showing that he has chosen the EXIT SYSTEM option on his (as yet) imaginary menu. Fred has decided to test this option first (a very good idea).

```
EXIT          OPTION
 N              X
```

Fig. 8-15. The main customer system menu.

```
 ------------------------------------------------------
 :                                                    :
 :          FRED'S FRIENDLY FISH MARKET               :
 :             CUSTOMER SYSTEM MENU                    :
 :                                                    :
 :                                                    :
 :         ENTER SELECTION ===>  __                   :
 :                                                    :
 :            1 - ADD CUSTOMER                        :
 :            2 - CHANGE CUSTOMER                     :
 :            3 - REMOVE CUSTOMER                     :
 :            4 - DISPLAY CUSTOMER                    :
 :                                                    :
 :            5 - PRINT MAILING LABELS                :
 :            6 - PRINT DIRECTORY                     :
 :                                                    :
 :            X - EXIT SYSTEM                         :
 :                                                    :
 ------------------------------------------------------
```

```
                    MENU PROGRAM

   SET EXIT TO "N"
   DISPLAY MENU SCREEN
   READ OPTION
   DOWHILE EXIT = "N"
     CASE
       WHEN OPTION = 1 PERFORM "ADD CUSTOMER"
       WHEN OPTION = 2 PERFORM "CHANGE CUSTOMER"
       WHEN OPTION = 3 PERFORM "REMOVE CUSTOMER"
       WHEN OPTION = 4 PERFORM "DISPLAY CUSTOMER"
       WHEN OPTION = 5 PERFORM "PRINT MAILING LABELS"
       WHEN OPTION = 6 PERFORM "PRINT MAILING LIST"
       WHEN OPTION = X SET EXIT TO "Y"
       OTHERWISE WRITE "INVALID OPTION"
       DISPLAY MENU SCREEN
       READ OPTION
     ENDCASE
   ENDDO
```

Fig. 8-16 Pseudocode for a menu selection.

The next statement to be performed is the DO WHILE. The condition asks if EXIT is equal to N. Looking at his sheet of paper, Fred sees that EXIT is equal to N, because N was assigned to it in the first statement; EXIT has not been changed by another assignment. "This isn't right," thought Fred. The program should not get into the loop if the X option was chosen. On close examination of the code, Fred

```
   SET EXIT TO "N"
   DOWHILE EXIT = "N"
     CASE
       DISPLAY MENU SCREEN
       READ OPTION
       WHEN OPTION = 1 PERFORM "ADD CUSTOMER"
       WHEN OPTION = 2 PERFORM "CHANGE CUSTOMER"
       WHEN OPTION = 3 PERFORM "REMOVE CUSTOMER"
       WHEN OPTION = 4 PERFORM "DISPLAY CUSTOMER"
       WHEN OPTION = 5 PERFORM "PRINT MAILING LABELS"
       WHEN OPTION = 6 PERFORM "PRINT MAILING LIST"
       WHEN OPTION = X SET EXIT TO "Y"
       OTHERWISE WRITE "INVALID OPTION"
     ENDCASE
   ENDDO
```

Fig. 8-17. Redesigning the pseudocode.

sees that the condition would be met on the next time through the loop, but only after the menu is displayed another time.

So, Fred makes a modification to the pseudocode as shown in Fig. 8-17.

Now when he chooses option X, the WHEN unit for the condition OPTION-X is performed, and the value of EXIT is changed to Y. Control jumps out of the CASE figure to the ENDDO, and the conditions is tested. Since EXIT now equals Y, the condition is no longer true, so control then passes out of the DO WHILE to the statement following the ENDDO.

THE FUNCTIONS

Now Fred begins to code the functions on the second level of the hierarchy chart. As he looks at the functions, Fred realizes that the add, change, remove, and display functions are probably performed easily in a powerful database manager like dBASE II.

Since the major purpose of a database management program is to add, change, delete, and display records in a database file, he can probably use very few dBASE III commands to perform these functions. His pseudocode for these functions look like this:

```
ADD A CUSTOMER

    ACCESS CUSTOMER FILE
    ADD CUSTOMER DATA IN LAST NAME ORDER
    CLOSE FILE
```

```
CHANGE A CUSTOMER

    ACCESS CUSTOMER FILE
    ENTER CUSTOMER NAME
    VERIFY AND RETRIEVE RECORD
    CHANGE CUSTOMER DATA
    CLOSE FILE
```

```
REMOVE CUSTOMER

    ACCESS CUSTOMER FILE
    ENTER CUSTOMER NAME
    VERIFY AND DELETE RECORD
    CLOSE FILE
```

```
DISPLAY CUSTOMER

    ACCESS CUSTOMER FILE
    ENTER CUSTOMER NAME
    VERIFY AND DISPLAY CUSTOMER
    CLOSE FILE
```

Fred has now pseudocoded all but the last two functions the system is to perform. These functions are a little more involved:

```
PRINT MAILING LABELS

    PERFORM "ALIGNMENT PRINT"
    ACCESS CUSTOMER FILE
    READ A CUSTOMER RECORD
    DOWHILE MORE RECORDS
    PERFORM "FORMAT FOR LABELS"
      IF LABEL COUNTER = 3
        THEN
            PRINT A ROW OF LABELS
            RESET LABEL COUNTER
      ENDIF
      READ NEXT RECORD
    ENDDO
    CLOSE FILE
```

In this program, notice that Fred has put off defining the two subfunctions in the PERFORM statements. No matter how simple they may be, they are still on the next level of the hierarchy, and the second level is not finished yet:

```
PRINT MAILING LIST

    ACCESS CUSTOMER FILE
    READ CUSTOMER RECORD
    DOWHILE MORE RECORDS
      PRINT DIRECTORY ENTRY
      READ NEXT RECORD
    ENDDO
    CLOSE FILE
```

Again, Fred has postponed the definition of the third-level modules until later. Notice that these programs will still be valid, no matter what format the final labels or directory take. This means that if Fred starts out using sheets that contain 3 labels across the page, *3-up labels* and later switches to 2-up labels, the only modules that need to be changed are the PRINT ALIGNMENT and FORMAT FOR LABELS modules. This is an advantage of modular programming—changes to the lower level functions do not require the recoding of any higher modules.

THE SUBFUNCTIONS

Now Fred turns to his third and final level:

```
PRINT ALIGNMENT LABELS

   ASK IF ALIGNMENT NEEDED
   DO WHILE ALIGNMENT NEEDED
      PRINT LABEL WITH X'S FILLING
        EVERY FIELD
      ADVANCE TO NEXT LABEL
      ASK IF ALIGNMENT IS NEEDED
   ENDDO


FORMAT FOR LABELS

   ADD 1 TO LABEL COUNTER
   MOVE CUSTOMER FIELDS TO LABEL 1, 2 OR 3,
      DEPENDING ON LABEL COUNTER
```

These two functions could probably be coded in the PRINT MAILING LABELS pseudocode. Do not be tempted to join short modules, however. Always break the process down into functional components, as Fred has done. Always traverse the module hierarchy from top to bottom; beware of short-cuts.

Fred now codes the final function:

```
PRINT DIRECTORY ENTRIES

   PRINT THE DIRECTORY ENTRIES
   BLANK OUT THE DIRECTORY FIELDS
   ADVANCE PAPER
   IF TOO CLOSE TO BOTTOM OF PAGE FOR MORE
      ENTRIES
      THEN ADVANCE TO TOP OF PAGE
   ENDIF
```

Notice that Fred did not say just exactly how he is going to know when the printer is nearing the bottom of the page. This will have to be done in dBASE III code, and Fred hasn't learned it yet. Therefore, he leaves the pseudocode statements deliberately vague; he will not be tied down to a particular method.

An important advantage of top-down coding is that the basic system can be made available quickly, before all the modules are coded in dBASE III. In the customer system example, the ADD CUSTOMER function could be the first one done. Then, while Fred is coding the other modules, someone else can be entering the customer data (Fred's wife Elsa, for instance). Then, when the PRINT functions are ready to be placed *on-line*, the data will be available to test them, and the system will be ready to go.

Chapter 9

Fred Gets Ambitious

Fred has finished the design for his customer information system. He is feeling very proud of himself but, he still doesn't feel perfect; it seems too easy! Fred wants to automate as much as he can. He thinks of other sections that he can automate most easily.

"Gee whiz, I should automate orders next. There are so many each day that we work many hours after the docks close just to do the paperwork. Also, we could do the daily inventories so we know what to order each day. My brother Frank always orders too much mackeral and not enough lobster. He says, 'Don't worry, what we sell, we sell.' But I do worry; we need to track our inventories so we don't run out. Murphy's Restaurant came to us for crab last week, and we were out; they haven't ordered from us since. So, I want to automate our customer orders and our inventories. That way I will know what my customers are ordering and what I need to have in our warehouse. Finally, I want to automate the payroll here. We are always paying too much to the dockhands or the checks are late or

something. I will do all these things."

Fred has gone off the deep end! Because of one success, he is ready to tackle the world (and all he has done is the design). The next logical step is to chart the whole system. This will become the new top level of the hierarchy chart, and everything else will move down one level. The customer system becomes part of a bigger system and will be represented as such. The resulting hierarchy chart is shown in Fig. 9-1, and the Main Menu screen is shown in Fig. 9-2.

After charting and designing his Main Menu screen, Fred thinks he is now ready to tackle the rest of the system. He remembers that a beginner should design a little at a time. One module can be finished before the others are started.

Fred is now ready to automate the next part of his system, the ordering system. When customers place orders with Fred, the smallest part of the process that he goes through is actually sending out the order. The rest of the process is filling out the order form, keeping track of the inventory, and

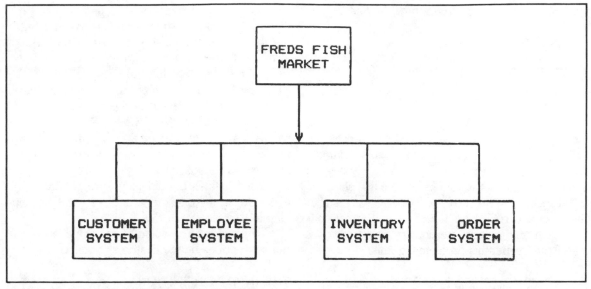

Fig. 9-1. Fred's Fish Market system hierarchy chart.

keeping orders on the file for long periods of time. Fred has just about outgrown his four-drawer file cabinet. In the fish business there are no backorders. If you don't have it, the customer will go somewhere else to get it. There are many standing orders. One of Fred's customers, The Fish Depot in Somersville, has a lobster special twice a week. They expect sixty-two 1-pound lobsters every Tuesday and Saturday. They don't even call in the order; the lobsters are expected to be there (and it's a long walk). They do call in other items each day, though. Fred and Frank (his brother) spend a lot of time remembering who gets what, and when.

So with one design already under his belt, Fred starts the design for the Customer Order System.

THE PROBLEM DEFINITION

Fred needs certain information to create this

Fig. 9-2. Fred's Fish Market main screen design.

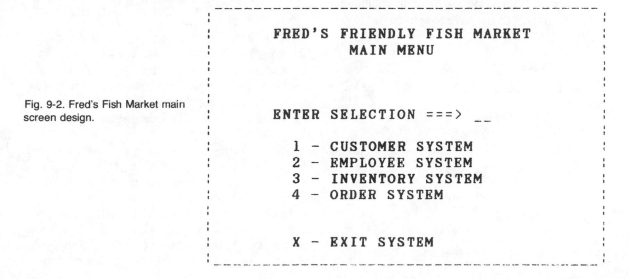

```
------------------------------------------------
|                                              |
|        FRED'S FRIENDLY FISH MARKET           |
|              MAIN MENU                        |
|                                              |
|                                              |
|                                              |
|    ENTER SELECTION ===>  __                  |
|                                              |
|        1 - CUSTOMER SYSTEM                    |
|        2 - EMPLOYEE SYSTEM                    |
|        3 - INVENTORY SYSTEM                   |
|        4 - ORDER SYSTEM                       |
|                                              |
|                                              |
|        X - EXIT SYSTEM                        |
|                                              |
------------------------------------------------
```

system. In processing orders now, he has

Customer information
An order number to uniquely identify orders
The date of the order
The quantity, description, and price of each
  item ordered

As Fred examined his current way of processing orders, he saw that there were two forms of output: the order form that goes to Fred's shipping department to indicate what is to be packed and shipped, and the shipping form (bill of lading), which is also the invoice (Fred's Fish is C.O.D. only—not codfish, cash on delivery—he doesn't give credit).

Fred defined his problem like this:

```
"I need to record and store
order information
to be used to produce
order forms and shipping labels.
The order forms should have:
    the order number and customer name
    each item and quantity number.
The shipping form should have:
    the order number and all customer
    information
    each item and quantity
    along with prices and a total."
```

Fred immediately noticed that the shipping form has some information on it that can be retrieved from the customer system he has just finished designing! That means that he will not have to reenter the information; he will just have to retrieve it when he wants.

THE OUTPUT DEFINITION

Now Fred defines the fields he will need for his output:

Field	Type	Length
FNAME	Character	20
LNAME	Character	20
ADDRESS	Character	25
CITY	Character	15
ST	Character	2
ZIP	Character	10
ORDER NUMBER	Numeric	5
DATE ORDERED	Character	8
QUANTITY	Numeric	3
ITEM	Character	25
PRICE	Numeric	5.2

Six out of the eleven items of output that Fred defined are fields from his previous system! Since that information will be available in computer-usable form, Fred doesn't have to worry about entering it again. Fred wonders how to retrieve it from the customer file, but he realizes that should be figured out as a part of the input design.

The length of the PRICE field is 5.2. This means it will contain a total of 5 digits, with two representing pennies. The largest price you could have would be 999.99.

Fred defines the shipping form so that it will look just like the ones he wrote by hand. The shipping form is shown in Fig. 9-3.

The order form would be the same but would not have prices or the customer's address.

THE INPUT DEFINITION

The total price fields including the TOTAL OWED would not be input fields. They can be calculated by multiplying QTY times PRICE as the items are printed on the form.

Fred now can define his input. The fields from the customer system can be retrieved, so the only fields that need to be input for the order system are

ORDER NUMBER	Numeric	5
DATE ORDERED	Character	8
QUANTITY	Numeric	3
ITEM	Character	25
PRICE	Numeric	5.2

Now Fred can address a question that has been bothering him. "How can I use my customer file with my new order file? Each order must be related to a unique customer, and if, at some point, I have two customers named Bill Smith; how could the program tell them apart using the information I have given it?"

A good question: as things are designed now, there is no unique identification for a customer, apart from the customers last and first names. When Fred was envisioning his customer system, it wasn't important. If he somehow asked to delete the wrong customer, he could always abort the delete and find the next record that had the name he entered. Now, however, when he will be accessing that file from a

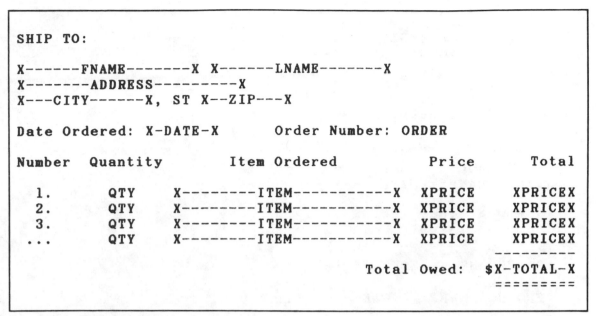

```
SHIP TO:

X------FNAME-------X X------LNAME-------X
X-------ADDRESS---------X
X---CITY------X, ST X--ZIP---X

Date Ordered: X-DATE-X        Order Number: ORDER

Number    Quantity           Item Ordered           Price        Total

   1.        QTY      X--------ITEM-----------X     XPRICE      XPRICEX
   2.        QTY      X--------ITEM-----------X     XPRICE      XPRICEX
   3.        QTY      X--------ITEM-----------X     XPRICE      XPRICEX
  ...        QTY      X--------ITEM-----------X     XPRICE      XPRICEX
                                                              ----------
                                            Total Owed:    $X-TOTAL-X
                                                              =========
```

Fig. 9-3. The shipping form field definition.

program, Fred cannot rely on his own judgment because a computer cannot make judgment of this type. Another way must be found.

Fred decides that he must change his customer system to include a field called Customer Number. This will be a unique indentifier, will be first on the record, and will be assigned by Fred when the customer data is initially added to the file.

Fred has also decided to add something he always wanted and never even did in the manual system—the customer's business name. When Fred started, he sold mainly to other distributors. He always dealt with the owner and would ship the items with the owners name on the label. As Fred has gotten larger (the business, not Fred: he only weighs 130 lbs), he has not been able to meet all of his customers. The business name is more important than the owner's or seafood buyer's name in a large supermarket chain.

Fred's new input description for the customer system looks like this:

Field	Data Type	Length
CUSTNO	Numeric	5
COMPANY	Character	20

Field	Data Type	Length
FNAME	Character	20
LNAME	Character	20
ADDRESS	Character	25
CITY	Character	15
STATE	Character	2
ZIP	Character	10
PHONE	Character	13

Fred makes this change to his customer system design, and looks for more changes. He knows that his customer information screens will change; for example, the Add Customer screen now will have to include customer number and company, as shown in Fig. 9-4.

Also, the screens for Change Customer, Delete Customer, and Display Customer can be changed to retrieve the customer record by the customer number, rather than by the more unreliable customer name. For example, the Change Customer screens would look like the one shown in Fig. 9-5.

Fred had to make these changes to the customer name screens for Delete Customer, and Display Customer as well. He also had to make the change to his directory format as shown in Fig. 9-6.

With these changes made, Fred feels that he

```
 _____
|                                                |
|    FRED'S FRIENDLY FISH MARKET                 |
|       CUSTOMER ADDITIONS                        |
|                                                |
|                                                |
|                                                |
|    CUSTOMER NUMBER: CUSTN                       |
|                                                |
|    COMPANY:      COMPANY------------X           |
|    LAST NAME:    LNAME--------------X           |
|    FIRST NAME:   FNAME--------------X           |
|                                                |
|    ADDRESS: ADDRESS-----------------X          |
|    CITY:      CITY----------X                   |
|                                                |
|    STATE: ST      ZIP: ZIP-----X                |
|                                                |
|    PHONE NUMBER: PHONE-------X                   |
|                                                |
 ------------------------------------------------
```

Fig. 9-4. A new customer additions screen.

can now produce an input definition for the order system:

Field	Type	Length
ORDER NUMBER	Numeric	5
CUST NUMBER	Numeric	5
DATE ORDERED	Character	8

Field	Type	Length
QUANTITY	Numeric	3
ITEM	Character	25
PRICE	Numeric	5.2

A TWO FILE SYSTEM

Now that Fred has decided on the input fields,

```
 _____
|                                                |
|    FRED'S FRIENDLY FISH MARKET                 |
|        CUSTOMER CHANGES                         |
|                                                |
|                                                |
|                                                |
|    CUSTOMER NUMBER: CUSTN                       |
|                                                |
|    LAST NAME:    LNAME--------------X           |
|    FIRST NAME:   FNAME--------------X           |
|                                                |
|    ADDRESS: ADDRESS-----------------X          |
|    CITY:      CITY----------X                   |
|                                                |
|    STATE: ST      ZIP: ZIP-----X                |
|                                                |
|    PHONE NUMBER: PHONE-------X                   |
|                                                |
 ------------------------------------------------
```

Fig. 9-5. A revised customer change screen.

```
Customer Number: CUSTN
X-----COMPANY------X
X------LNAME-------X,  X------FNAME-------X
                      X------ADDRESS----------X
                      X----CITY-----X  ST  X--ZIP--X

                   Phone: X-PHONE--X
```

Fig. 9-6. A revised directory format.

he looks at the design of the data. One order record, as just defined has one item associated with it. "This is no good," Fred thought. "Most of the orders I process are for more than one item." He could put ITEM1, ITEM2, etc., directly on the order record, but this would make the record very large and difficult to use. This would also limit the number of items that could be assigned to one order number. Fred is about to experience the realities of relational database design, (and he doesn't even know what that means—yet).

In the Database section of this book, you will learn in detail how to analyze and design databases. For now, only a brief mention of the *two-file* system is necessary.

The solution is for Fred to create two files: one for order number, customer number, and date; and another for the quantities, items, and prices. The "bridge" between the files is the order number which will appear in both. In the order file one record will appear for each order. In the order items file, one record will appear for each different item ordered. The order number will be placed in the order items file, and all item records with the same order number will be the corresponding order on the order file.

The order file itself will be a bridge between the customer file and the order items file, because of the inclusion of the customer number. The definitions that Fred has arrived at are:

ORDER FILE

Field	Type	Length
ORDER NUMBER	Numeric	5
CUST NUMBER	Numeric	5
DATE ORDERED	Character	8

ORDER ITEMS FILE

ORDER NUMBER	Numeric	5
QUANTITY	Numeric	3
ITEM	Character	25
PRICE	Numeric	5.2

By using the two-file approach, Fred has made his system easier to use. Also, he can have any number of items on a single order. This has made the system more flexible.

THE FUNCTION HIERARCHY

Fred's major function is called the Order System. What would an order system consist of? Well, Fred has a good example of an order system right now—the one he uses currently. So, he examines what exactly it is that he does now with orders. Figure 9-7 presents a comparison between a manual order system and an automated order system.

One thing he does now is write new orders as they come in. Therefore, the system will need a function for ENTER ORDERS.

Now, when a customer calls to change an order, Fred makes the correction using a pencil, crossing off and adding items in the list. Also, if a customer calls and says "Forget it," he just throws that order form away (after a few choice words). So, his system will need to perform the functions CHANGE ORDERS, and DELETE ORDERS.

Another thing that Fred does is look up an order in that old four-drawer file cabinet when there is a question about it. A DISPLAY ORDER function is also necessary. Fred also needs to have standing orders on the system. These are orders that are basically the same each week. Fred decides to input those once and use the order number over and over

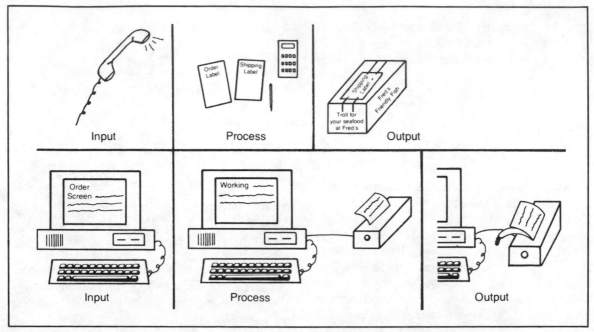

Fig. 9-7. A comparison between a manual order system and an automated order system.

again, changing the date.

Finally, the system will need a function to print the order forms that are to be sent to the shipping department and the shipping forms with the prices that Fred has already defined in his output definition. The shipping department will enter the prices and make any changes for any out-of stock items after the order has been packed. Remember, there are no backorders in the fresh fish business—only lost sales—and Fred doesn't want to see any get away! The function hierarchy chart, showing the main functions, is presented in Fig. 9-8. Now, Fred can design his main menu for the order system as shown in Fig. 9-9.

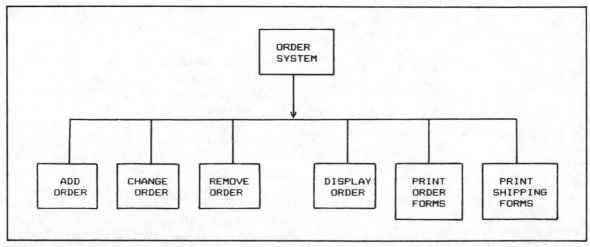

Fig. 9-8. An order system hierarchy chart.

```
----------------------------------------------------------------------
|                                                                      |
|        FRED'S FRIENDLY FISH MARKET                                   |
|           ORDER SYSTEM MENU                                          |
|                                                                      |
|                                                                      |
|                                                                      |
|     ENTER SELECTION ===>  __                                         |
|                                                                      |
|        1 - ADD ORDERS                                                |
|        2 - CHANGE ORDERS                                             |
|        3 - REMOVE ORDER                                              |
|        4 - DISPLAY ORDER                                             |
|                                                                      |
|        5 - PRINT ORDER FORMS                                         |
|        6 - PRINT SHIPPING FORMS                                      |
|                                                                      |
|        X - EXIT SYSTEM                                               |
|                                                                      |
----------------------------------------------------------------------
```

Fig. 9-9. The order system main menu.

All system functions are available from this menu—or will be when Fred gets the system coded and tested!

Fred's pseudocode for the menu program looks like this:

```
SET EXIT TO "N"
DISPLAY MENU SCREEN
DOWHILE EXIT = "N"
  READ OPTION
  CASE
    WHEN OPTION = 1 PERFORM "ADD ORDERS"
    WHEN OPTION = 2 PERFORM "CHANGE ORDER"
    WHEN OPTION = 3 PERFORM "REMOVE ORDER"
    WHEN OPTION = 4 PERFORM "DISPLAY ORDER"
    WHEN OPTION = 5 PERFORM "PRINT ORDER
      FORMS"
    WHEN OPTION = 6 PERFORM "PRINT
      SHIPPING FORMS
    WHEN OPTION = X SET EXIT TO "Y"
    OTHERWISE WRITE "INVALID OPTION"
  ENDCASE
ENDDO
```

With the menu out of the way, Fred moves to the next level of his hierarchy chart. The establishment of an add order function is the first and most important step in creating an order system, so Fred tackles this function first.

THE ADD ORDER FUNCTION

Something about this system has been bother-ing Fred. Each time an order is entered, one or more items are going to be entered. How can the items be entered at the same time as the order is created?

Fred can land this fish by accessing both files in his program. The first screen will ask for information that is specific to that order; in other words, the customer number and order date. When this information is entered, the program will display a second screen for adding items.

The second screen will have room for the operator to enter ten items. If there are more than ten items, the screen will be redisplayed with enough space for the next ten items. Each screen will allow ten items to be entered under that order number; by redisplaying the screens, the operator can add any number of items.

What if the order number that is entered already exists on the order file? This would be an invalid condition, since according to Fred's design, the order number is supposed to be unique. It would be irritating to enter the customer number and date, just to find out that the order number already exists, and the information must be reentered.

One way of eliminating this problem is to use an entry screen. An entry screen is a preliminary screen that would ask for the order number and

```
--------------------------------------------------------
|                                                        |
|          FRED'S FRIENDLY FISH MARKET                   |
|               ORDER ADDITIONS                          |
|                                                        |
|                                                        |
|    ORDER NUMBER:        ORDRN                           |
|                                                        |
|    CUSTOMER NUMBER:   CUSTN                             |
|                                                        |
|                                                        |
|                                                        |
--------------------------------------------------------
```

Fig. 9-10. The order additions preliminary screen.

customer number. Then, if an order with that number already exists, an error could be displayed. Otherwise the order would be new (and valid), and the customer number could be used to pull the necessary customer fields from the customer file. The customer number would be checked to make sure that it did exist on the customer file, as the system can't retrieve information that is not there. By adding this entry screen, Fred makes his system more reliable, because duplicate orders would not be possible.

Fred's first input screen, the entry screen, is shown in Fig. 9-10.

He can then create the next screen in the sequence, the order additions screen shown in Fig. 9-11.

In this figure, you can see the customer infor-

mation that was drawn from the customer file. This information is displayed on the add order screen so that the operator can judge whether or not the correct customer number was chosen. If the customer did not exist on the customer file, an error message would be displayed, but there is no way that Fred can guard against an incorrect customer number entry. The computer can't read minds! Therefore Fred displays the customer information immediately, so the operator will be able to double check to see that the customer's name matches what he believes is the customer number.

Finally, Fred creates the add items screen as shown in Fig. 9-12.

Notice that the company and name information is displayed on this screen, also. This is another double-check; if the operator gets confused about

Fig. 9-11. The order additions screen.

```
----------------------------------------------------------------
|                                                                |
|            FRED'S FRIENDLY FISH MARKET                         |
|                 ORDER ADDITIONS                                |
|                                                                |
|                                                                |
|      ORDER NUMBER:        ORDRN                                |
|                                                                |
|      CUSTOMER NUMBER:   CUSTN                                  |
|                                                                |
|      COMPANY:        COMPANY---------------X                   |
|      LAST   NAME:  LNAME-----------------X                     |
|      FIRST  NAME:  FNAME-----------------X                     |
|                                                                |
|                                                                |
|      DATE ORDERED:  MM/DD/YY                                   |
|                                                                |
----------------------------------------------------------------
```

```
        FRED'S FRIENDLY FISH MARKET
            ORDER ITEM ADDITIONS


    ORDER NUMBER:        ORDRN

    COMPANY:        COMPANY-------------X
    LAST   NAME:    LNAME-------------X
    FIRST NAME:     FNAME-------------X


      #   QUANTITY   ITEM NUMBER

      1     QTY        ITEMN
      2     QTY        ITEMN
      3     QTY        ITEMN
     ...    QTY        ITEMN
     10     QTY        ITEMN
```

Fig. 9-12. The order items additions screen.

which order is being entered, the name information will help figure it out.

The quantity and item number for ten items can be entered on this screen. If there are less than ten items, the operator enters the orders and enters blanks on the next line (actually just presses the enter key again), and the order is filed. If there are more than ten items, the operator fills up the ten items on the first screen, presses enter, and receives a fresh screen with room to add ten more items. The # field changes to show records eleven to twenty. When a blank line is entered on the screen, the program will know that the operator is finished adding items.

Fred is almost ready to begin pseudocoding the add order function, but first, he notices that he needs to make a small change to the hierarchy chart. The add items function would go under the add order function in the hierarchy chart.

Fred has broken this function into its smallest parts. He can now design the process of adding items. The pseudocode Fred created for add order is shown in Fig. 9-13.

In this program, Fred decides that the operator entering of a blank order number will signal the end of the process. As long as the operator continues to enter order numbers and customer numbers on the screen, the program will continue to add orders to the file. This is done with the DO WHILE loop in conjunction with the IF statement; each time the screen is displayed, the IF statement checks for an order number. If it is blank, control shuttles around the processing to the end of the loop. The DO WHILE condition then becomes false, and control passes out of the loop to the end of the program.

Within the first IF statement, "verify order number" means to check the order file for an identical order number.

The IF NEW NUMBER statement following the VERIFY order number statement sees if a duplicate order number is found. If a duplicate is found, control passes to the ELSE unit, which causes an error message to be displayed. Within the THEN unit of the IF NEW NUMBER statement, the customer number is treated in much the same way.

Once the order number and the customer number are verified, the display screen for add order is presented. The operator can see the customer information that was retrieved from the customer file and can enter the order date. When this

```
ADD AN ORDER

    ACCESS ORDER FILE
    SET ORDER NUMBER TO NOT BLANK
    DO WHILE ORDER NUMBER NOT BLANK
       DISPLAY SCREEN
       ENTER ORDER NUMBER AND CUSTOMER NUMBER
       IF ORDER NUMBER NOT BLANK
          VERIFY ORDER NUMBER
          IF NEW NUMBER
             THEN
                ACCESS CUSTOMER FILE
                VERIFY CUSTOMER NUMBER
                IF FOUND
                   THEN
                      DISPLAY CUSTOMER DATA
                      ENTER DATE FIELD
                      ADD TO ORDER FILE
                      PERFORM "ADD ITEMS"
                   ELSE
                      WRITE "CUSTOMER NUMBER NOT FOUND"
                ENDIF
             ELSE
                WRITE "ORDER NUMBER ALREADY ON FILE"
          ENDIF
       ENDIF
    ENDDO
```

Fig. 9-13. The add order pseudocode.

screen is entered correctly, control passes to the add items function for the addition of items to the order.

Satisfied with this pseudocode, Fred moves on to define the add items process as shown in Fig. 9-14.

In this program, the add items screen has ten lines for item numbers and quantities. Each time a line is entered, the program verifies that the item number exists on the item file, and if it does, it retrieves the price. It then places the newly ordered item into the order items file. If the item number is not on the file, an appropriate error message is displayed.

As long as the item number entered is not blank, the system will continue to add records to the file. Each time the operator has entered ten records an IF statement will clear the display and update the item number counter.

THE CHANGE ORDER FUNCTION

Fred is now ready for the next leg on the hierarchy—the change order function. In this function, Fred envisions that the only changes that should be necessary will be changes to the items. The customer number should never be incorrect as it is double checked at entry time. Fred has learned that some controls are necessary, but too many

```
ADD ITEMS

    ACCESS ORDER FILE
    ACCESS ORDER ITEM FILE
    SET ITEMCOUNT TO 1
    SET QUANTITY TO NOT BLANK
    DO WHILE QUANTITY NOT BLANK
       DISPLAY SCREEN AND EXISTING ITEM NUMBERS
       ENTER QUANTITY AND ITEM NUMBER
       IF QUANTITY NOT BLANK
          VERIFY ITEM NUMBER
          IF FOUND
             THEN
                RETRIEVE PRICE
                WRITE RECORD TO ORDER ITEM FILE
                INCREMENT ITEMCOUNT BY 1
             ELSE
                WRITE "ITEM NUMBER NOT ON FILE"
          ENDIF
       ENDIF
       IF ITEMCOUNT IS A MULTIPLE OF 10
          THEN REDISPLAY ITEM SCREEN
       ENDIF
    ENDDO
```

Fig. 9-14. The add items pseudocode.

controls or redundant controls only slow down processing and make the system overly complicated.

Other functions that come under the change order heading are: add items, change the quantity of an item, change an item number, and remove an item. On the advice of a friend, Fred has decided to combine them into one function. Fred's new hierarchy chart for the change order items function is shown in Fig. 9-15.

Now Fred can create the screens that the pro-

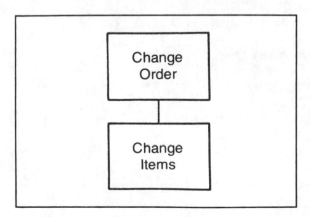

Fig. 9-15. The updated change order hierarchy.

```
 ┌─────────────────────────────────────────┐
 │                                         │
 │    FRED'S FRIENDLY FISH MARKET          │
 │         ORDER CHANGES                   │
 │                                         │
 │                                         │
 │                                         │
 │    ORDER NUMBER:       ORDRN            │
 │                                         │
 │                                         │
 │                                         │
 └─────────────────────────────────────────┘
```

Fig. 9-16. The order changes preliminary screen.

gram will use. He again uses the entry screen method, but with a minor difference as shown in Fig. 9-16.

On this entry screen, Fred does not ask for the customer number. Why not? Because it already exists on the order file, thus there is no need to enter it again! The customer number had to be entered on the add order entry screen because the order did not exist yet and the customer number was needed to retrieve the customer information. Now the order record already exists on the file and can provide the customer number.

The next screen to develop is the order changes screen. This screen is merely a *pass-through* to the change order items function. A pass-through screen is one that is displayed but allows no input to the system. The screen in Fig.

9-17 allows Fred to make sure that he has the right order before moving on to the change items function.

When this screen is displayed, the program asks the operator if there are changes to be made to the items in the order. If there are, and the operator answers affirmatively, Fred will have the program display the change items screen.

Since the change items function seems a little tricky to Fred, he decides to first pseudocode the change order pass-through screen. The pseudocode is shown in Fig. 9-18.

Fred first verifies that the order exists, and if it does, he has the program display the order changes screen. The customer's number, company name, and contact's name are displayed to make sure that the right order has been retrieved. Then the

Fig. 9-17. The order changes screen.

```
 ┌─────────────────────────────────────────────────────────┐
 │                                                         │
 │        FRED'S FRIENDLY FISH MARKET                      │
 │              ORDER CHANGES                              │
 │                                                         │
 │        CHANGE ITEMS? ===>  __                           │
 │     ENTER <cr> TO CONTINUE,  X TO ABORT                 │
 │                                                         │
 │     ORDER NUMBER:       ORDRN                           │
 │                                                         │
 │     CUSTOMER NUMBER:    CUSTN                           │
 │                                                         │
 │     COMPANY:        COMPANY--------------X             │
 │     LAST  NAME:  LNAME----------------X                │
 │     FIRST NAME:  FNAME----------------X                │
 │                                                         │
 │     DATE ORDERED:  MM/DD/YY                             │
 │                                                         │
 └─────────────────────────────────────────────────────────┘
```

```
CHANGE AN ORDER

    ACCESS ORDER FILE
    SET ORDER NUMBER TO NOT BLANK
    DO WHILE ORDER NUMBER NOT BLANK
       DISPLAY SCREEN
       ENTER ORDER NUMBER
       IF ORDER NUMBER NOT BLANK
          VERIFY ORDER NUMBER
          IF FOUND
            THEN
                ACCESS CUSTOMER FILE
                RETRIEVE CUSTOMER INFORMATION
                DISPLAY "CHANGE ITEMS" MESSAGE
                READ CHOICE
                IF CHOICE NOT X
                   THEN PERFORM "CHANGE ITEMS MENU"
                ENDIF
            ELSE WRITE "ORDER NUMBER NOT FOUND"
          ENDIF
       ENDIF
    ENDDO
```

Fig. 9-18. The pseudocode for the change order screen.

operator can enter a carriage return to continue (<cr>), or an X to abort changing that particular order number. When the operator enters a blank order number, the system will return to the main order menu. After a carriage return is entered the order items change screen is displayed.

Originally, Fred was going to have functions that would add, change, and remove items. After thinking about it for several days, in between his arguments with Frank, the only design he could envision was a simple design that would show one item at a time and allow it to be changed. Fred knows he can improve on this. He doesn't want to watch each and every item appear before him just to change the twenty-second item. He wants a system that allows him to enter the quantity and item number he wants to change or delete. He will worry about adding items later. He finished his design just as a friend of his named Myron strolled into the retail area of Fred's Friendly Fish. He showed his design

to Myron who promptly talked him into trading three lobsters and a pound of scallops for a more difficult-to-implement but easier-to-use design. (Myron already computerized his business, a local personnel agency that does some computer work too.)

Fred had explained to Myron that it was important that the operator be able to see all the items at once and be able to add, change, or remove items from the same screen. Myron told Fred that because of the screen size limitations the addition of only 10 items could be displayed at a time. Through a *scroll* function, more items could be displayed after the first ten. The resulting screen is shown in Fig. 9-19.

Myron also explained that there is a difference between adding items to a new order and adding items to an existing order. The change items menu displays ten items at a time, like the add items menu. However, only the items that already exist for that

```
 --------------------------------------------------
|                                                  |
|       FRED'S FRIENDLY FISH MARKET                |
|          ORDER ITEM CHANGES                      |
|                                                  |
|       ENTER SELECTION ===>  __                   |
|       C/CHANGE,S/SCROLL,X/EXIT                    |
|                                                  |
|    ORDER NUMBER:        ORDRN                     |
|                                                  |
|    COMPANY:       COMPANY-------------X          |
|    LAST   NAME:   LNAME---------------X          |
|    FIRST  NAME:   FNAME---------------X          |
|                                                  |
|       #  QUANTITY  ITEM NUMBER                    |
|                                                  |
|       1    QTY        ITEMN                       |
|       2    QTY        ITEMN                       |
|       3    QTY        ITEMN                       |
|      ...   QTY        ITEMN                       |
|      10    QTY        ITEMN                       |
|                                                  |
 --------------------------------------------------
```

Fig. 9-19. The order items changes screen.

order will be placed on the change items menu for review and selection. Fred wondered how an item could be added. The answer struck him like a ton of mackerel. "If there are less than ten items on the screen, there will be some blank lines on the menu." If the operator (probably Fred or Elsa) asks to change a blank line, the item number and quantity that are typed for that line will be added to the file.

The best way to handle the change, or removal of items was to think of each function as a variety of the change function. The easiest way to do that was to make changes or deletions one part of an IF statement and the additions another part. Myron impatiently explained to Fred: "If you retrieve an item that exists on the file, you can do two things to it; change the quantity, item number, or both, or you could remove the item by changing the quantity to zero.

Fred understands, Myron leaves. He can use the record numbers shown on the screen to retrieve the data. If there is no data for that record number, the record will be added. If there is data, the item is changed if the quantity is set to anything besides zero. The item is deleted if the quantity is set to

zero. The first option listed on the menu is C for change, which means add, change, or delete items. The S will allow Fred to page forward through the displayed items ten at a time. The X function will allow Fred to exit this function and return to the main order change screen to change other orders.

The next logical step is to design the screen to be displayed when the C option, change an item, is requested. The screen is shown in Fig. 9-20.

This screen allows the operator to specify the record number of the items they wish to change. The record number is the first field on the item list. The user must choose one of the record numbers displayed or an error message will be displayed. Once the record number is entered and the record found, the next screen, shown in Fig. 9-21, will display the item to be changed.

Fred can now enter any changes he wishes. He can also not enter changes, which will leave the item as is. Fred decides that there is no need for a delete confirmation. If the operator changes the quantity to 0, that is a very conscious decision. Fred is beginning to understand the use of controls.

These are all the screens needed for the

```
------------------------------------------
:                                          :
:      FRED'S FRIENDLY FISH MARKET         :
:          ORDER ITEM CHANGES              :
:                                          :
:      RECORD NUMBER ==>  __               :
:    ENTER RECORD NUMBER TO BE CHANGED     :
:                                          :
:    ORDER NUMBER:        ORDRN            :
:                                          :
:    COMPANY:        COMPANY------------X  :
:    LAST  NAME: LNAME---------------X     :
:    FIRST NAME: FNAME--------------X      :
:                                          :
:       #   QUANTITY   ITEM NUMBER         :
:                                          :
:       1     QTY        ITEMN             :
:       2     QTY        ITEMN             :
:       3     QTY        ITEMN             :
:      ...    QTY        ITEMN             :
:      10     QTY        ITEMN             :
:                                          :
------------------------------------------
```

Fig. 9-20. The order items change screen.

```
-----------------------------------------------
:                                               :
:         FRED'S FRIENDLY FISH MARKET           :
:             ORDER ITEM CHANGES                :
:                                               :
:      QUANTITY: QTY   ITEM NUMBER:  ITEMN      :
:                ENTER CHANGES                  :
:                                               :
:       ORDER NUMBER:        ORDRN              :
:                                               :
:       COMPANY:        COMPANY------------X    :
:       LAST   NAME: LNAME---------------X      :
:       FIRST NAME: FNAME-------------X         :
:                                               :
:          #   QUANTITY   ITEM NUMBER           :
:                                               :
:          1     QTY        ITEMN               :
:          2     QTY        ITEMN               :
:          3     QTY        ITEMN               :
:         ...    QTY        ITEMN               :
:         10     QTY        ITEMN               :
:                                               :
-----------------------------------------------
```

Fig. 9-21. The order items change screen.

change items function. Figure 9-22 shows a sample of the screen that would be displayed if the S command were entered. It shows a screen with items 11, 12, and 13. The operator would have to enter a number greater than 13 to add an item to the file.

Prior to pseudocoding the change items subfunction, Fred comes up with the final hierarchy chart for the order system as shown in Fig. 9-23.

Fred starts the pseudocoding with the main part of the menu for changing items. He builds the menu just like other menus he has built before, using the CASE statement:

```
CHANGE ITEMS

   SET EXIT TO 'N'
   DISPLAY MENU SCREEN
   DOWHILE EXIT = 'N'
     DISPLAY ITEMS
     DISPLAY SELECTION
     READ SELECTION
     CASE
       WHEN SELECTION = 'X'
         SET EXIT TO 'Y'
       WHEN SELECTION = 'C'
         CHANGE RECORDS
       WHEN SELECTION = 'S'
         ADD 10 TO SCROLL COUNTER
     ENDCASE
   ENDDO
```

Here, Fred has the program look for C, S, or X. Option C causes the section used to change the items to be accessed. Option S will add ten to the counter that keeps track of the record numbers displayed and causes the next ten to be displayed the next time the screen is shown. The X option is chosen when the operator wants to leave the menu and return to the change order function.

Pseudocoding the Change Items Menu

Now that Fred is finished with screen design for the change order items function, he feels he understands the process better. With a little help from his friend, he will turn his hand to pseudocoding; Myron gets more lobsters. The resulting code is shown in Fig. 9-24.

Fred performs all three functions (add, change, and delete) in this one piece of pseudocode. This may or may not be a good idea, from the standpoint of modularity, because the fewer functions a module is to perform, the easier it is to code later. However, Fred does (wisely) separate the functions within the pseudocode with some extra comments.

The first step in the pseudocode is to display

```
FRED'S FRIENDLY FISH MARKET
       ORDER ITEM CHANGES

     RECORD NUMBER ==>  __
  ENTER RECORD NUMBER TO BE CHANGED

  ORDER NUMBER:        ORDRN

  COMPANY:        COMPANY-------------X
  LAST   NAME:    LNAME---------------X
  FIRST NAME:     FNAME---------------X

     #   QUANTITY   ITEM NUMBER

    11     QTY        ITEMN
    12     QTY        ITEMN
    13     QTY        ITEMN
```

Fig. 9-22. The order items scroll screen.

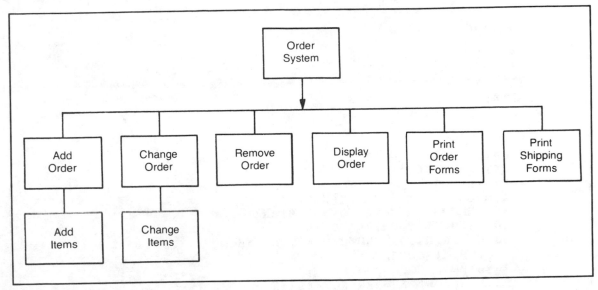

Fig. 9-23. The order system hierarchy chart.

the screen that requests the record number. All functions require the record number, and it is immediately checked to determine if that record number is currently displayed on the screen. If that record is not displayed, an error message is sent to the operator and another record number can be entered.

If the record is currently displayed on the screen, the change item panel is displayed, allowing the operator to change the quantity and item number shown on the screen. The program determines whether or not the line for that record number was blank by checking to see if the old fields were blank. If they are, this item is to be added and after verifying the item number, the record is added to the item file.

If the quantity of the chosen item is changed to zero, Fred has the program recognize this as a delete function, and the record is removed from the order items file.

If the item number is changed, Fred's program decides that this is a change to the item, checks to make sure that the new item number is on the item file, and retrieves the price. Finally the changed record is updated in the order item file.

Now, Fred adds pseudocode for the scroll function to the bottom of the pseudocode, and he is

done. In this small program, Fred creates a *scroll counter* to keep track of the top item on the menu screen. The scroll counter is set to one in the change order program. The first item and the following nine items are then displayed on the menu. When the S option is chosen, this program adds ten to the scroll counter, and the eleventh through twentieth items are displayed. No matter how many items are in the file for this order, the scroll program will display ten at a time, scrolling forward only.

Fred has completed the toughest design he has had to tackle so far in his short data processing career, and he is now free to move on to the next function in the system.

THE REMOVE ORDER FUNCTION

For the remove order function, Fred again decided to use an entry screen to confirm that the order exists before any processing is performed. In the case of a delete operation, this is particularly important. It is easier to go through an extra confirmation step than it is to reenter an entire order that was deleted by mistake.

The entry screen looks like the change order entry screen and is shown in Fig. 9-25.

Figure 9-26 shows the next screen that Fred designs, the confirmation screen for the delete.

71

```
CHANGE ITEMS

  SET EXIT TO 'N'
  DISPLAY MENU SCREEN
  DOWHILE EXIT = 'N'
    DISPLAY ITEMS
    DISPLAY SELECTION
    READ SELECTION
    CASE
      WHEN SELECTION = 'X'
        SET EXIT TO 'Y'
      WHEN SELECTION = 'C'
        ACCESS ORDER ITEM FILE
        SET RECORD NUMBER TO NOT BLANK
        SET SCROLL COUNTER TO 10
        DO WHILE RECORD NUMBER NOT BLANK
          DISPLAY SCREEN
          ENTER RECORD NUMBER
          IF RECORD NUMBER NOT BLANK
            THEN
              VERIFY RECORD NUMBER IN THE 10 DISPLAYED
              IF IN THE 10
                THEN
                  RETRIEVE RECORD
                  DISPLAY QTY AND ITEMN
                  IF BLANK
                    THEN
                      DISPLAY ADD MESSAGE
                  ENDIF
                  ENTER CHANGES
                  IF QTY AND ITEMN NOT BLANK
                    THEN                              /* ADD RECORD */
                      IF OLD QUANTITY BLANK
                        THEN
                          VERIFY ITEM NUMBER
                          IF FOUND
                            THEN
                              RETRIEVE PRICE
                              WRITE RECORD TO ORDER ITEM FILE
                            ELSE
                              WRITE "ITEM NUMBER NOT ON FILE"
                          ENDIF
                      ENDIF
                  IF QTY OR ITEM NUMBER DIFFERENT THEN ORIGINAL
                    THEN                              /* DELETE RECORD */
                      IF QTY = 0
                        THEN
                          REMOVE RECORD FROM ORDER ITEM FILE
                        ELSE                          /* CHANGE RECORD */
```

72

```
                                   VERIFY ITEM NUMBER
                                   IF FOUND
                                      THEN
                                          RETRIEVE PRICE
                                          WRITE RECORD TO ORDER ITEM FILE
                                      ELSE
                                          WRITE "ITEM NUMBER NOT ON FILE"
                                   ENDIF
                             ENDIF
                         ENDIF
                       ENDIF
                       ELSE
                           WRITE "RECORD NUMBER NOT ON DISPLAY"
                 ENDIF
            ENDIF
         ENDDO
    WHEN SELECTION = 'S'
         ADD 10 TO SCROLL COUNTER
    ENDCASE
ENDDO
```

Fig. 9-24. The order item changes pseudocode.

This screen looks like the other item screens; however, only the first ten items are displayed. Fred has decided not to give the delete function a scrolling capability. "Anyone can tell if the order is the correct one from the first ten items," said Fred. "Why bother with unnecessary processing?"

So Fred pseudocodes the delete order function as shown in Fig. 9-27.

After the order number is entered from the entry screen, the order is looked up in the order file. If it does not exist, an error message is displayed. If it does exist, the order, customer, and ordered items information is retrieved from their respective files, and the delete order confirmation screen is displayed. If a D is entered from this screen, the order will be removed from the order file, and all items with that order number will be removed from the ordered items file.

Fred is satisfied with the documentation of his system so far. He is ready to dive into the next function.

THE DISPLAY ORDER FUNCTION

Fred can now design the display order function, and he designs it almost like the remove order function. If you look closely at the screens and pseudocode, you can see many similarities. Instead

Fig. 9-25. The preliminary order removal screen.

```
-----------------------------------------
:                                       :
:        FRED'S FRIENDLY FISH MARKET     :
:             ORDER REMOVAL              :
:                                       :
:                                       :
:     ORDER NUMBER:      ORDRN          :
:                                       :
:                                       :
:                                       :
-----------------------------------------
```

```
 ------------------------------------------
|                                          |
|      FRED'S FRIENDLY FISH MARKET          |
|           ORDER DISPLAY                   |
|                                          |
|        ENTER <cr> TO CONTINUE            |
|                                          |
|                                          |
|   ORDER NUMBER:        ORDRN              |
|                                          |
|   CUSTOMER NUMBER:   CUSTN                |
|                                          |
|   COMPANY:       COMPANY-------------X    |
|   LAST   NAME:  LNAME-------------X       |
|   FIRST  NAME:  FNAME-------------X       |
|                                          |
|   DATE ORDERED:  MM/DD/YY                 |
|                                          |
|                                          |
|      #   QUANTITY   ITEM NUMBER           |
|                                          |
|      1      QTY        ITEMN              |
|      2      QTY        ITEMN              |
|      3      QTY        ITEMN              |
|     ...     QTY        ITEMN              |
|     10      QTY        ITEMN              |
|                                          |
 ------------------------------------------
```

Fig. 9-26. The order removal screen.

of deleting orders, Fred just has the program display the information on the screen. He also allows scrolling forward through the items by pressing the enter key. The screens are shown in Figs. 9-28 and 9-29. The pseudocode is shown in Fig. 9-30.

First, the order number is entered and checked against the order file. If the order exists, the order and customer information is displayed, along with the first ten item records for that order. By placing the item displays within a DO WHILE loop, Fred has taken care of the scrolling facility. When the enter key is pressed, more items are looked for in the order items file, and if found, they are displayed. When there are no more item records for that order, the process is complete, and the entry screen is displayed again.

Now Fred has all the administrative functions out of the way. The add, change, delete, and display functions all exist for only one purpose: to add and manipulate the information necessary to produce the output, the order form and the shipping form.

THE PRINT ORDER FORM FUNCTION

To print the order form, Fred uses the entry screen concept to find the order in the file. If the order is not present, an error message is displayed. The entry screen, shown in Fig. 9-31, looks almost like the other order number entry screens.

Another design consideration is the way the printed order form will appear on paper. Fred will use the form he uses now, so he defines his output to assure that he remembers all the fields and can easily code the line and column numbers in his final program. The layout of the form is shown in Fig. 9-32.

Since this function does not require a "confirm"

```
REMOVE ORDERS

    ACCESS ORDER FILE
    SET ORDER NUMBER TO NOT BLANK
    DO WHILE ORDER NUMBER NOT BLANK
       DISPLAY SCREEN
       ENTER ORDER NUMBER
       IF ORDER NUMBER NOT BLANK
          VERIFY ORDER NUMBER
          IF FOUND
             THEN
                RETRIEVE ORDER
                ACCESS CUSTOMER FILE
                RETRIEVE CUSTOMER INFORMATION
                DISPLAY ORDER
                ACCESS ORDER ITEMS FILE
                DISPLAY 1ST 10 ITEMS
                ENTER DELETE CONFITMATION
                IF CONFIRM = D
                   THEN
                      DELETE MAIN ORDER RECORD
                      DELETE ALL ITEM RECORDS
                ENDIF
             ELSE
                WRITE "ORDER NOT ON FILE"
          ENDIF
```

Fig. 9-27. The delete order pseudocode.

screen, like remove order, Fred can jump right into his process definition as shown in Fig. 9-33.

In this program, the entry screen is displayed, and the order number is entered by the operator. The program searches the order file for that order number and when it is found, the program retrieves the customer information. The order and customer information is printed, and then the order item file is searched for all items belonging to that order. As each item record is retrieved, the item file is

```
FRED'S FRIENDLY FISH MARKET
      ORDER DISPLAY



ORDER NUMBER:      ORDRN
```

Fig. 9-28. The preliminary order display screen.

```
-------------------------------------------------
:         FRED'S FRIENDLY FISH MARKET             :
:                ORDER REMOVAL                    :
:                                                 :
:  ENTER D TO CONFIRM DELETE ==> __               :
:                                                 :
:                                                 :
:    ORDER NUMBER:        ORDRN                   :
:                                                 :
:    COMPANY:       COMPANY-------------X         :
:    LAST   NAME:   LNAME---------------X         :
:    FIRST  NAME:   FNAME---------------X         :
:                                                 :
:    DATE ORDERED:  MM/DD/YY                       :
:                                                 :
:       #  QUANTITY   ITEM NUMBER                 :
:                                                 :
:       1    QTY        ITEMN                      :
:       2    QTY        ITEMN                      :
:       3    QTY        ITEMN                      :
:      ...   QTY        ITEMN                      :
:      10    QTY        ITEMN                      :
:                                                 :
:                                                 :
-------------------------------------------------
```

Fig. 9-29. The order display screen.

Fig. 9-30. The pseudocode for the
display order function.

```
DISPLAY ORDERS

    ACCESS ORDER FILE
    SET ORDER NUMBER TO NOT BLANK
    DO WHILE ORDER NUMBER NOT BLANK
      DISPLAY SCREEN
      ENTER ORDER NUMBER
      IF ORDER NUMBER NOT BLANK
        VERIFY ORDER NUMBER
        IF FOUND
          THEN
             RETRIEVE ORDER
             ACCESS CUSTOMER FILE
             RETRIEVE CUSTOMER INFORMATION
          DISPLAY ORDER
          ACCESS ITEM FILE
          DO WHILE MORE RECORDS
             DISPLAY 10 ITEMS
             ENTER CONTINUE CONFIRMATION
          ENDIF
        ELSE
          WRITE "ORDER NOT ON FILE"
      ENDIF
    ENDIF
  ENDDO
```

```
┌───────────────────────────────────────────────────┐
│                                                   │
│          FRED'S FRIENDLY FISH MARKET              │
│             ORDER FORMS PRINT                     │
│                                                   │
│                                                   │
│       ORDER NUMBER:          ORDRN                │
│                                                   │
│                                                   │
└───────────────────────────────────────────────────┘
```

Fig. 9-31. The print order forms screen.

searched for that item number so that the item description may be printed on the order form. The program then loops back, using the inner DO WHILE loop, to search for more items.

THE PRINT SHIPPING LABEL FUNCTION

The last function of Fred's order system is to print the shipping label for an order from the stored order information. Again, the entry screen concept is used, as it was in the print order form function. The screen is shown in Fig. 9-34.

The final design consideration is the way the printed shipping form will appear on paper. Fred will use the form he uses now so he defines his output to assure that he remembers all the fields and can

easily code the line and column numbers in his final program. The format of the output is shown in Fig. 9-35. The pseudocode is shown in Fig. 9-36.

In this process, the order number is searched for on the order file, and if it is not present, an error message is displayed. If an order is on file, however, the order and customer fields are retrieved and printed on the shipping form. Then, Fred has the program search for the items that belong to the order. As each item is found, the item description and its price are retrieved from the item file. The program calculates the price to the customer for each item by multiplying quantity times the item price. The total is accumulated, so that the bottom line, the total cost can be printed on the form. The

```
┌───────────────────────────────────────────────────────────────┐
│                                                               │
│        Order Number: ORDRN                                    │
│                                                               │
│        X-----COMPANY------X                                   │
│        X------FNAME-------X X-------LNAME-------X             │
│                                                               │
│        Order Date: MM/DD/YY                                   │
│                                                               │
│ ITEM #       QUANTITY      ITEM NUMBER       DESCRIPTION      │
│    1           QTN           ITEMN      X----------DESC---------X │
│    2           QTN           ITEMN      X----------DESC---------X │
│    3           QTN           ITEMN      X----------DESC---------X │
│    4           QTN           ITEMN      X----------DESC---------X │
│    5           QTN           ITEMN      X----------DESC---------X │
│    6           QTN           ITEMN      X----------DESC---------X │
│    7           QTN           ITEMN      X----------DESC---------X │
│    8           QTN           ITEMN      X----------DESC---------X │
│                                                               │
└───────────────────────────────────────────────────────────────┘
```

Fig. 9-32. The order form print layout.

77

```
PRINT ORDER FORM

    STORE BLANK TO ORDER NUMBER
    DO WHILE ORDER NUMBER NOT BLANK
      DISPLAY SCREEN
      ENTER ORDER NUMBER
      IF ORDER NUMBER NOT BLANK
        ACCESS ORDER FILE
        VERIFY ORDER NUMBER
        IF FOUND
          THEN
            PRINT HEADER OF ORDER
            ACCESS CUSTOMER FILE
            RETRIEVE CUSTOMER INFORMATION
            DISPLAY ORDER INFORMATION
            ACCESS ORDER ITEM FILE
            DO WHILE MORE RECORDS
              RETRIEVE QUANTITY AND ITEM NUMBER
              ACCESS ITEM FILE
              RETRIEVE DESCRIPTION
              PRINT RECORD
            ENDDO
          ELSE
            WRITE "ORDER NUMBER NOT ON FILE"
        ENDIF
      ENDIF
    ENDDO
```

Fig. 9-33. The pseudocode for the print order form.

program then loops to get any further items for the order.

If Fred has decided that a particular customer rets a discount, the discount percentage is retrieved from the customer file; the amount of the discount is then calculated and subtracted from the total price of all items on the order. Last the total cost is printed at the bottom of the form.

```
-----------------------------------------------
|                                             |
|     FRED'S FRIENDLY FISH MARKET             |
|       SHIPPING FORMS PRINT                  |
|                                             |
|                                             |
|                                             |
|   ORDER NUMBER:      ORDRN                   |
|                                             |
|                                             |
-----------------------------------------------
```

Fig. 9-34. The print shipping forms screen.

```
         Order Number: ORDRN

         X-------FNAME-------X X------LNAME-------X
         X-----COMPANY-----X
         X--------ADDRESS--------X
         X-----CITY----X, ST
         X--ZIP--X

         Order Date: MM/DD/YY

Quantity              Description              Price Each        Amount

   QTN      X---------DESC----------X           999.99       $99,999.99
   QTN      X---------DESC----------X           999.99       $99,999.99
   QTN      X---------DESC----------X           999.99       $99,999.99
   QTN      X---------DESC----------X           999.99       $99,999.99
   QTN      X---------DESC----------X           999.99       $99,999.99
   QTN      X---------DESC----------X           999.99       $99,999.99
   QTN      X---------DESC----------X           999.99       $99,999.99
   QTN      X---------DESC----------X           999.99       $99,999.99
                                                            ----------
                                  Total Amount:        $999,999.99

                                  Discount: (xx%) ($ 99,999.99)
                                                            ------------
                                  Amount Due:          $999,999.99
                                                            ============
```

Fig. 9-35. The shipping forms print layout.

```
        PRINT SHIPPING FORM

            STORE BLANK TO ORDER NUMBER
            DO WHILE ORDER NUMBER NOT BLANK
              DISPLAY SCREEN
              ENTER ORDER NUMBER
              IF ORDER NUMBER NOT BLANK
                ACCESS ORDER FILE
                VERIFY ORDER NUMBER
                IF FOUND
                  THEN
                      PRINT HEADER OF ORDER
                      ACCESS CUSTOMER FILE
                      RETRIEVE CUSTOMER INFORMATION
                      PRINT ORDER INFORMATION
                      ACCESS ORDER ITEM FILE
                      SET TOTAL TO 0
                      DO WHILE MORE RECORDS
                        RETRIEVE QUANTITY AND ITEM NUMBER
                        ACCESS ITEM FILE
                        RETRIEVE DESCRIPTION AND PRICE
                        AMOUNT = QUANTITY X PRICE
                        ADD AMOUNT TO TOTAL
                        PRINT RECORD
```

```
            ENDDO
            WRITE TOTAL
            DISCOUNT AMOUNT = DISCOUNT/100 X TOTAL
            WRITE DISCOUNT
            SUBTRACT DISCOUNT FROM TOTAL
            WRITE AMOUNT DUE
         ELSE
            WRITE "ORDER NUMBER NOT ON FILE"
      ENDIF
   ENDIF
ENDDO
```

Fig. 9-36. The print shipping form pseudocode.

THE INVENTORY SYSTEM

Fred's friend Myron made some other suggestions for Fred to try. One of these is to incorporate an inventory system. This is a logical extension of the item file that Fred would like to build. Fred hasn't realized yet, but he has to find a way to add, change, or delete items in the item file. Fred has produced the design shown in Fig. 9-37 and will tackle it in the future. For now, Fred will simply establish the item file using the dBASE III user functions.

SUMMARY

In the last two chapters, you have followed Fred as he designed systems for his business. You saw the logical constructs at work in his pseudocode, saw him develop his systems from scratch, and you saw his documentation package slowly grow as he aimed to automate his entire business.

Fred had to change his original design for the customer system as other systems started to need access to that data. His design was growing and evolving, bending to his needs as he defined his business problems.

You will be seeing more of Fred in the next two sections of this book, as he learns dBASE III, and sees how to turn his designs into working reality.

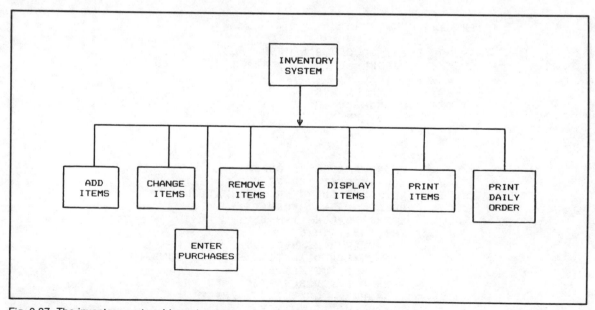

Fig. 9-37. The inventory system hierarchy chart.

Section II

DATABASE FUNDAMENTALS

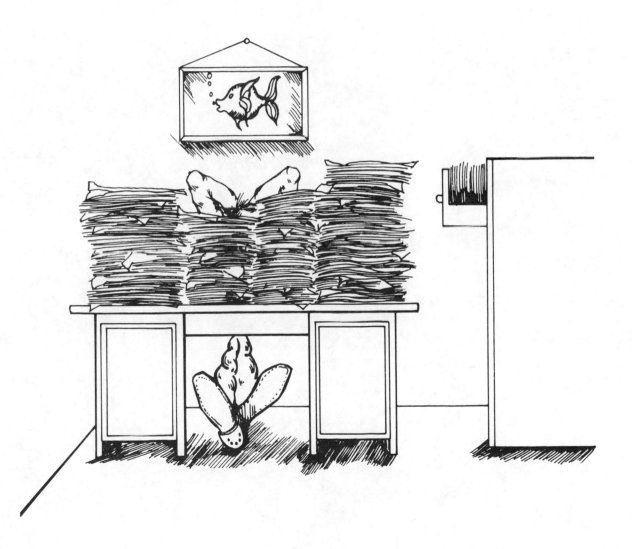

Chapter 10

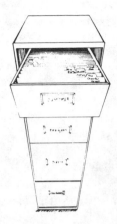

What is a Database?

Database is a term given to the physical area and logical means of storing your data in a computer system. A database is simply data that has been transformed into meaningful information by logically grouping and storing it.

There are endless numbers of databases in the world. One of the more common databases in any-business is the file of customers. This file in its simplest form would contain the customer's name, address, and phone number. The database might contain many other files such as customer accounts, and lists of items the customers have purchased. In a retail business there would be other files such as inventory files, price files, stock number files, and description files. Together, all these files make up the database for the business. The terms *database* and *files* are used interchangeably in this book, although you could think of all related files as being a database.

Another example of a database is a dictionary system. The files that make up the database would include the dictionary file and the thesaurus file. The dictionary file would include a single entry for each word. The entry would contain three fields: the word, the type (noun, verb, etc.), and the definition. The thesaurus file would contain many entries for each word. Each entry would contain the word from the dictionary file along with other words that mean the same thing.

A database is an organized collection of records. Such things as newspapers or magazines are not databases. An index of magazine articles that tells the subject, magazine name, and date is a database. Information must be in some order and must be retrievable by some orderly means. This is the difference between information and chaos.

Why would you need a database? This is a commonly asked question. A database will allow you to ask questions and quickly receive answers about your data. "How many customers bought $200 worth of product this month? "Which customers live in Connecticut?" "How many customers in New England pay their bills?" These are all typical questions that you might ask if you had a database.

What can a database management system like dBASE III do for you? Besides being able to allow you to easily enter, change, and delete data, it allows you to change the description of your records at any time. For example, for ten years you have had two stores in Connecticut. Now you are adding stores in Massachusetts, Rhode Island, and New York. Your database has a place for store name and city but not state. If you have many records already on a computer, would you have to change them all? The answer is yes. With most languages this would be a difficult process. With a database manager like dBASE III it is simple and easy.

A database manager can also let you ask questions in many forms. "How many fish did we sell this month? the last 3 months? how about all year?." "How many customers live outside of CT?" Questions such as these are simple to ask using dBASE III. It's almost as simple as asking them in English! dBASE III also lets you produce reports with just one command. The true beauty of dBASE III, however, is that apart from being a database manager, it is also a programming language.

In the first section, you learned about how to program. That section discussed the proper design of a program and all the logical constructs. In this chapter, you will learn more about how to plan your database and use dBASE III programming commands to manipulate the database. First, let's learn a little bit more about databases.

dBASE III is a relational database management system. This means that each record is stored just as you entered it. Each record is the same size and has the same fields, each the same size. The records are collections of related fields. Each file is a collection of records; one or several files can constitute a database. With microcomputers you can think of a database as being all the files on your disk. If these terms still confuse you, read the explanations on the following pages carefully.

Usually, when you are using several files in a database system, you have to have some way to use them together. This is where the concept of a *common key* comes in. In the customer example a key might be the customer name. If you had one file with the customer name, addresses, and phone num-

bers, while another file had the customer names and account balances, you could use the name as a key to retrieve information from both files.

These keys allow you to tie many files together. For example, a parts file from a typical business might look like this:

```
         DESCRIPTION FILE
PART_NO  WEIGHT      DESCRIPTION
6HD      6oz.        Heavy Duty Nails
8LT      8oz.        Light Weight Nails
8LTS     8oz.        Light Weight Screws
6BT      6oz.        Light Weight Bolts
10WA     10oz.       Heavy Duty Washers
6RN      6oz.        Roofing Nails
ES-28    -           28 in. Electric Saw
```

This file can be accessed, and information concerning the part number and its corresponding description can be retrieved. But in this example, there are two other pieces of information needed: the price of a part and the number in stock. This company has several files in their databases; the other files are shown in Fig. 10-1.

To produce a report that will include the part number, description, price per item, and quantity in stock, you would have to check three different files. Here, you see that each file contains the same part numbers, but they have no other common information. This is one way to organize your information. The part number is called the key; all other information is related to it.

The part number need not be the only key field in the database. For example, in the inventory file, location may also be used as a key field. This file might have the building location, the hours the building is open, and the state it is in. The concept of key fields is an important one in organizing your data and retrieving it again later.

Files

In dBASE III, a file is synonymous with a database. Figure 10-2 is an example of a file. This one is aptly named CUSTOMER FILE. All the information in the file makes up the file, or as some people refer to it, the database. As described above, there really is no key associated with this file. A

```
                    PRICE FILE
    PART_NO         UNIT          PRICE_EA    PRICE_10    PRICE_100
     6HD            1000            22.34      182.30      1595.00
     8LT            1000            22.34      162.70      1256.00
     8LTS            100             3.56       33.50       295.00
     6BT             100             4.35       41.30       386.00
    10WA            1000            18.45      174.50      1663.00
     6RN            1000            22.34      162.70      1200.00
    ES-28              1            89.50      695.00      5950.00


                    INVENTORY FILE
    PART_NO     QTY_INSTK    ORDER_QTY     ORDER_LVL    LOCATION
     6HD          63000        50000         10000       WHSE1
     8LT          56000        50000         15000       WHSE2
     8LTS          3000         5000          4000       BIN37
     6BT           5000         5000          4000       WHSE4
    10WA           6000        20000         10000       WHSE2
     6RN          12000        10000          5000       WHSE3
    ES-28            78           50            25       STORE
```

Fig. 10-1. Sample price and inventory files.

likely key would be name; however, if you are interested in location, state, or zip codes, any of these might be keys instead.

Records

A database file is made up of records. Each record would be a line in the table. In the customer file, each record consists of a name, several address fields, and the phone number. There are three records in this file: one each for Joe Smith, Bill Jones and Mark Ames.

Fields

Each field is a column in the table and has its own title. The customer file has the following fields: NAME, STREET, CITY, ST, ZIP, and PHONE. These fields are defined when the database is created. Whenever you wish to use this data you must call each field by its name. Later, if you want to print the information, you could change the column header from NAME to PERSON'S NAME or anything else you want. The field names exist only to help you use the data in the program.

```
                       CUSTOMER FILE
    NAME            STREET            CITY      ST     ZIP      PHONE
    Joe Smith    23 Daring Lane    Enfield     CT    06268    5552345
    Bill Jones   156 East St       Windsor     CT    06234    5551645
    Mark Ames    10 South Rd       Branford    CT    05455    5553774
```

Fig. 10-2. An example of a file.

DATABASE STRUCTURES

The *database structure* is the dictionary to your data. You will sometimes hear the database structure referred to as the *data dictionary*. The database structure is made up of several elements including the database name, the name of each field, the maximum size each of field, and the field type.

Database Names

The database name should be something meaningful. Actually all names you use in a computer system should be meaningful. Remember, some day someone else may have this program. Even though you have two lovely children named Sue and Bobby, these names are inappropriate in your computer system. Choose names that will indicate what the database contains. In dBASE III there are four rules for creating the database name:

1. A maximum of eight characters may be used.
2. The first character must be a letter.
3. The other nine characters may be letters, numbers, or underscores.
4. No "blanks" allowed in the name.

Good database names include: CUSTOMER for a customer file, INVNTORY for an inventory file, and SALE_OCT for an October sales file. Examples of illegal names are 1957SALE (the name must start with a letter), CUSTOMERS (the name is too long), and CAR PART (no blanks are allowed).

By properly naming your files, you will be able to easily recognize and use your databases—and so will everybody else!

Field Names

Records do not have names. They can be identified by their record number; each record is assigned a number by dBASE III. Usually this number reflects the sequence of creation. The first record entered is record 1, the next record 2, and so on. When the records are sorted they will have different numbers—but more about that later.

Each field has a field name. It is this name that you use to search, sort, report, change, or do anything to the database. Each file name in a file must be unique; that is, no two can be the same. You can use the same name in different files; when two files share a common key, the same field name should be used.

As with database names, each field name should be meaningful. Use NAME to represent a person's name, and ZIP_CODE for the zip code. Remember, these names will be used extensively in your program so they should be easily recognizable, and if possible, short. When a short field name is used in calculations or expressions, they won't go on forever.

Field names have rules just like database names:

1. A maximum of ten characters may be used.
2. The first character must be a letter.
3. The other nine characters may be letters, numbers, or underscores
4. No "blanks" are allowed in the name.

Examples of good names include CUSTOMER, QTY, CITY_ST. Unacceptable names include CUSTOMER NAME (more than ten characters), CITY ST (no blanks allowed), or 52_WKS (must start with a letter).

Fields

Field names allow us to identify a column of data, such as NAME or ZIP_CODE, but what is actually in those columns? Why the data, of course. Each data item is called a field, or variable. This is because the NAME in record 3 may be changed at any time. Its value can vary. The program will never change the value unless you tell it to.

You will find there are many ways to change a field. You can directly input data into the field; you can edit a value already there—an assignment statement can be used to change it. No matter what, you always have control over the contents of a field.

Field Types

There are five types of fields:

1. Character
2. Date
3. Logical
4. Memo
5. Numeric

Character fields are fields that will not be used in mathematical expressions. Character fields may contain any value—letters, numbers, special characters, anything! Don't forget that values of all numbers, such as zip codes and social security numbers, should also be character fields because they will never be used in calculations.

Data fields are special fields used for date calculations. They are in the form of mm /dd /yy (month,day,year). Date fields are always eight characters long which includes the separating slashes.

Logical fields are data items that have only two possible values—true or false (T or F). They are always one position in length. A logical field is used as a "check-list" type of variable. A field name of VETERAN may be a logical field. If the person is a veteran the field is set to T; if not, it is set to F.

Memo fields are variable width fields. They vary from 10 to 4000 characters long. They are used to hold large amounts of text that is to be stored in a record.

Numeric fields are just that—they contain numbers. The numbers may include decimal points

and even negative signs on the left side. These are values that might be used in calculations. Amounts of any kind are numbers.

Field Rules

As with field names the fields themselves have a few rules to follow:

CHARACTER	maximum length of 254 characters
DATE	always 8 characters in the form mm /dd /yy
LOGICAL	maximum length of 1 (T or F)
MEMO	varible length up to 4000 characters
NUMERIC	maximum length of 19 digits

In the next chapter, you will learn how dBASE III allows you to create your "data dictionary." There are a few things to remember first.

1. Every database has a name of 8 or less characters.
2. Fields are the columns of your database. Each field has a name of 10 characters or less. Each field has a type and a length.
3. Together, the fields make up the rows, which are the records.
4. Make your names mean something!

Chapter 11

Creating and Using the Database Structure

The first thing you will do after your program design is completed is to begin the database design. Your database should have all the fields needed for your program. Output fields are of no concern at this point; you have already used the output fields to determine the input fields. These input fields are the only fields that belong on your database. Any fields that can be calculated should not be on the database; they can be calculated at any time.

DESIGNING THE DATABASE

When you are creating a database, keep these limits in mind:

1. Databases can have a maximum of 128 fields.
2. The total length of a record cannot exceed 4000 characters.
3. Databases can have an unlimited number of records, up to the physical size of the floppy disk or hard disk.

Let's take our small businessman Fred. The first task that Fred has decided to computerize is his customer file. So far you know that Fred has decided to include the customer's name, address, and phone number. Should his database look like this?

Fieldname	Type	Length
NAME	CHAR	20
ADDRESS	CHAR	29
PHONE	CHAR	10

Total		59

No, of course not! If you had defined your database this way, it would be very difficult to ask questions of it and to group common types of customers. Rather, let's divide up the database into a format that is easier to *query;* that is, get answers from:

Fieldname	Type	Length
LAST_NAME	CHAR	10
FIRST_NAME	CHAR	10
STREET	CHAR	12
CITY	CHAR	10
STATE	CHAR	2
ZIP_CODE	CHAR	5
AREA_CODE	CHAR	3
NUMBER	CHAR	7

Total		59

You can see that the size of the total database has not changed, but it is now easier to use if you wish to see a list of all customers in Connecticut or Massachusetts. This method of breaking each field into the smallest part is important in database design. Note that there is a field called STREET. You could have divided it into STREET#, STREETNAME, and STREETTYPE, but this would not have made any sense. You would never care how many people lived on lanes as opposed to streets and roads. You would never ask to see customers who lived at addresses whose number was 32. You might, however, ask to see a list of all customers who live on Main Street. This can be done regardless of the street number, and you will see how later in this chapter.

The next activity is to create your database. When you run dBASE III, you will see a period on the screen. This dot is where you will type in dBASE III commands. The dot or period is called a *prompt* character; it appears when dBASE III is waiting for you to enter a command. The first command you will learn to use is the CREATE command.

CREATING THE DATABASE

Once you have entered dBASE III from your operating system, you type the CREATE command. This will allow you to create your database.

```
. CREATE
     Enter the name of the new file:
```

dBASE III now asks you for the filename or database name. You must provide a name for dBASE III to store the database. The filename on your disk will be the name that you enter followed by the .DBF suffix. If you name your database CUSTOMER, you will see the dataset CUSTOMER.DBF when you list a directory of your disk. If you want your database on your default disk drive you would enter it as follows:

```
Enter the name of the new file: CUSTOMER
```

If you want the file on the B drive, you would enter the name with the drive specification:

```
Enter the name of the new file: B:CUSTOMER
```

Either way, this will set up the file CUSTOMER.DBF on the drive that was specified or on the default drive if no drive was specified.

After you type the filename, the screen will change to the one shown in Fig. 11-1.

dBASE III is now ready for you to describe the file. Notice there are four items to enter for each field. The first three have been mentioned (NAME, TYPE, and WIDTH). The fourth is the number of decimal places in a field that is declared as numeric. Unless you need pennies in a dollar amount or decimal places, you can ignore this item. If you need two decimal places in a field that can have amounts up to 99,999, you would want to describe the field as width of 7 and DECIMAL of 2. The WIDTH is the total width of the field including the decimals.

You are now ready to enter your fields. Enter each field's name, type, width, and optionally, decimal places. Enter the field descriptions using your machine's cursor keys to move between fields. Use commas between items. You can change fields you have already defined by using the cursor keys to go back up or back over. You can also move between fields by pressing the ENTER key.

Press the ENTER key after completing the field description. You may then enter the description for the next field. Figure 11-2 shows a valid entry for the customer record:

If you need help remembering which keys to press to change entries or add or delete fields, press the F1 function key. This will change the display as shown in Fig. 11-3. To turn off the display, press F1 again.

After entering the eight fields and pressing the enter key after each one, the information above should be on your screen. When dBASE III displays the line for the ninth entry, you just press the enter key to tell dBASE III you are done. dBASE III gives you the opportunity to enter data right away if you want. You can type N at this time and enter your data later.

USING THE DATABASE STRUCTURE

Once you have created the database, you can begin to use it. The first command you need is the command to OPEN the database. Opening the

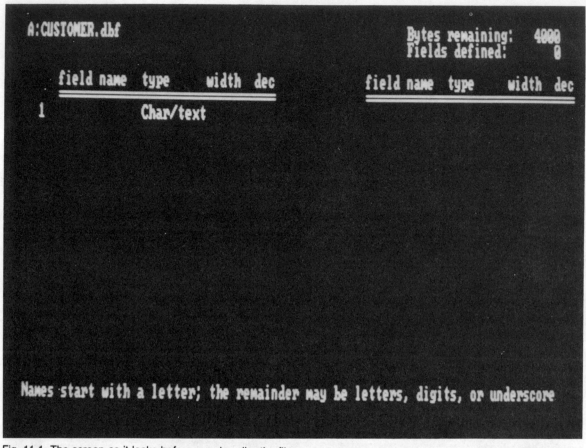

```
       field name  type    width dec         field name   type     width dec
    1               Char/text



















Names start with a letter; the remainder may be letters, digits, or underscore
```

Fig. 11-1. The screen as it looks before you describe the file.

database means choosing the database you wish to use. When you have many databases this will become more important than when you only have one.

To use the database, you must enter the appropriate dBASE III command. This command is USE. Below you see an example of this command:

. USE CUSTOMER

dBASE III knows to go to the default disk drive and open the file called CUSTOMER.DBF. In opening the database, dBASE III checks to make sure the file exists and then positions a pointer at the first record. You can always return to the top of a database with the USE command.

If the database is not on the default drive, that is, if your system is displaying the A > prompt but the database is on the B drive, you would open the database like this:

. USE B:CUSTOMER

The extension of DBF is used only by DOS. dBASE III knows that a file that is to be USEd must be a database file. Later, you will learn of other file extensions that dBASE III uses.

When you are done with the database you should close it. This will free memory and allow you to access other databases. In dBASE III, you don't have to CLOSE your database, but it is a good idea. dBASE III performs some of its updating only at the time the file is closed. If an error occurs while a file is open there can be problems.

To close a database, simply type USE by itself. dBASE III remembers the database in the original USE and closes it for you, for example

. USE

VIEWING THE DATABASE STRUCTURE

Now that you have learned how to USE a database, let's look at the one you've created. You can see it on your screen with a very simple command, DISPLAY STRUCTURE. Figure 11-4 shows the display.

As you can see, the database structure is displayed for you. In addition to the structure, the number of records that are in the file and the last update are displayed. The date is taken from DOS.

CHANGING THE DATABASE

Up to this point, you have seen how to create a database and open it for use. You have not yet learned how to put data into it nor how to use this data. First, a very important subject is the problem of changing the database once it is defined. For now, assume there is no data in the database. Later you will learn how to change a full database without losing any of the records already in it.

So far, you have only created the database structure, the data dictionary if you will. Now you will see how to make a small change to it.

Fred decides that the street address is not enough. Some of his customers have internal mail addresses; some have post office boxes; others have apartment numbers or other secondary addresses. Fred realizes he needs a second address

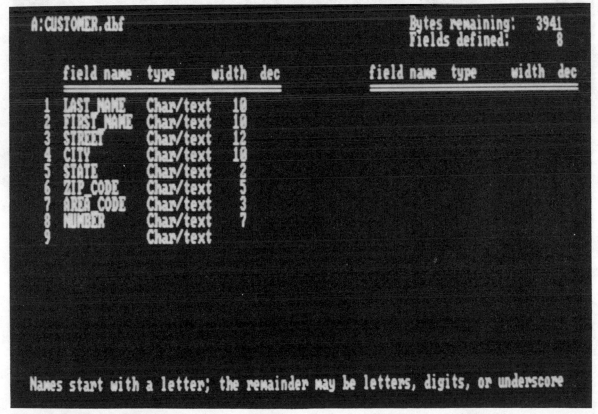

Fig. 11-2. The screen after the fields have been entered.

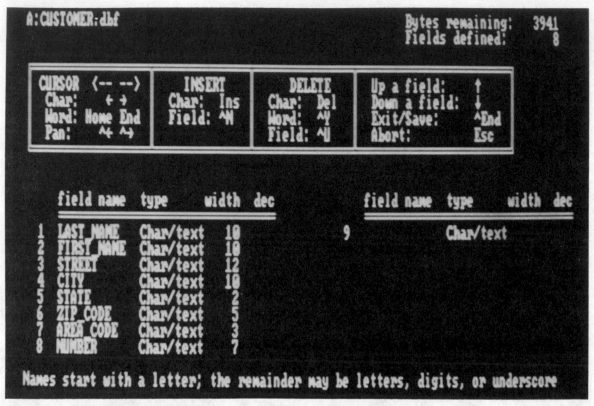

Fig. 11-4. The results of pressing the f1 key.

```
. DISPLAY STRUCTURE
Structure for database : a:CUSTOMER
Number of data records :        0
Date of last update    : 08/13/84
Field  Field name     Type       Width    Dec
    1  LAST_NAME      Character     10
    2  FIRST_NAME     Character     10
    3  STREET         Character     12
    4  CITY           Character     10
    5  STATE          Character      2
    6  ZIP_CODE       Character      5
    7  AREA_CODE      Character      3
    8  NUMBER         Character      7
** Total **                        60
```

Fig. 11-4. The database structure.

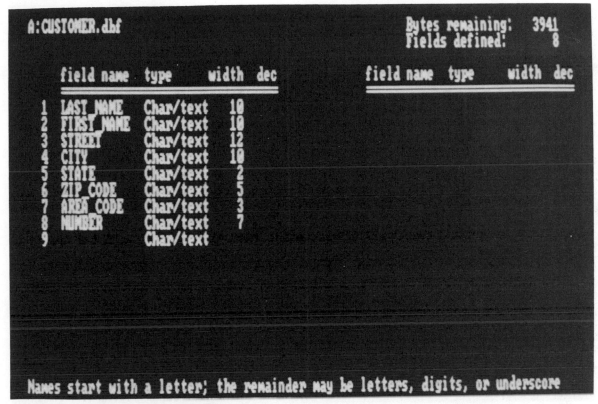

```
A:CUSTOMER.dbf                                   Bytes remaining:   3941
                                                 Fields defined:       8

        field name   type      width  dec        field name   type      width  dec
        =================================        =================================
      1 LAST_NAME    Char/text     10
      2 FIRST_NAME   Char/text     10
      3 STREET       Char/text     12
      4 CITY         Char/text     10
      5 STATE        Char/text      2
      6 ZIP_CODE     Char/text      5
      7 AREA_CODE    Char/text      3
      8 NUMBER       Char/text      7
      9              Char/text




 Names start with a letter; the remainder may be letters, digits, or underscore
```

Fig. 11-5. Changing the database structure.

field. He will use the MODIFY STRUCTURE command to add the field. The screen will look like this:

. USE CUSTOMER
. MODIFY STRUCTURE

Figure 11-5 shows the screen you would get. The first nine fields are listed including the field name, type, length, and number of decimal places. You now have the opportunity to change any existing field, add or insert a field, or delete a field. Adding or deleting fields require a special series of keys. These are known as *control keys*. On some computers there is a control key marked CTRL or CONTROL; on other computers the control symbol is above the 6 and looks like this: ^ . The most common control sequences are:

```
CTRL-N Insert Field above cursor
CTRL-T Delete Field at cursor
```

```
CTRL-W Save changes and exit
CTRL-Q Quit without saving
```

The cursor can be moved normally around the display. Fred moves the cursor to FIELD 05 and types CTRL-N. Instantly the screen changes to prepare for the insertion of a new field as shown in Fig. 11-6.

Fred puts in the description of his new field and types CTRL-W. This will save his additions. He now uses the DISPLAY STRUCTURE command to review the change. The result is shown in Fig. 11-7.

Notice that the total reflects the change to the apartment number. There is no limit to the number database structure. Fred now has enough room to put both the street address and a post office box or of changes that can be made to a database structure, as long as the total number of fields is 128 or less and the total record length is 4000 characters or less.

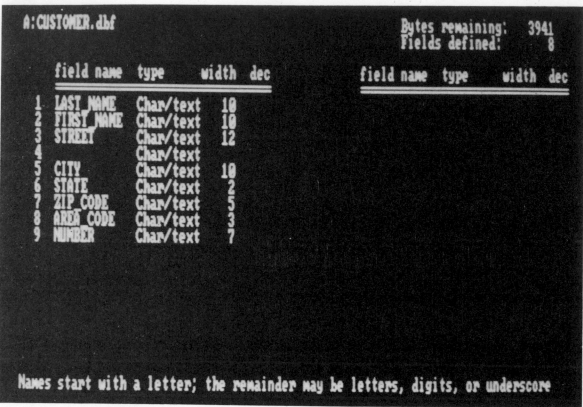

Fig. 11-6. Inserting a new field.

```
.  USE CUSTOMER
.  DISPLAY STRUCTURE

Structure for database : a:CUSTOMER
Number of data records :        0
Date of last update    : 08/13/84
Field   Field name    Type        Width      Dec
    1    LAST_NAME     Character      10
    2    FIRST_NAME    Character      10
    3    STREET        Character      12
    4    POBOX_APT     Character       7
    5    CITY          Character      10
    6    STATE         Character       2
    7    ZIP_CODE      Character       5
    8    AREA_CODE     Character       3
    9    NUMBER        Character       7
** Total **                          67
```

Fig. 11-7. The updated database.

Chapter 12

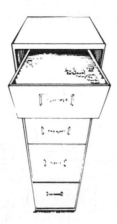

Database Records

Once the database structure has been created, you can begin to input records. When you first create the database structure, dBASE III asks you if you wanted to begin to input records immediately. If you had replied Y to that question, the screen shown in Fig. 12-1 would have appeared.

ADDING RECORDS

dBASE III automatically generates a form for you. You can fill in the form just like you would fill in any other form. You can now begin to input your data. As you press the enter key, the cursor will skip to the next field. After you enter the last field (NUMBER) and press the enter key, the record counter will be incremented by 1 and a new blank form will be displayed if you are in the add (AP-PEND) mode. To quit entering records, you would simply enter a blank record. This would return you to the "." prompt. You can enter as many records as you wish.

Entering character data is the easiest. Whatever you place in a field will be its value. Numeric fields work a little differently. As you enter the value, the number appears in the exact spaces that you type it into. When you press enter key, however, dBASE III will *right justify* the number. The number simply shifts to the right side of the bucket; whatever you typed is still there, just shifted over a little so that the rightmost figure is in the rightmost position.

This procedure takes care of entering data when you create the database, but how do you add data at other times? To add data at other times you use the APPEND command. The APPEND command allows you to enter data to the end of an existing database whenever you want. The append screen is shown in Fig. 12-2.

The procedure for entering data is the same whether you enter it after creating the database or use the APPEND command. If there are already records in the database, dBASE III will position the record pointer to the last record on the file, and the new records will be placed after the existing ones. dBASE III takes care of adding the records regard-

```
Record No.        1

LAST_NAME    :_            :
FIRST_NAME   :            :
STREET       :                :
POBOX_APT    :        :
CITY         :            :
STATE        :  :
ZIP_CODE     :      :
AREA_CODE    :    :
NUMBER       :          :
```

Fig. 12-1. The blank additions screen.

Fig. 12-2. The additions screen with APPEND.

```
. USE CUSTOMER
. APPEND

Record No.          1

LAST_NAME    :_            :
FIRST_NAME   :          :
STREET       :                :
POBOX_APT    :          :
CITY         :          :
STATE        :  :
ZIP_CODE     :      :
AREA_CODE    :    :
NUMBER       :        :
```

```
Record No.        1

LAST_NAME    :SMITH      :
FIRST_NAME   :JOHN       :
STREET       :PILGRIM WAY :
POBOX_APT    :          :
CITY         :PLYMOUTH   :
STATE        :MA:
ZIP_CODE     :05634:
AREA_CODE    :617:
NUMBER       :3442654:
```

Fig. 12-3. Entering the first record.

```
Record No.          2

LAST_NAME    : _            :
FIRST_NAME   :              :
STREET       :                   :
POBOX_APT    :            :
CITY         :              :
STATE        :    :
ZIP_CODE     :         :
AREA_CODE    :    :
NUMBER       :            :
```

Fig. 12-4. The screen display for Record #2.

less of the number of records in the database.

Figure 12-3 shows a sample record that has been added to the file.

After the first record has been entered, the screen will change to look like the one shown in Fig. 12-4. The first record has been added, and the second record is ready to be entered.

Assume that 15 records are now in the database. These records will be used to demonstrate some of the capabilities of the dBASE III database manager.

DISPLAYING RECORDS

There are many ways to display records. The easiest is to ask dBASE III to list all records. There are two ways to do this. The LIST command tells dBASE III to list all the records in the database. If you have a lot of records, you'd better be quick because dBASE III will roll them right off the screen. A better way to display the records is with the DISPLAY command. This command by itself will display only the record that the record pointer is currently pointing to. Let's use the DISPLAY ALL OFF option to list the records in the database. The OFF option will suppress the display of the record numbers. The ALL option will cause all the records to be displayed. Figure 12-5 shows the resulting display. For the purpose of simplicity, the

```
     . USE CUSTOMER
     . DISPLAY ALL OFF
SMITH      JOHN      PILGRIM WAY           PLYMOUTH    MA 05634 617 3442654
JONES      BILL      15 SAMOAN DR APT # 7  WESTVILLE   CT 04663 203 4662837
WILLIAMS   DANNY     17 ALOHA DR.          HONOLULU    HA 67355 808 1257688
SMITH      ROBERT    15 APPIAN DR BOX 7    TRENTON     NJ 16645 207 5663343
ROBERTS    PHIL      GEORGIA LANE          HARTFORD    CT 06105 203 4662777
CHARLES    LARRY     45 DOG LANE           HARTFORD    CT 06105 203 2663885
CLARK      SEYMOUR   26 WHITE LN.          E.HARTFORD  CT 06034 203 7546663
SMITH      KIRK      27 INN AVE.           SPRINGS     MA 16646 413 2774883
YOUNG      SUE       27 VISTA DR. APT #7   WESTVIEW    MA 16646 413 3664828
JOHNSON    GEORGE    3445 OHIO LA          DETROIT     MI 35535 574 2553773
MITCHELL   HENRY     23 DENNIS DR          W.HARTFORD  CT 06117 203 7333232
YORK       JOHN      34 CAPE DR.           HARTFORD    CT 06334 203 3664773
BATES      MARK      CHARLES RD.           BOSTON      MA 46638 617 3552626
JAMES      GEORGE    24 PIE LANE           S. WINDOW   CT 47744 203 3665737
SHERRI     JOE       14 CUP ROAD           BUCKSVILLE  CT 46627 203 2663737
```

Fig. 12-5. Displaying Records.

```
         LAST          FIRST                           POBOX                            ZIP  AREA
         NAME          NAME             STREET          APT          CITY      STATE   CODE CODE NUMBER
         ----          -----            ------          -----        ----      -----   ---- ---- ------

         SMITH         JOHN          PILGRIM WAY                  PLYMOUTH      MA   05634 617 3442654
         JONES         BILL          15 SAMOAN DR   APT # 7       WESTVILLE     CT   04663 203 4662837
         WILLIAMS      DANNY         17 ALOHA DR.                 HONOLULU      HA   67355 808 1257688
         SMITH         ROBERT        15 APPIAN DR   BOX 7         TRENTON       NJ   16645 207 5663343
         ROBERTS       PHIL          GEORGIA LANE                 HARTFORD      CT   06105 203 4662777
         CHARLES       LARRY         45 DOG LANE                  HARTFORD      CT   06105 203 2663885
         CLARK         SEYMOUR       26 WHITE LN.                 E.HARTFORD    CT   06034 203 7546663
         SMITH         KIRK          27 INN AVE.                  SPRINGS       MA   16646 413 2774883
         YOUNG         SUE           27 VISTA DR.   APT #7        WESTVIEW      MA   16646 413 3664828
         JOHNSON       GEORGE        3445 OHIO LA                 DETROIT       MI   35535 574 2553773
         MITCHELL      HENRY         23 DENNIS DR                 W.HARTFORD    CT   06117 203 7333232
         YORK          JOHN          34 CAPE DR.                  HARTFORD      CT   06334 203 3664773
         BATES         MARK          CHARLES RD.                  BOSTON        MA   46638 617 3552626
         JAMES         GEORGE        24 PIE LANE                  S. WINDOW     CT   47744 203 3665737
         SHERRI        JOE           14 CUP ROAD                  BUCKSVILLE    CT   46627 203 2663737
```

Fig. 12-6. The main database.

field names are displayed.

As you can see, all the records have been displayed as they were entered, records to 15. Later you will see how to sort these records by any of the fields. Now you will see some of the power of the display command. You can use the DISPLAY command to selectively display certain records, and at the same time, display only certain columns.

The complete database is shown in Fig. 12-6. Using other options of the DISPLAY command you can change the looks of the display. First, Fig. 12-7 shows only those customers with addresses in the state of CT.

The phrase FOR STATE = "CT" means to choose records that contain "CT" in the state field.

Why is "CT" enclosed in quotation marks? This is to identify it as a literal value. "CT" is the value of STATE in the records to be displayed. If you wished to compare the variable STATE to a variable named CT the quotation marks would not be used with CT. When referring to a character value (also known as a *character literal*), you should enclose the value in quotation marks. Numbers do not have to be enclosed in quotation marks because variable names cannot begin with a number. With character fields, the quotation marks are the only way to tell the difference between a variable or field name and a character literal.

Figure 12-8 shows the display of only the names and phone numbers from all the records.

```
      . DISPLAY ALL OFF FOR STATE = 'CT'

      JONES     BILL      15 SAMOAN DR APT # 7 WESTVILLE    CT   04663 203 4662837
      ROBERTS   PHIL      GEORGIA LANE          HARTFORD    CT   06105 203 4662777
      CHARLES   LARRY     45 DOG LANE           HARTFORD    CT   06105 203 2663885
      CLARK     SEYMOUR   26 WHITE LN.          E.HARTFORD  CT   06034 203 7546663
      MITCHELL  HENRY     23 DENNIS DR          W.HARTFORD  CT   06117 203 7333232
      YORK      JOHN      34 CAPE DR.           HARTFORD    CT   06334 203 3664773
      JAMES     GEORGE    24 PIE LANE           S. WINDOW   CT   47744 203 3665737
      SHERRI    JOE       14 CUP ROAD           BUCKSVILLE  CT   46627 203 2663737
```

Fig. 12-7. The Connecticut records only.

```
. DISPLAY ALL OFF FIRST_NAME,LAST_NAME,AREA_CODE,NUMBER

    JOHN      SMITH      617 3442654
    BILL      JONES      203 4662837
    DANNY     WILLIAMS   808 1257688
    ROBERT    SMITH      207 5663343
    PHIL      ROBERTS    203 4662777
    LARRY     CHARLES    203 2663885
    SEYMOUR   CLARK      203 7546663
    KIRK      SMITH      413 2774883
    SUE       YOUNG      413 3664828
    GEORGE    JOHNSON    574 2553773
    HENRY     MITCHELL   203 7333232
    JOHN      YORK       203 3664773
    MARK      BATES      617 3552626
    GEORGE    JAMES      203 3665737
    JOE       SHERRI     203 2663737
```

Fig. 12-8. Limiting the scope of the display.

Notice that you are able to show only four of the fields by listing the names of the fields you want. Simply type the field names separated by commas to suppress the listing of all the fields. Also, you will notice that the fields are listed in the order you have specified.

Figure 12-9 shows how you can combine the two DISPLAY commands to list only those records that are from the state of CT. Notice that you are able to display the Connecticut records without showing the state in the display.

Let's learn one more way of selecting records using the DISPLAY command along with the string command. The $ is a special symbol to dBASE III. It is used to search for partial matches. Let's assume that Fred wants to see his customers who live in any city that contains the word HARTFORD. Fred would type the command like this:

```
. DISPLAY ALL OFF FOR STATE = 'CT' FIRST_NAME,
  LAST_NAME,AREA_CODE,NUMBER

    BILL      JONES     203 4662837
    PHIL      ROBERTS   203 4662777
    LARRY     CHARLES   203 2663885
    SEYMOUR   CLARK     203 7546663
    HENRY     MITCHELL  203 7333232
    JOHN      YORK      203 3664773
    GEORGE    JAMES     203 3665737
    JOE       SHERRI    203 2663737
```

Fig. 12-9. Limiting the search and the scope.

```
. DISPLAY ALL OFF FOR 'HARTFORD'$CITY

ROBERTS     PHIL        GEORGIA LANE      HARTFORD    CT 06105 203 466277
CHARLES     LARRY       45 DOG LANE       HARTFORD    CT 06105 203 266388
CLARK       SEYMOUR     26 WHITE LN.      E.HARTFORD  CT 06034 203 754666
MITCHELL    HENRY       23 DENNIS DR      W.HARTFORD  CT 06117 203 733323
YORK        JOHN        34 CAPE DR.       HARTFORD    CT 06334 203 366477
```

Fig. 12-10. Searching for a field.

DISPLAY ALL OFF
FOR "HARTFORD" $CITY

The resulting display is shown in Fig. 12-10.

This form of DISPLAY command allowed Fred to display all the records in the database whose city field included the word HARTFORD.

The DISPLAY command is extremely important for ad-hoc reports. In later chapters you will learn how to save these reports with the REPORT command and how to add titles, column headers, totals, and subtotals (for your numeric fields). You will also learn some other commands for quick reporting, and learn how to use all these commands in *compound phrases*. A compound phrase provides ways of asking compound questions; for example, you could use a compound phrase if you want to see the names of people from Connecticut only if they live in Hartford. Compound phrases can produce very specific extractions from the database.

CHANGING RECORDS

After adding records, you might discover a mistake has been made. This is when the correction of records is necessary. To change a record you use the EDIT command. This command identifies the record by its record number. If you notice a record that has to be changed, you must find out its record number; then you may change the record as shown in Fig. 12-11.

After changing the record, move the cursor to the last field and press the ENTER key. The display will change to show RECORD 7. If you want to edit more records, you can continue until the end of the file, or you can end the process by hitting the "ESC" key.

```
. EDIT 6

RECORD # 6
LAST_NAME    :CHARLES    :
FIRST_NAME   :LARRY      :
STREET       :45 DOG LANE :
POBOX_APT    :           :
CITY         :HARTFORD   :
STATE        :CT:
ZIP_CODE     :06105:
AREA CODE    :203:
NUMBER       :2663885:
```

Fig. 12-11. Editing a record.

```
                DISPLAY ALL OFF
  SMITH      JOHN       PILGRIM WAY              PLYMOUTH    MA 05634 617 3442654
 *JONES      BILL       15 SAMOAN DR APT # 7     WESTVILLE   CT 04663 203 4662837
 *WILLIAMS   DANNY      17 ALOHA DR.             HONOLULU    HA 67355 808 1257688
  SMITH      ROBERT     15 APPIAN DR BOX 7       TRENTON     NJ 16645 207 5663343
 *ROBERTS    PHIL       GEORGIA LANE             HARTFORD    CT 06105 203 4662777
 *CHARLES    LARRY      45 DOG LANE              HARTFORD    CT 06105 203 2663885
 *CLARK      SEYMOUR    26 WHITE LN.             E.HARTFORD  CT 06034 203 7546663
  SMITH      KIRK       27 INN AVE.              SPRINGS     MA 16646 413 2774883
  YOUNG      SUE        27 VISTA DR. APT #7      WESTVIEW    MA 16646 413 3664828
  JOHNSON    GEORGE     3445 OHIO LA             DETROIT     MI 35535 574 2553773
 *MITCHELL   HENRY      23 DENNIS DR             W.HARTFORD  CT 06117 203 7333232
 *YORK       JOHN       34 CAPE DR.              HARTFORD    CT 06334 203 3664773
  BATES      MARK       CHARLES RD.              BOSTON      MA 46638 617 3552626
 *JAMES      GEORGE     24 PIE LANE              S. WINDOW   CT 47744 203 3665737
 *SHERRI     JOE        14 CUP ROAD              BUCKSVILLE  CT 46627 203 2663737
```

Fig. 12-12. Showing deleted records.

DELETING RECORDS

In most computer systems, deleting records is a slow and arduous process, because as records are deleted, the file must somehow regain the use of the recovered space. In dBASE III, deleting records is a two-step process. First, you will use the DELETE command. This is very similar to the DISPLAY command; if you type the DELETE command, it will delete the record the pointer is currently pointing to. Giving the command DELETE FOR STATE = "MA" will delete only the first occurrence of a record with the state of MA. The most effective form is DELETE ALL FOR . . . .. This command will delete all the records for the given condition. For example, you may type

```
DELETE FOR AREA_CODE = '808'
    1 record deleted
```

and

```
DELETE FOR STATE = 'CT'
    8 records deleted
```

Figure 12-12 shows how the sample database will look after you have entered these two commands.

You will notice that all the records are there, but how can that be? You just deleted 9 of them! Notice the * in front of some records. The * indicates the records that are marked for deletion. Remember, this is a two-step process. The records won't physically disappear until the PACK command is issued. This command copies the file over without the deleted records. It takes a fair amount of time and should be done only after all deletions are completed. Do all your deletions first; then use PACK once! If you decide against deleting all the records marked with asterisks, you can issue the RECALL command. Let's bring back the records from Connecticut before packing the file:

```
. RECALL ALL FOR STATE = 'CT'
     8 records recalled
. PACK
    14 records copied
```

Now, all of the unmarked records are copied. Notice that only 14 records were kept. The customer from Hawaii is gone. This is how dBASE III takes care of freeing up the space that was used by the now deleted records in the file. The use of the PACK command actually causes the unmarked records to be copied to a new file. The old file is then deleted, and the new file renamed.

Chapter 13

Sorting the Database

Most of the time you will want the records in your database in a certain order. You may want to see your customers in alphabetical order by last name; maybe you may want them listed according to the state they live in. There are even times you might want a list of your customers starting with the customer who owes the most money and ending with the one who owes the least money. No matter what order you wish to see the records in the database, some type of arrangement will be necessary.

A NEW ORDER

The most common way to rearrange data in a file is to sort the data. This, however, means physically moving the records each time you want to change the way you see the data. This takes a great deal of computer time. To sort one thousand records using dBASE III will take several minutes or more. This is unacceptable to most people. Unless you have very small databases that do not have too many fields, sorting the database takes too long.

There is also the problem caused by the need for multiple sorts. If you need to see your data in many different orders you will constantly be sorting your files.

There is a solution to the sorting dilemma. *Indexing* is a method that utilizes a separate list of pointers. This list contains the order of the records in the database based upon the sort criteria you have specified. A database can be indexed far more quicker than it can be sorted. This is because indexing a database means assigning values to a list of pointers, while sorting means physically rearranging the data. Updating indexes is also very quick as no physical rearrangement of the data is necessary.

To illustrate the concept of pointers, let's assume that you have the following data:

NAME	TEST SCORE
WILLIAM	85
SAMUEL	57
FRED	63
GEORGE	98
ADAM	91
JOHN	89
ZACHARY	76
CORY	34

You can see that there is no special order to this sample file. A database can be sorted in ascending or descending order. If a database is sorted by an ascending key, the record with the lowest value in the field is the first record, and the record with the highest value in the key field is the last record. In a descending sort, the highest values come first. Character values are sorted from Z to A, and numbers from the largest positive value to the largest negative value; the opposite is true for an ascending sort.

Let's look at the data as if it had been sorted by name in ascending order. The data would be physically rearranged and would now look like this:

NAME	TEST SCORE
ADAM	91
CORY	34
FRED	63
GEORGE	98
JOHN	89
SAMUEL	57
WILLIAM	85
ZACHARY	76

Sorting it by descending score yields:

NAME	TEST SCORE
GEORGE	98
ADAM	91
JOHN	89
WILLIAM	85

NAME	TEST SCORE
ZACHARY	76
FRED	63
SAMUEL	57
CORY	34

Notice that in these two examples, the data itself was physically rearranged. Figure 13-1 shows a conceptual model of the same two sorts done with indexes.

As you can see there is a separate field (actually a separate field with the extension .NDX) that contains the order of each record for the sort desired. In this case there are two separate index files.

For a final analogy describing the index pointers, imagine what you would do when you want to see a product that you know is in a software catalog, but you cannot remember the product name. The product you are searching for is indexed in several ways in the back of the catalog. Usually these indexes are in order by the product type, manufacturer, and by the product name itself. There are three separate indexes all pointing to the same page in the catalog.

SORTING THE DATABASE

The database above consisted of two fields; NAME and SCORE. If you wish to SORT the database by name, you would issue the SORT command. Assume that the database name is TESTS:

NAME	TEST SCORE	ASCENDING NAME INDEX	DESCENDING TEST SCORE INDEX
WILLIAM	85	7	4
SAMUEL	57	6	7
FRED	63	3	6
GEORGE	98	4	1
ADAM	91	1	2
JOHN	89	5	3
ZACHARY	76	8	5
CORY	34	2	8

Fig. 13-1. The database with index pointers.

```
. USE TESTS
. SORT ON NAME TO TESTSORT
   100% Sorted          15 Records sorted
. USE TESTSORT
```

Now there is a sorted copy of the database known as TESTSORT. The original database known as TESTS still exists in its original form. It is advisable to not sort your database into itself as you will lose your data if an error occurs while copying and rearranging the database. Since SORTing is a special form of copying, the original data is always safe.

To sort the database by descending test score you would enter the following:

```
. USE TESTS
. SORT ON TEST TO TESTSOR2/D
   100% Sorted          15 Records sorted
. USE TESTSOR2
```

The problem of multiple keys has not yet been addressed. Using the customer file for example, how would you sort the file if you later wanted to report by STATE, and within the report for each state, you wished to see the people sorted by name. This would allow you to group the people from Connecticut, then those from Massachusetts, and so on. Within Connecticut you wish to find individual people in alphabetical order.

```
. USE CUSTOMER
. SORT ON STATE,LAST_NAME TO CUSTSORT
   100% Sorted          15 Records sorted
```

The data is first sorted by state, and then people within each state are sorted by name. The sorted database is called CUSTSORT and must be referenced this way:

```
          . USE CUSTSORT
```

INDEXING THE DATABASE

Indexing the database is a much simpler task. Let's first look at the code to INDEX the TESTS database:

```
     . USE TESTS
     . INDEX ON NAME TO TESTSRT1
         15 records indexed
     . USE TESTS INDEX TESTSRT1
```

In order to index the database, you simply use the INDEX command. When you want to use the database with the index, you will USE it with the index file. Unlike the sort, which must be redone every time a record is added, the index is automatically updated as you add records.

Let's look at the sort that was done by descending test score, this time using an index:

```
     . USE TESTS
     . INDEX ON -TEST TO TESTSRT2
         15 records indexed
     . USE TESTS INDEX TESTSRT2
```

Here you see that, to index on a descending key, you place a "-" before the field name being indexed. This indicated to dBASE III to create the descending index. Both of the previous examples produce the same result as the SORT—only much faster.

Finally, you must learn how to do a multiple sort. You will use the CUSTOMER database and sort by STATE, and within each state the names will be sorted by LAST:NAME:

```
   . USE CUSTOMER
   . INDEX ON STATE + LAST_NAME TO CUSTSORT
       15 records indexed
   . USE CUSTOMER INDEX CUSTSORT
```

Using Indexes

You can see how much simpler it is to index a database rather than to sort it. You can have one database of records and many different indexes that you can use. The example above shows indexing with multiple keys but using only one index file. You will always USE the database file; only the index will change!

When you search for records in a nonindexed file, dBASE III will check every record sequentially until it finds a match or reaches the end of the file. If there are thousands of records to search, this may take a long while. dBASE III will read the whole file just to find a single record. Using a database that has been sorted will not improve the situation. Sorting the database only rearranges the data; it does nothing to help dBASE III locate records faster.

Indexing, on the other hand, helps dBASE III locate records quickly. The typical find time on an indexed file is only two seconds when you are using a floppy disk system. Not only are indexes a better way to sort your data, they are also necessary for speed in your system.

Chapter 14

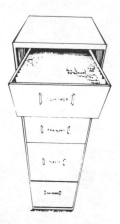

Searching the
Database—A Second Look

In this chapter you will see some advanced ways to search a database and begin to see the differences between using dBASE III as a database manager and using the dBASE III programming statements.

COMPOUND EXPRESSIONS

Compound expressions involve the use of connectors, such as AND, OR, and NOT. These allow you to ask far more specific questions than just querying the state someone lives in. With compound expressions, you can ask questions such as "Which of my customers live in apartments that are not in Connecticut or Massachusetts?" "How many customers do I have that have not made an order in two years but whose last order was over $20.00?" "Which of my largest ten customers owes the most money for more that 60 days?"

Obviously these pieces of data would have to be on the database in order for you to get a response to these types of questions, but without the compound expression, they could not be asked.

Let's discuss the first two connectors AND,

and OR. AND is a connector that allows you to evaluate several comparisons and make a positive decision only if all the comparisons are true. (If you are asked to compare the variable AMT_SPENT to "less than 500" and the value of AMT_SPENT is less than 500, the expression is true. If AMT_SPENT is equal to or greater than 500, the expression is false.) Using AND you may ask a question such as the following:

```
IF AMT_SPENT < 500 .AND. STATE = 'CT'
    THEN PRINT THE CUSTOMER
```

This pseudocode representation illustrates the use of AND. Only if the customer has both spent less than 500 and been a resident of Connecticut will his name be printed. Merely living in Connecticut is not enough, the customer must also have spent less than 500.

The connector OR allows you to evaluate several expressions and take a certain course of action if any of the comparisons are true.

```
IF AMT_SPENT < 500 .OR. STATE = 'CT'
   THEN PRINT THE CUSTOMER
```

This pseudocode representation shows the use of OR. If the customer has spent less than 500 the expression is true regardless of the state he or she lives in. Likewise if he or she lives in Connecticut the expression is true regardless of the amount spent. Only if both parts of the expression are false is the expression false. For the expression in this example to be false, the person must not live in Connecticut and must have spent at least 500.

The final connector, NOT is always used only in conjunction with the expression itself. It does not allow two expressions to be combined. NOT causes the opposite of the expression to be true. For example

```
IF AMT_SPENT .NOT. < 500
   THEN PRINT THE CUSTOMER
```

is the same as:

```
IF AMT_SPENT >= 500
   THEN PRINT THE CUSTOMER
```

You might notice that there are periods surrounding the AND, OR, and NOT connectors. This is the real syntax that dBASE III uses. This allows dBASE III to recognize these three words as connectors rather than as variable names.

DISPLAYING SELECTED RECORDS

Assume the database shown in Fig. 14-1. Let's take a look at several examples of DISPLAY command using compound expressions.

```
. DISPLAY ALL OFF FOR STATE = 'CT'
   .AND. BUY_THISYR = 'Y'
```

. You have asked for dBASE III to display all records for customers in Connecticut who have bought from you this year. Figure 14-2 uses italic type to indicate the records that were selected and dieplayed.

```
. DISPLAY ALL OFF FOR STATE = 'CT'
   .OR.  BUY_THISYR = 'Y'
```

Now you have changed what you are asking for. You want to see a customer's name if he or she lives in Connecticut or if he or she has bought from you this year. It doesn't matter which of those conditions were met; even if a given customer meets both requirements, you want to see his or her name. The results are shown in Fig. 14-3.

```
DISPLAY ALL OFF FOR STATE .NOT. = 'CT' .OR.
   AMOUNT < 10000
```

Using the NOT expression, you will be able to see a customer's name if he or she has spent less than

LAST_NAME	FIRST_NAME	STATE	CUST_SINCE	BUY_THISYR	AMOUNT
SMITH	JOHN	MA	1981	Y	2356
JONES	BILL	CT	1979	Y	21533
ROBERTS	PHIL	NJ	1975	N	0
CLARK	SEYMOUR	CT	1973	Y	35689
SMITH	KIRK	MA	1975	N	0
YOUNG	SUE	MA	1971	Y	45680
JOHNSON	GEORGE	MI	1982	N	0
MITCHELL	HENRY	CT	1967	Y	8390
YORK	JOHN	CT	1969	Y	33612
JAMES	GEORGE	CT	1982	N	0

Fig. 14-1. A sample database.

```
           SMITH      JOHN        MA        1981          Y          2356
===>       JONES      BILL        CT        1979          Y         21533
           ROBERTS    PHIL        NJ        1975          N             0
===>       CLARK      SEYMOUR     CT        1973          Y         35689
           SMITH      KIRK        MA        1975          N             0
           YOUNG      SUE         MA        1971          Y         45680
           JOHNSON    GEORGE      MI        1982          N             0
===>       MITCHELL   HENRY       CT        1967          Y          8390
===>       YORK       JOHN        CT        1969          Y         33612
           JAMES      GEORGE      CT        1982          N             0
```

Fig. 14-2. Using the AND connector.

$10,000 or if he or she is not from Connecticut. Note that you want to see the names of those not residing in Connecticut no matter how much they have spent. The resulting display is shown in Fig. 14-4.

```
. DISPLAY ALL OFF FOR STATE = 'CT' .AND.
(CUST_SINCE <= 1980 .OR. AMOUNT > 1000)
```

In this example you see a *double compound* expression. Though there are three conditions, STATE ="CT" CUST_SINCE<= 1980, and AMOUNT > 1000, the expression is reduced to two conditions, because of the placement of the parentheses. The first condition is simply that the customer must live in Connecticut (STATE="CT"); the second is a complex expression itself and must be evaluated before being evaluated in conjunction with the first condition.

The second expression is true if the customer has been a customer since 1980 or before. The second expression is also true if the customer has spent $1000 or more. Finally, it is true if the customer has both been a customer since 1980 or before and has spent $1000 or more. Only if the customer meets neither condition is the second expression false.

After evaluating the simple first expression and the compound second expression, you can evaluate the expression as a whole. Since there is an AND clause between them, both sides must be true to be true.

After careful examination, you realize that only people in Connecticut who have been customers since 1980 or have spent $1,000 or more should be listed. Figure 14-5 shows the resulting display. George James is not selected.

```
===>       SMITH      JOHN        MA        1981          Y          2356
===>       JONES      BILL        CT        1979          Y         21533
           ROBERTS    PHIL        NJ        1975          N             0
===>       CLARK      SEYMOUR     CT        1973          Y         35689
           SMITH      KIRK        MA        1975          N             0
===>       YOUNG      SUE         MA        1971          Y         45680
           JOHNSON    GEORGE      MI        1982          N             0
===>       MITCHELL   HENRY       CT        1967          Y          8390
===>       YORK       JOHN        CT        1969          Y         33612
===>       JAMES      GEORGE      CT        1982          N             0
```

Fig. 14-3. Using the OR Connector.

===>	SMITH	JOHN	MA	1981	Y	2356
	JONES	BILL	CT	1979	Y	21533
===>	ROBERTS	PHIL	NJ	1975	N	0
	CLARK	SEYMOUR	CT	1973	Y	35689
===>	SMITH	KIRK	MA	1975	N	0
===>	YOUNG	SUE	MA	1971	Y	45680
===>	JOHNSON	GEORGE	MI	1982	N	0
===>	MITCHELL	HENRY	CT	1967	Y	8390
	YORK	JOHN	CT	1969	Y	33612
===>	JAMES	GEORGE	CT	1982	N	0

Fig. 14-4. Using the NOT connector.

	SMITH	JOHN	MA	1981	Y	2356
===>	JONES	BILL	CT	1979	Y	21533
	ROBERTS	PHIL	NJ	1975	N	0
===>	CLARK	SEYMOUR	CT	1973	Y	35689
	SMITH	KIRK	MA	1975	N	0
	YOUNG	SUE	MA	1971	Y	45680
	JOHNSON	GEORGE	MI	1982	N	0
===>	MITCHELL	HENRY	CT	1967	Y	8390
===>	YORK	JOHN	CT	1969	Y	33612
	JAMES	GEORGE	CT	1982	N	0

Fig. 14-5. A Double Compound Expression.

. DISPLAY ALL OFF FOR BUY:THISYR = 'Y' .OR. AMOUNT = 0

===>	SMITH	JOHN	MA	1981	Y	2356
===>	JONES	BILL	CT	1979	Y	21533
===>	ROBERTS	PHIL	NJ	1975	N	0
===>	CLARK	SEYMOUR	CT	1973	Y	35689
===>	SMITH	KIRK	MA	1975	N	0
===>	YOUNG	SUE	MA	1971	Y	45680
===>	JOHNSON	GEORGE	MI	1982	N	0
===>	MITCHELL	HENRY	CT	1967	Y	8390
===>	YORK	JOHN	CT	1969	Y	33612
===>	JAMES	GEORGE	CT	1982	N	0

Fig. 14-6. An example of conflicting search criteria.

.DISPLAY ALL OFF FOR BUY_THISYR = "Y"; .OR. AMOUNT = 0

In the final example two opposite possibilities have been used. Logically, if someone has bought this year, their amount cannot be 0. Conversely, if their amount is 0 they could not have bought this year. By using the OR clause all records are selected, as shown in Fig. 14-6.

What would happen if you change this expression to AND? That's right—none of the records would have been selected.

LOCATE

When you are using dBASE III as a database manager and are querying your data with commands such as LIST and DISPLAY, you are asking dBASE III to search for records that meet a certain criteria and then show them to you on the screen. When you are using dBASE III as a programming language you will not use those commands as they do not give you very much flexibility when displaying the records on the screen.

When programming, you will want to know where it exists on the file. If it does exist, you will want to know where it exists. Once you determine the location of a record, you can use a standard programming techniques to retrieve the record and display it any way you want.

The LOCATE command is used to help you to see if a record exists. The LOCATE command should only be used with nonindexed databases. It is used just like the DISPLAY command except all you can specify is the *search criteria* that is the characters the desired entry should contain. LOCATE will search the file beginning with the first record and continuing until it either finds the record or reaches the bottom of the file. If your file is very large, it may take a long time to go through it as every record must be read. If the desired record is on the bottom or not there at all, you will be in for a long wait.

LOCATE does not show you the record. If it finds the record, it responds by telling you the record number. If it doesn't find the record, it will tell you "END of locate scope" for example:

```
. LOCATE FOR NAME = 'SMITH'
  Record =      25
```

and

```
. LOCATE FOR NAME = 'JONES' AND STATE='MO'
  End of locate scope
```

LOCATE also allows you to continue the search without returning to the *top* of the database.

As you find a record, the record pointer moves to the record and the record number is displayed. If you issued another LOCATE command, dBase III would start again at the top of the file and only find the first occurrence of the record. The CONTINUE command allows you to keep searching:

```
. LOCATE FOR NAME = 'SMITH'
  Record =      25

. CONTINUE
  Record =     104

. CONTINUE
  Record =     684

. CONTINUE
  End of locate scope
```

In this example, records with the name of SMITH can be found in record numbers 25, 104, and 684. You can then use the location number to display those records, or in programs, you would display each record before using the CONTINUE phrase. In programming, you would have to check to see if the record information was equal to the information you were searching for after using the LOCATE or CONTINUE phrases. When End of locate scope scope is displayed, the record pointer is pointing to the bottom of the file.

FIND

The FIND command is used in the same manner as the locate command but is used with indexed databases to determine whether or not the indexed key exists. The FIND command knows what the indexed key is. You do not have to specify the field name or names that were used in the creation of the key. The FIND command will only tell you if the record was not found. You must query the record pointer variable. This is an internal variable known to dBASE III as RECNO ( ) for instance, consider:

```
FIND

. USE CUSTDATA INDEX CUST
. FIND 'SMITH'
. ? RECNO()
       25
```

and

```
.  USE CUSTDATA INDEX CUST
.  FIND 'JONES'
   No find
.  ? RECNO()
        300
```

In the first example, the first occurrence of SMITH is in record number 25. The ? RECNO ( ) command allowed you to see whether or not there was a SMITH in the database and to display the record number. The ? RECNO( ) command could have been followed by a DISPLAY command, which would have showed you record number 25, at which the record pointer is currently pointing.

In the second example, the record was not in the database. The pointer is set to the last record in the data save, and no record could be displayed.

When you used the LOCATE command you were able to see subsequent occurrences of matching records by using the CONTINUE phrase. When using the FIND command, you must program this function. Since each keyed record is sequentially connected you can use SKIP commands and check the data:

```
.  USE CUSTDATA INDEX CUST
.  FIND 'SMITH'
.  DISPLAY NAME,STATE
      SMITH   CT
.  SKIP
   Record No.    12
.  DISPLAY NAME,STATE
      SMITH   VT
```

```
.  SKIP
   Record No.    56
.  DISPLAY NAME,STATE
      SMITH   MA
.  SKIP
   Record No.    12
.  DISPLAY NAME,STATE
      STEBBINS AZ
.  SKIP
   Record no.     8
.  DISPLAY NAME,STATE
      ZEBULAH MO
.  SKIP
   End of file encountered
```

As you can see, dBASE III does not know if it has found other occurrences of SMITH. The SKIP command simply runs through the database sequentially according to the indexed key, one record per SKIP. The FIND command lets you position the pointer and then search until there is no longer a match. However, you must use programming to determine when there is no longer a match, as shown below:

```
USE INDEXED DATABASE
FIND RECORD
IF # NOT 0
   THEN
      DO WHILE SEARCHFIELD = INDEXKEY
         DISPLAY RECORD
         SKIP
      ENDDO
   ELSE
      RECORD NOT FOUND
ENDIF
```

```
.  USE CUSTOMER INDEX CUSTOMER
.  DISPLAY ALL OFF

JONES        BILL       CT     1979        Y        21533
CLARK        SEYMOUR    CT     1973        Y        35689
MITCHELL     HENRY      CT     1967        Y         8390
YORK         JOHN       CT     1969        Y        33612
JAMES        GEORGE     CT     1982        N            0
SMITH        KIRK       MA     1975        N            0
YOUNG        SUE        MA     1971        Y        45680
SMITH        JOHN       MA     1981        Y         2356
JOHNSON      GEORGE     MI     1982        N            0
ROBERTS      PHIL       NJ     1975        N            0
```

Fig. 14-7. A look at the database.

```
. USE CUSTHIST INDEX CUSTST
. CREATE REPORT
  ENTER REPORT FORM NAME: CUST1
```

Fig. 14-8. The report command.

CREATE REPORT and REPORT COMMANDs

You have already seen how to use the DIS-PLAY command to display your records. The DIS-PLAY command allows you to display some or all of your records and allows you to display some or all of your records and also allows you to display only certain fields. The REPORT command will enable you to do all that, but with a more formal display. The CREATE REPORT command also allows you to save the format so you can see the formatted report whenever you want without having to redefine the format.

The REPORT command uses the FOR phrase, as does the DISPLAY command, to choose which records will be selected for display.

Before using the REPORT command you must use the CREATE REPORT command to define the report. After you type CREATE REPORT, dBASE III asks you for the name in which to store the report definition. This will be the name you will later use to

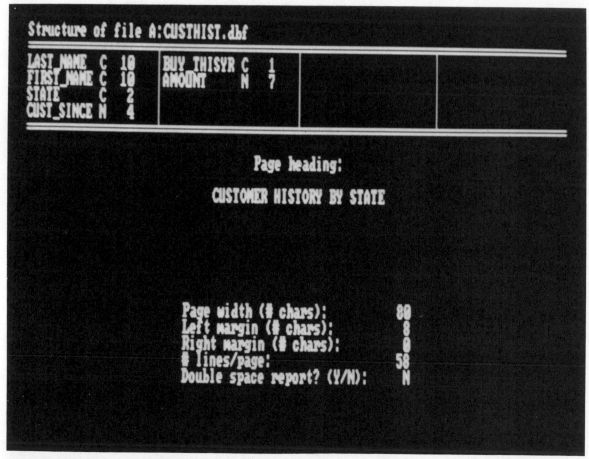

Fig. 14-9. The first screen in the preparation of the report.

print the report again and again.

Let's first "USE" and DISPLAY our database; as shown in Fig. 14-7 and 14-8.

You can see there are three screens that appear after typing the CREATE REPORT command. These questions allow you to decide how your report will look. In this case you have chosen for your report to have subtotals by state, have a title called "CUSTOMER HISTORY BY STATE", have totals which you later defined to be of amount, and to have no options, no double spacing, and no new pages after each subtotal. You also told dBASE III you did not want a summary report.

The CREATE REPORT command permits a simple interface for column headers, subtotals, and totals. It allows the freedom to move fields and records almost anywhere on a page. Customized reporting will be demonstrated later in the programming section.

The report in Fig. 14-12 was produced by filling in the three screens in Figures 14-9, 10, and 11.

REPORT

The "REPORT FORM" command will work with any database. It permits a simple interface for column headers, subtotals, and totals. It does not allow the freedom to move fields and records anywhere on a page.

If you wanted to print this report you could have used the following command:

. REPORT TO PRINT

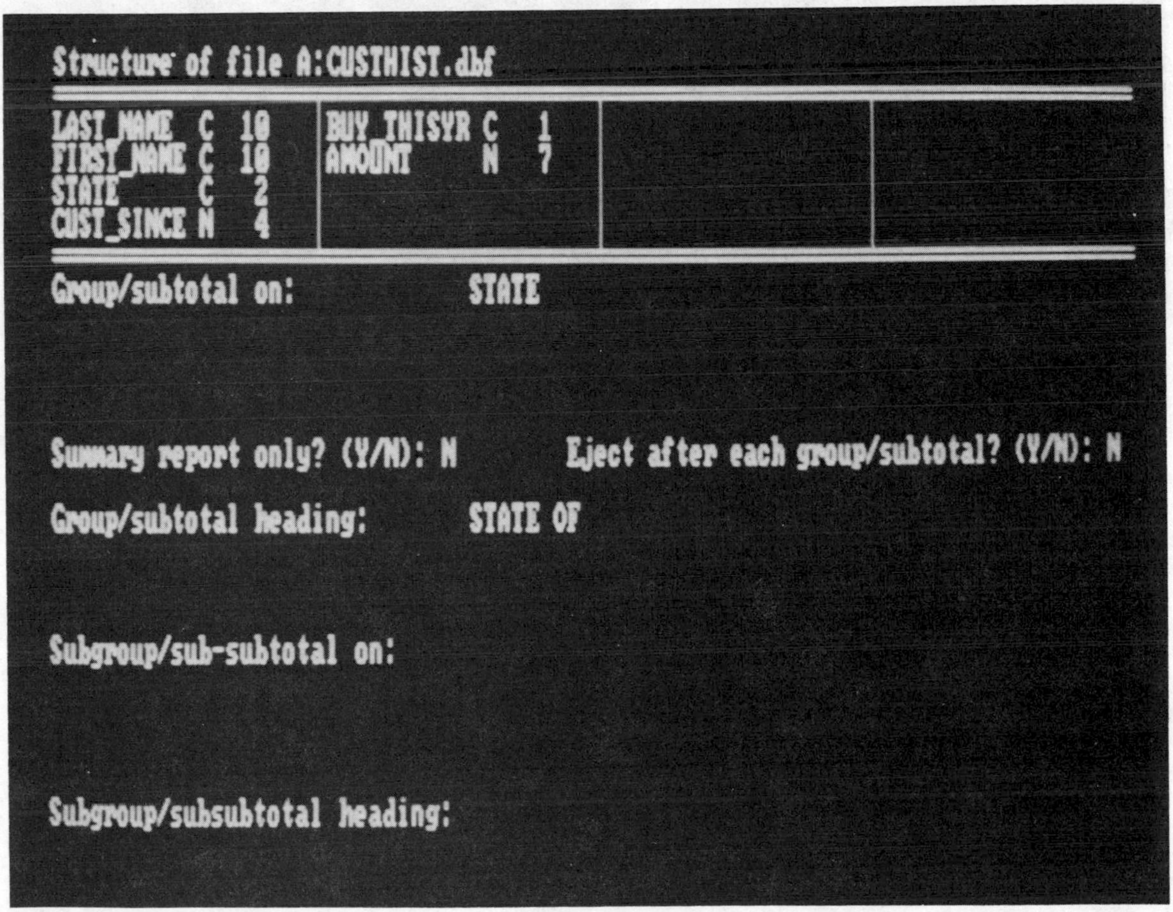

Structure of file A:CUSTHIST.dbf

LAST_NAME C 10   BUY_THISYR C 1
FIRST_NAME C 10   AMOUNT N 7
STATE C 2
CUST_SINCE N 4

Group/subtotal on: STATE

Summary report only? (Y/N): N   Eject after each group/subtotal? (Y/N): N

Group/subtotal heading: STATE OF

Subgroup/sub-subtotal on:

Subgroup/subsubtotal heading:

Fig. 14-10. The second screen in the preparation of the report.

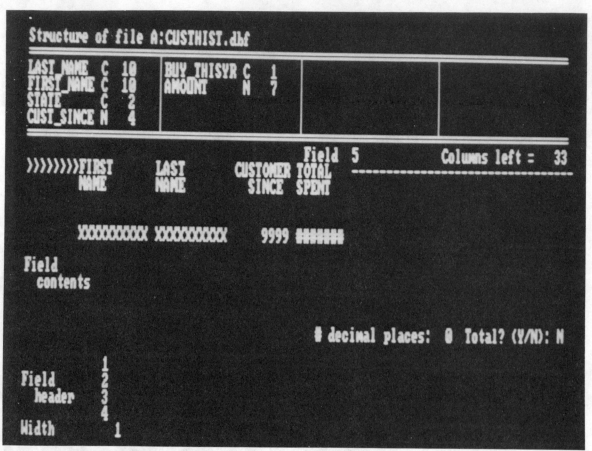

Fig. 14-11. The third screen in the preparation of the report.

```
.  REPORT FORM CUST1

Page No.          1
08/26/84
               CUSTOMER HISTORY BY STATE

       FIRST          LAST         CUSTOMER       TOTAL
       NAME           NAME           SINCE        SPENT

   ** STATE OF CT
      BILL           JONES          1979          21533
      SEYMOUR        CLARK          1973          35689
      HENRY          MITCHELL       1967           8390
      JOHN           YORK           1969          33612
      GEORGE         JAMES          1982              0
   ** Subtotal **
                                                  99224
```

```
    ** STATE OF MA
      KIRK        SMITH              1975        45680
      JOHN        SMITH              1981         2356
    ** Subtotal **
                                                48036


    ** STATE OF MI
      GEORGE      JOHNSON            1982            0
    ** Subtotal **
                                                    0


    ** STATE OF NJ
      PHIL        ROBERTS            1975            0
    ** Subtotal **
                                                    0

    *** Total ***
                                               147260
```

Fig. 14-12. The report command output.

CUSTOMER HISTORY BY STATE

```
          FIRST       LAST      CUSTOMER     TOTAL
          NAME        NAME       SINCE       SPENT


    ** STATE OF CT
      GEORGE      JAMES              1982            0
    ** Subtotal **
                                                    0

    ** STATE OF MI
      GEORGE      JOHNSON            1982            0
    ** Subtotal **
                                                    0


    ** STATE OF NJ
      PHIL        ROBERTS            1975            0
    ** Subtotal **
                                                    0

    *** Total ***
```

Fig. 14-13. The final report.

If you had already defined the report format:

```
. REPORT FORM CUST1 TO PRINT
```

Finally, if you had only wanted those customers who haven't bought anything this year:

```
. REPORT FORM CUST1 TO PRINT FOR BUY:
     THISYR = 'N'
```

This would have produced the report in Fig. 14-13.

Chapter 15

Data Relations

So far you have learned about using one database at a time. You have examined a customer database used to store such things as name, address, and phone number. You also examined a database that contained customers' names, and some history about their buying levels and longevity. These could easily fit in a single database. But, what about a file of customer purchases? One record could consist of all the items shown in Fig. 15-1.

What is shown is a symbolic record that has the customer name and address information along with shipping information and complete information concerning the 12 items on the order.

DATA REDUNDANCY

Can a record like this be created using a relational database manager such as dBASE III? Of course, but it would not be an efficient approach. Having a record like this would:

1. require that every record have twelve different quantity, item number, list price, discount, net price, and amount fields whether there were twelve items on the order or one.

2. limit the record to twelve items. If the order had twenty items, you would have to split it up.

3. make querying difficult. Each quantity, item number, and so on would have a different field name.

The way you can implement this type of data structure is by establishing a record for each quantity, item number, and so on. The record might contain the following fields:

```
ORDER_NO
CUST_NAME
BILL_STREET
BILL_CITY
BILL_STATE
BILL_ZIP
SHIP_STREET
SHIP_CITY
```

```
SHIP_STATE
SHIP_ZIP
PHONE
DATE
QTY
ITEM_NO
LIST_PRICE
DISC
NET_PRICE
AMOUNT
```

There will be a separate record for each item ordered. Notice the new field called ORDER_NO. This is the key. Each record that belongs to the order will have the same order number (along with all the same customer information). With the database structured in this fashion, you can easily query the database to see the items for each order number.

This database design solves the previous problems. You can query the database; and most importantly, if you have one item on the order, there will be only one record. You also have the ability to have an endless (or almost endless) number of items. If there are 75 items there would be 75 records. This, however, poses another problem **data redundancy.**

Data redundancy occurs when *normalization* has not taken place. Normalization is a fancy term applied to database design. Simply put, normalization means having one data field in one place unless it is the key. You do have a key in your database— ORDER_NO. Each record for a specific order will have the same order number. But, look at the begining of each record; the name, billing and shipping addresses, phone number, and date will be the same for each record with the same order number. Only the fields that contain the quantity, item number, discount, and prices will be different. This is data redundancy at its worst.

There is a solution. Through the use of multiple databases, you will see how to transform this record structure into several smaller ones, save a lot of storage space, and eliminate data redundancy.

MULTIPLE DATABASES

Let's first define the present structure:

```
ORDER_NO,     CHAR   005   000
CUST_NAME     CHAR   015   000
BILL_STREET   CHAR   015   000
BILL_CITY     CHAR   015   000
BILL_STATE    CHAR   002   000
BILL_ZIP      CHAR   005   000
SHIP_STREET   CHAR   015   000
SHIP_CITY     CHAR   015   000
SHIP_STATE    CHAR   002   000
SHIP_ZIP      CHAR   005   000
PHONE         CHAR   013   000
DATE          CHAR   008   000
QTY           NUM    003   000
ITEM_NO       CHAR   006   000
LIST_PRICE    NUM    005   002
DISC          NUM    003   000
NET_PRICE     NUM    005   002
AMOUNT        NUM    008   002

**TOTAL**            145
```

Each record is 145 characters long. If an order has 15 items this will produce 15 records, each 145 characters long. Each record will have the same customer information with only the actual quantity and item information different. Looking at this, you will see that 15 records will cause 2175 characters to be added to the database. When you realize that the customer information, which includes name, addresses, phone number, and order date, need only be entered once, you will realize that of the 2175 characters added to the database, 1575 are redundant.

The solution is to break up this record structure and place portions of it in two databases. The first database will contain the order number and customer information. The second will contain the order number and order information:

```
CUSTOMER DATABASE
ORDER_NO      CHAR   005   000
CUST_NAME     CHAR   015   000
BILL_STREET   CHAR   015   000
BILL_CITY     CHAR   015   000
BILL_STATE    CHAR   002   000
BILL_ZIP      CHAR   005   000
SHIP_STREET   CHAR   015   000
SHIP_CITY     CHAR   015   000
SHIP_STATE    CHAR   002   000
SHIP_ZIP      CHAR   005   000
PHONE         CHAR   013   000
DATE          CHAR   008   000

**TOTAL**            115
```

```
CUST_NAME
BILL_STREET
BILL_CITY
BILL_STATE
BILL_ZIP
SHIP_STREET
SHIP_CITY
SHIP_STATE
SHIP_ZIP
PHONE
DATE

    QTY              QTY              QTY              QTY
    ITEM_NO          ITEM_NO          ITEM_NO          ITEM_NO
    LIST_PRICE       LIST_PRICE       LIST_PRICE       LIST_PRICE
    DISC             DISC             DISC             DISC
    NET_PRICE        NET_PRICE        NET_PRICE        NET_PRICE
    AMOUNT           AMOUNT           AMOUNT           AMOUNT

    QTY              QTY              QTY              QTY
    ITEM_NO          ITEM_NO          ITEM_NO          ITEM_NO
    LIST_PRICE       LIST_PRICE       LIST_PRICE       LIST_PRICE
    DISC             DISC             DISC             DISC
    NET_PRICE        NET_PRICE        NET_PRICE        NET_PRICE
    AMOUNT           AMOUNT           AMOUNT           AMOUNT

    QTY              QTY              QTY              QTY
    ITEM_NO          ITEM_NO          ITEM_NO          ITEM_NO
    LIST_PRICE       LIST_PRICE       LIST_PRICE       LIST_PRICE
    DISC             DISC             DISC             DISC
    NET_PRICE        NET_PRICE        NET_PRICE        NET_PRICE
    AMOUNT           AMOUNT           AMOUNT           AMOUNT
```

Fig. 15-1. A sample database.

```
ORDER DATABASE
    ORDER_NO        CHAR    005    000
    QTY             NUM     003    000
    ITEM_NO         CHAR    006    000
    LIST_PRICE      NUM     005    002
    DISC            NUM     003    000
    NET_PRICE       NUM     005    002
    AMOUNT          NUM     008    002

    **TOTAL**               35
```

Now there are two databases. The CUS-TOMER database will have only the record for each order, while the ORDER database will have one record for each item in the order. This procedure illustrates how large applications are designed using relational databases. This technique allows you to program large applications very efficiently.

The next step is to further eliminate redundancy. If there are many repeat customers who will have many different orders on the database, it would make a lot of sense to have a separate customer file. You could create a third database called CUSTOMER, while renaming the existing databases ORDER and ORDERITM. This would produce the following databases:

```
CUSTOMER DATABASE
   CUST_NO       CHAR   005   000
   CUST_NAME     CHAR   015   000
   BILL_STREET   CHAR   015   000
   BILL_CITY     CHAR   015   000
   BILL_STATE    CHAR   002   000
   BILL_ZIP      CHAR   005   000
   SHIP_STREET   CHAR   015   000
   SHIP_CITY     CHAR   015   000
   SHIP_STATE    CHAR   002   000
   SHIP_ZIP      CHAR   005   000
   PHONE         CHAR   013   000

   **TOTAL**            107

ORDER DATABASE
   ORDER_NO      CHAR   005   000
   DATE          CHAR   008   000
   CUST_NO       CHAR   005   000

   **TOTAL**            18

ORDERITM DATABASE
   ORDER_NO      CHAR   005   000
   QTY           NUM    003   000
   ITEM_NO       CHAR   006   000
   LIST_PRICE    NUM    005   002
   DISC          NUM    003   000
   NET_PRICE     NUM    005   002
   AMOUNT        NUM    008   002

   **TOTAL**            35
```

Let's do a quick analysis. Assuming 15 orders per customer with each order having 15 items, it would take the following amount of space to store the records:

ONE DATABASE
32,625 bytes

TWO DATABASES
9,600 bytes

THREE DATABASES
8,252 bytes

Let's not stop here. If you analyze the ORDERITM database, you can see some redundancies. The LIST:PRICE can be found on a separate file. The key for this file could be ITEM:NO. Creation of this file will save additional resources. Another possible reduction in storage space is to delete the NET:PRICE and AMOUNT fields. These fields are calculated and have no business being on the database. NET:PRICE is really LIST:PRICE × DISC; AMOUNT is really QTY × NET:PRICE. Let's make these changes and see the final database solution. The databases would look like this:

```
CUSTOMER DATABASE
   CUST_NO       CHAR   005   000
   CUST_NAME     CHAR   015   000
   BILL_STREET   CHAR   015   000
   BILL_CITY     CHAR   015   000
   BILL_STATE    CHAR   002   000
   BILL_ZIP      CHAR   005   000
   SHIP_STREET   CHAR   015   000
   SHIP_CITY     CHAR   015   000
   SHIP_STATE    CHAR   002   000
   SHIP_ZIP      CHAR   005   000
   PHONE         CHAR   013   000

   **TOTAL**            107

PRICE DATABASE
   ITEM_NO       CHAR   006   000
   LIST_PRICE    NUM    005   002

   **TOTAL**            11

ORDER DATABASE
   ORDER_NO      CHAR   005   000
   DATE          CHAR   008   000
   CUST_NO       CHAR   005   000

   **TOTAL**            18

ORDERITM DATABASE
   ORDER_NO      CHAR   005   000
   QTY           NUM    003   000
   ITEM_NO       CHAR   006   000
   DISC          NUM    003   000

   **TOTAL**            17
```

Let's do some more analysis. Assuming 15 orders per customer with each order having 15 items that are the same items each time, it would take the following amounts of space to store the records:

ONE DATABASE	TWO DATABASES
32,625 bytes	9,600 bytes
THREE DATABASES	FOUR DATABASES
8,252 bytes	4,213 bytes

This division would totally eliminate any redundancies. Notice that the amount of space necessary to store the 15 orders has been reduced from 32,625 characters to 4,213 characters. To put this in a better perspective, with a 320K disk you could have the following number of orders on a disk:

ONE DATABASE	151 orders
TWO DATABASES	512 orders
THREE DATABASES	596 orders
FOUR DATABASES	1,166 orders

You can see that the savings from the original design to the final design represents an almost eight-fold increase in space savings. The savings in disks alone would be worth the few minutes it might take to do a good database analysis.

JOINING MULTIPLE DATABASES

With dBASE III, commands such as DISPLAY, LIST, or REPORT usually only work with one database at a time. In relational database management, there is a command that allows the merging or JOINing of databases.

There are several ways you can join databases together in order to use your data effectively. In the third section of this book, you will learn the proper programming techniques to accomplish this without creating one large database from the small ones.

Even without programming you can merge separate databases in order to use the dBASE III query commands. The JOIN command allows you to combine databases. Let's assume the databases and data shown in Fig. 15-2.

Let's define a report you might wish to see. What about a report of all the orders in the file? You might want to see the customer's number, the date, and the quantity of each item, and the item number. You could use the following dBASE III commands shown in Fig. 15-3.

You will first notice the command SELECT.

This command allows you to activate or USE a second database. To join two databases it is necessary to SELECT a primary database and a secondary database.

The JOIN command allows you to take all the records from one database and merge the fields into the fields of another database. In the previous case the condition that the order numbers must be the same was imposed. Therefore, there are records in common in each of the database as shown in Fig. 15-2.

ITEM NO is common to the ITEM and ORDERITM databases. CUSTNO is common to the CUSTOMER and ORDER databases. ORDNO is common to the ORDER and ORDERITM databases.

This result is accomplished using the dBASE III commands in Fig. 15-3.

This report was sufficient, but there were too many codes. Let's get rid of those codes through a series of JOINs. Suppose you want to see the order number along with customer name, date, quantity, description, and cost of each item.

This task began with joining the ORDER and ORDERITM databases. As can be seen in Fig. 15-3, this allows you to combine the order number, customer number, and date with the order number, quantity, and item number. You will notice the ORDNO field is specifically identified in the FIELDS portion of the JOIN statement to the ORDER database; this ORDNO field does not appear in the display twice.

Next, the new database is joined to the ITEM database. This allows the ITEM records to be attached to the ORDER records. As shown in Fig. 15-4, the resulting database has order number, customer number, date, quantity, and item number, and has now had the description, and price added from the ITEM file.

The last JOIN involves JOINing the ORDREP2 database to the CUSTOMER database to translate the customer number into the customer name.

Finally, you have the final database. The required fields were specified, the previous database was joined to the CUSTOMER database, and unneeded fields have been eliminated.

```
ITEM DATABASE

    ITEMNO       DESC       PRICE

    0001        HAMMERS      5.63
    0002        PLIERS       7.94
    0003        SCREWS        .04
    0004        STAPLERS    17.46
    0005        KNIVES       2.98


CUSTOMER DATABASE

    CUSTNO      NAME        STREET         CITY         STATE    ZIP

    0001    Fred Smith  24 Hall Blvd   Yalesville     CT     06354
    0002    Bill Jones  19 Dry Gulch   Berlin         NH     07242
    0003    John Wille  7 Seaton Rd.   Salem          NC     96738
    0004    Susan James 41 Knott Dr.   Branford       MI     64483
    0005    George Ho   63 Oahu Dr.    Maui           HA     82267

ORDER DATABASE

    ORDNO      CUSTNO      DATE

    0001        0003     6/15/83
    0002        0005     6/15/83
    0003        0001     6/16/83
    0004        0002     6/16/83
    0005        0003     6/17/83

ORDERITM DATABASE

    ORDNO       QTY       ITEMNO

    0001         15        0001
    0001          9        0005
    0001        100        0003
    0002          3        0002
    0002         16        0004
    0003         23        0001
    0003          7        0004
    0003         20        0005
    0003        800        0003
    0003         35        0002
    0004         40        0001
    0005         12        0005
    0005         15        0003
```

Fig. 15-2. A sample database.

```
.   SELECT 2
.   USE ORDERITM
.   SELECT 1
.   USE ORDER
.   JOIN WITH ORDERITM TO ORDREP   FOR ORDNO=ORDER-->ORDNO ;
       FIELDS ORDER->ORDNO, CUSTNO, DATE, QTY, ITEMNO
.   USE ORDREP
.   DISPLAY ALL OFF

      0001   0003   06/15/83         15      0001
      0001   0003   06/15/83          9      0005
      0001   0003   06/15/83        100      0003
      0002   0005   06/15/83          3      0002
      0002   0005   06/15/83         16      0004
      0003   0001   06/16/83         23      0001
      0003   0001   06/16/83          7      0004
      0003   0001   06/16/83         20      0005
      0003   0001   06/16/83        800      0003
      0003   0001   06/16/83         35      0002
      0004   0002   06/16/83         40      0001
      0005   0003   06/17/83         12      0005
      0005   0003   06/17/83         15      0003
```

Fig. 15-3. The JOIN Command.

```
.   SELECT 2
.   USE ITEM
.   SELECT 1
.   USE ORDEREP
.   JOIN WITH ITEM TO ORDREP2 FOR ITEMNO=ITEM->ITEMNO ;
       FIELDS ORDNO, CUSTNO, DATE, QTY, ITEM->ITEMNO, DESC, PRICE
.   USE ORDREP2
.   DISPLAY ALL OFF


   0001 0003 06/15/83     15 0001   HAMMERS        5.63
   0001 0003 06/15/83      9 0005   KNIVES         2.98
   0001 0003 06/15/83    100 0003   SCREWS         0.04
   0002 0005 06/15/83      3 0002   PLIERS         7.94
   0002 0005 06/15/83     16 0004   STAPLERS      17.46
   0003 0001 06/16/83     23 0001   HAMMERS        5.63
   0003 0001 06/16/83      7 0004   STAPLERS      17.46
   0003 0001 06/16/83     20 0005   KNIVES         2.98
   0003 0001 06/16/83    800 0003   SCREWS         0.04
   0003 0001 06/16/83     35 0002   PLIERS         7.94
```

```
0004 0002 06/16/83      40 0001   HAMMERS        5.63
0005 0003 06/17/83      12 0005   KNIVES         2.98
0005 0003 06/17/83      15 0003   SCREWS         0.04
```

Fig. 15-4. The second JOIN.

```
. SELECT 2
. USE CUSTOMER
. SELECT 1
. USE ORDEREP2
. JOIN WITH CUSTNO TO ORDREP3 FOR CUSTNO=CUSTOMER->CUSTNO ;
    FIELDS ORDNO, NAME, DATE, QTY, DESC, PRICE

. USE ORDREP2
. DISPLAY ALL OFF


  0001   John Wille    06/15/83    15 HAMMERS       5.63
  0001   John Wille    06/15/83     9 KNIVES        2.98
  0001   John Wille    06/15/83   100 SCREWS        0.04
  0002   George Ho     06/15/83     3 PLIERS        7.94
  0002   George Ho     06/15/83    16 STAPLERS     17.46
  0003   Fred Smith    06/16/83    23 HAMMERS       5.63
  0003   Fred Smith    06/16/83     7 STAPLERS     17.46
  0003   Fred Smith    06/16/83    20 KNIVES        2.98
  0003   Fred Smith    06/16/83   800 SCREWS        0.04
  0003   Fred Smith    06/16/83    35 PLIERS        7.94
  0004   Bill Jones    06/16/83    40 HAMMERS       5.63
  0005   John Wille    06/17/83    12 KNIVES        2.98
  0005   John Wille    06/17/83    15 SCREWS        0.04
```

Fig. 15-5. The final JOIN.

```
                        ORDER REPORT


   DATE      CUSTOMER NAME    QTY     DESCRIPTION      PRICE     AMOUNT

* ORDER NUMBER 0001
06/15/83    John Wille        15 HAMMERS              5.63      84.45
06/15/83    John Wille         9 KNIVES               2.98      26.82
06/15/83    John Wille       100 SCREWS               0.04       4.00
** Subtotal **

                                                               115.27
```

```
* ORDER NUMBER 0002
06/15/83    George Ho            3 PLIERS            7.94        23.82
06/15/83    George Ho           16 STAPLERS         17.46       279.36
** Subtotal **
                                                                303.18


* ORDER NUMBER 0003
06/16/83    Fred Smith          23 HAMMERS           5.63       129.49
06/16/83    Fred Smith           7 STAPLERS         17.46       122.22
06/16/83    Fred Smith          20 KNIVES            2.98        59.60
06/16/83    Fred Smith         800 SCREWS            0.04        32.00
06/16/83    Fred Smith          35 PLIERS            7.94       277.90
** Subtotal **
                                                                621.21


* ORDER NUMBER 0004
06/16/83    Bill Jones          40 HAMMERS           5.63       225.20
** Subtotal **
                                                                225.20


* ORDER NUMBER 0005
06/17/8     John Wille          12 KNIVES            2.98        35.76
06/17/83    John Wille          15 SCREWS            0.04         0.60
** Subtotal **
                                                                 36.36

*** Total ***
                                                               1301.22
```

Fig. 15-6. A report with subtotals.

Though the JOIN command is very powerful and allows you to connect many databases together, there are better techniques to use to prepare reports in dBASE III. You will see many of these in the third section of this book.

THE REPORT COMMAND REVISITED

Using the database created before, you can get a useful report. Let's prepare a report shows that the totals for each order. If you look at database in Fig. 15-5 you will see that there is no amount field because the amounts can be calculated by multiplying QTY times PRICE. Using amount as a field in the CREATE REPORT sequence of three screens, we can produce the report shown in Fig. 15-6.

Chapter 16

Fred's Friendly Fish Market

In the Programming Fundamentals section, you learned about program design. Throughout Chapters 8 and 9 our small businessman, Fred, defined his problems. As you may remember, Fred wants to computerize his customer lists so he can have a directory at his fingertips. He wants to maintain a mailing list so he can print labels each month to send his monthly "fish specials" circular to his customers. He also wants a customer order system to keep track of his customer's orders, to help his shipping department ship the orders, and to help his billing department price and bill the orders.

FRED AND THE DATABASE DESIGN

Fred spent a lot of time defining the input data that he would need to produce his reports and forms. Without knowing it, Fred did most of his database design! However, Fred still needs to look at the big picture. Can he design even more flexibility into his programs with the database design? If there are some special ways Fred may want to use his data in ad-hoc reports, he may want to add some

fields to his database even if the defined reports don't need them.

For example, Fred could put a field called CREDIT in his customer file. This field would be maintained as a credit rating. Though Fred uses a cash-on-delivery system now, with a computer he could begin to extend credit to some customers. If a customer always pays his or her bills, he could put a 1 in the field. If he or she is always 30 days behind, perhaps a 2 could be placed there. He could set up the rating system any way he wants. Later, he could look up people that have bad ratings to see how much they buy. A customer who pays only twice a year but buys hundreds of dollars worth of fish may be worth having as a customer. The restaurant that buys only two lobsters every other month and then pays 6 months later may not be.

When designing a database, you should look at all aspects of the database. You should begin by listing all the input files you have so far defined and deciding if there are any more fields that are necessary and if there are any fields that can be eliminated because of redundancy or because they can be calculated. Check to see if any databases can be split by a common key to create a new file and if any new files must be created (apart from keyed files). You should determine your indices or sorts for the file. Finally, you should calculate the amount of storage needed for your system before purchasing the hardware. dBASE III will run on almost any system, but you may want to buy a specific system for your own reasons.

FRED DEFINES HIS CUSTOMER DATABASE

There is little left to do in this area. Fred has done a wonderful job of defining his customer database. In Chapter 8, he used his head and was able to define his customer database almost perfectly. The record structure looks like this:

Fieldname	Data type	Length
FNAME	C	20
LNAME	C	20
ADDRESS	C	25
CITY	C	15
STATE	C	2
ZIP	C	10
PHONE	C	13

Fred could create his customer database right now, but remember that he must look at the big picture first.

In Chapter 9 Fred looked at the order system. When deciding on his input formats for his order system, he realized the need for a two-file system. He also realized the need for a key to the customer file. This meant rewriting the customer file to include the customer number. Fred discovered that without a customer number he could not tell the difference between John Smith of John's Seafood and John Smith of Smiths Dairy Bar. Fred decided that it would also be nice to have the customer's business name in the file. As long as he only had to enter it once and could retrieve it at any time using the customer number, he decided that he would add the business name. Fred redefined his customer database like this:

CUSTOMER DATABASE

Fieldname	Data type	Length
CUSTNO	N	5
COMPANY	C	20
FNAME	C	20
LNAME	C	20
ADDRESS	C	25
CITY	C	15
STATE	C	2
ZIP	C	10
PHONE	C	13

He could enter this database into the system now, but Fred knows that he still hasn't finished looking at the big picture. As Fred continues there may be more to change.

FRED DEFINES HIS ORDER DATABASES

In Chapter 9, Fred defined his order databases. He began with the following conceptual design:

ORDER DATABASE

Fieldname	Data type	Length
FNAME	C	20
LNAME	C	20
ADDRESS	C	25
CITY	C	15
STATE	C	2
ZIP	N	9
ORDER NUMBER	C	5
DATE ORDERED	C	8
QUANTITY	N	3
ITEM	C	25
PRICE	N	5.2

The price field's length is 5.2, which means a total of five digits with two decimal places. Fred quickly realized that there were too many fields to enter each time. So he divided the fields into two databases. One of these is the customer database he had already defined. "Wow," thought Fred, "I am automating already! I can use the customer file for the orders. It takes me almost two hours each night just to write the names and addresses on the shipping forms and order forms. I can't wait until this is done. Elsa and Fred Jr. will be happy too."

Fred redefined his databases as follows:

```
              CUSTOMER DATABASE
  Fieldname          Data type          Length
    CUSTNO              N                  5
    COMPANY            C                 20
    FNAME              C                 20
    LNAME              C                 20
    ADDRESS            C                 25
    CITY               C                 15
    STATE              C                  2
    ZIP                N                  9
    PHONE              C                 10

              ORDER DATABASE

    ORDER NUMBER       N                  5
    CUSTOMER NUMBER    N                  5
    DATE ORDERED       C                  8
    QUANTITY           N                  3
    ITEM               C                 25
    PRICE              N                  5.2
```

He now has his order file keyed to his customer file by the customer number. All Fred has to do is enter the customer's number, and the customer information will be retrieved when it is time to print the orders.

During the last analysis that Fred performed (described in Chapter 9) he realized that he would have many order-items records (one for each item ordered) for each order number. Though each order-items record has quantity, item description, and price fields, as well as the order number field, there is no need for each record to also have the customer number and date ordered. In more complex applications, there would probably be other information that is only in one file, such as shipping address, customer purchase order number, and shipping method.

Fred realizes that he can save some space with the two-file system. He therefore has divided his order file into two files—an Order file and an Order Items file.

```
              ORDER DATABASE
  Fieldname          Data type          Lengt

    ORDER NUMBER       N                  5
    CUSTOMER NUMBER    N                  5
    DATE ORDERED       C                  8

          ORDER ITEMS DATABASE

    ORDER NUMBER       N                  5
    QUANTITY           N                  3
    ITEM               C                 25
    PRICE              N                  5.2
```

The order file contains only the data needed for each order, while the order-items database contains only the data needed for each item of the order. Instead of each record having the extra burden of the customer number and date ordered, there is one record in the order file for each order, and as many records in the order-items file as there are items ordered.

FRED REDESIGNS THE ORDER FILES

So far, Fred has done a good job. He has almost normalized his data fully. He is able to analyze what he has done, and he says, "When I create an order I will add the main part of the order record to the order file and each item to the order-items file. When I add the order records the only other file that will be accessed will be the customer file (to obtain the customer information) and that is only accessed once for each record. I can add items to the order-items file about as fast as I can type. All I have to add is the quantity, item number, and price for each item. I can get the order number for each record from the main order file."

But wait! Fred is still thinking: "This still doesn't seem right. Why can't I make another file called item. This file can contain all the item descriptions and prices. I wouldn't have to look up the prices each day, since some change every week as the different boats bring different types of seafood to market. Why not set up a new file with the prices in it? That way we could enter any changes in prices in the morning, and as the orders came in, the new prices would be put on the orders. This would prevent us from undercharging or overcharging our customers."

Fred designs the new databases:

```
              ORDER DATABASE
  Fieldname          Data type          Length

    ORDER NUMBER       N                  5
    CUSTOMER NUMBER    N                  5
    DATE ORDERED       C                  8

          ORDER ITEMS DATABASE

    ORDER NUMBER       N                  5
    QUANTITY           N                  3
    ITEM               C                 25
```

```
        ITEM DATABASE

ITEM                    C           25
PRICE                   N            5.2
```

It is time for Fred to get some help. Do you see what is wrong? Sure, though Fred has made a new database, he didn't use his head. His key is a twenty-five character field, which is actually the item description. Fields like that do not make good keys. They are too long and are often entered incorrectly; they must be reentered when the data entry screen tells the operator "ITEM NOT FOUND." What about changing the order files to look like this:

```
            ORDER DATABASE

Fieldname       Data type       Length

ORDER NUMBER        N              5
CUSTOMER NUMBER     N              5
DATE ORDERED        C              8

        ORDER ITEMS DATABASE

ORDER NUMBER        N              5
ITEM NUMBER         N              5
QUANTITY            N              3

            ITEM DATABASE

ITEM NUMBER         C              5
ITEM DESC           C              25
PRICE               N               5.2
```

Now Fred thinks he has the final order file design. The item file can now be used by the order system and can be updated separately. Look at the order-items database. All that will be stored is the order number, item number, and quantity. What happens if Fred wishes to do some analysis in later weeks? The price that would be retrieved from the item file would be the present price, instead of the price on the day the order was shipped. Fred realizes this, and after taking a nice break for a bowl of Elsa's clam chowder, he has an idea: "I will retrieve the price from the item file when the order is shipped, and then store the price in the order-items database. That way I will have the price that is correct for that day, and I still won't have to enter it each time I ship an order."

Fred is learning. Sometimes in the ever-changing world of data management, you must store something even though it exists somewhere else. There is a difference between storing data because a master file like the item file changes all the time, and storing data such as the customer information redundantly. If a customer changes the name of the company, you would still keep the same customer information. If a customer goes out of business, you might still keep the customer data for a while, or you could mark that customer by putting "out of business" in the company name field.

FRED GETS THE BIG PICTURE

Fred looks at his present database structures. He is again trying to get the big picture. He has made one subtle change. He has increased the size of the PHONE field to 13 characters. He has decided to display and store the phone number as (AAA) NNN-NNNN for easier readability.

```
            CUSTOMER DATABASE
Fieldname       Data type       Length
CUSTNO              N              5
COMPANY             C              20
FNAME               C              20
LNAME               C              20
ADDRESS             C              25
CITY                C              15
STATE               C              2
ZIP                 N              10
PHONE               C              13

            ORDER DATABASE

ORDER NUMBER        N              5
CUSTOMER NUMBER     N              5
DATE ORDERED        C              8

        ORDER ITEMS DATABASE

ORDER NUMBER        N              5
ITEM NUMBER         N              5
QUANTITY            N              3
PRICE               N               5.2

            ITEM DATABASE

ITEM NUMBER         C              5
ITEM DESC           C              25
PRICE               N               5.2
```

Fred is satisfied. He thinks he is ready to think about the rest of the system. As he thinks, he realizes that he can make one more enhancement to the database and he decides to incorporate some new ideas.

Fred thinks aloud. "Ok, I have my customer file that will be used by both the customer system and the order system, and I have the item file that will be used by the order system. Am I missing anything? Oh, customer discounts! Each customer gets a discount on his order. Different customers get different discounts; That means that I can add DISCOUNT to the main customer file. When I retrieve the information for an order, I can retrieve the discount too. I will have to change my screen design again to input the discount, but at this time that's easy!"

Fred is performing good design analysis. You won't think of everything at once. Even though this is the final design phase, you may still think of new things. As long as your original design is good, additions are no problem.

FRED REMEMBERS THE INVENTORY SYSTEM

Fred also thought about two other systems, an inventory system and an employee system. Fred decides that the employee system is totally separate from the rest of his system and can wait until later. The inventory system, however, can use the item file. Fred decides to design the database now and design the rest of the system later.

The inventory system should have the quantity-on-hand of each item, and the quantity to be ordered when the on-hand amount drops below a certain number. Fred thinks quickly and decides that his inventory file will just be a reworking of his item file. He won't need to design a whole system to keep track of the items, descriptions, and prices. Just as the customer file is a file used by the order system but maintained by the customer system, which also uses it, the item file can be used by the order system but maintained by the inventory system. By doing the inventory system now, Fred will "catch two fish with one hook" (Is that how it goes?). He can add, change, and delete the items in the inventory system as well as alter the other inventory information. He redesigns the item database as follows:

ITEM DATABASE

Fieldname	Data type	Length
ITEM NUMBER	C	5
ITEM DESC	C	25
PRICE	N	5.2
ON HAND	N	5
STOCK LEVEL	N	5
ORDER AMOUNT	N	5
ORDER FLAG	L	1

The item number is the key that the order file uses to retrieve descriptions and prices. The ON HAND amount indicates what the present inventory is. Fred will use this file to determine when an item is out of stock, rather than checking the warehouse. The system can automatically subtract the amount of an order from the amount-on-hand and add to the on-hand amount when new seafood is delivered. The STOCK LEVEL is the amount of inventory that Fred wishes to maintain. If the STOCK LEVEL is 500, Fred wants to have at least 500 of that item at all times. STOCK LEVEL is sometimes called *EOQ* or *economic order quantity* when it is computed using a scientific method. In Fred's case, the quantity is selected based on years of experience. The ORDER AMOUNT is the amount Fred wants to buy when the ON HAND amount drops below the STOCK LEVEL. The ORDER FLAG is a logical field that indicates whether or not an order has been placed for the item. Fred has designed the inventory system in his head! Each day he will run a program that will run through all the items on the file and place orders for those whose ON HAND amount has fallen below the STOCK LEVEL. The ORDER FLAG is then turned on or changed to Y to indicate that an order has been placed with the fishermen. This is done just in case the delivery takes a few days. Fred does not want to order the same thing twice!

FRED CALCULATES HIS STORAGE SIZE

Fred's final database design for the system (after all those changes) is the following:

CUSTOMER DATABASE

Fieldname	Data type	Length
CUSTNO	N	5
COMPANY	C	20

```
FNAME            C        20
LNAME            C        20
ADDRESS          C        25
CITY             C        15
STATE            C         2
ZIP              C        10
PHONE            C        13
DISCOUNT         N         2
                        -----
                         131
```

ITEM DATABASE

```
ITEM NUMBER      C         5
ITEM DESC        C        25
PRICE            N        5.2
ON HAND          N         5
STOCK LEVEL      N         5
ORDER AMOUNT     N         5
ORDER FLAG       L         1
                        -----
                          51
```

ORDER DATABASE

```
ORDER NUMBER        N       5
CUSTOMER NUMBER     N       5
DATE ORDERED        C       8
                          -----
                            18
```

ORDER ITEMS DATABASE

```
ORDER NUMBER        N       5
ITEM NUMBER         N       5
QUANTITY            N       3
PRICE               N      5.2
                          -----
                            18
```

The last step is to determine the storage requirements for the system. Fred estimates the following:

```
200 Customers in the CUSTOMER file
300 Items in the ITEM file
```

```
500 Orders per month in the ORDER file
 10 Items per Order in the ORDER ITEMS
    file
```

Fred wants to keep the last three month's orders in the order files. The following calculations determine storage requirements:

```
200 Customers x   131 bytes/
    customer                    =  26,200b

300 Items     x    51 bytes/
    item                        =  15,300b

500 Orders/month x 18 bytes/
    order x 3 months
                                =  27,000b

10 Items/order x 500 orders/
   month x 18 bytes/order
   item x 3 months              = 270,000b
                                  --------


Total Storage Needed for 3      338,500 bytes
Months Data                     ========
```

Fred has now finished his database design. He calls the local computer stores and each assures him that they have a storage medium that will hold 338,000 bytes. Fred's only problem is that they gave him 338,000 different prices and choices too. Oh, well, if the fish don't byte, Fred will. He makes a firm decision based on his resources and his needs.

In the final section of this book you will see Fred's entire design again, and you will see Fred program his design. Fred's fish are moving closer to the computer age!!!

Section III

PROGRAMMING USING dBASE III

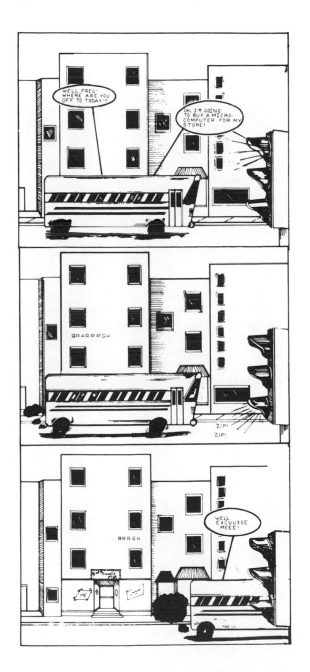

Chapter 17

Reexamining Fred's Fish Markets Design

In the first two sections of this book, you saw how to go about producing a business design, a database design, and a programming design. The next step is to begin the actual coding using dBASE III. A good place to start is to examine the final design. In the first two sections, the design was scattered throughout several chapters. In Appendix A of this book, you can find the design of Fred's Fish Market System in its entirety. In Appendix B, you can find all the programs that make up Fred's system.

In this section you will see Fred, as he begins to code his system. Fred will start with the customer system, then do the order system, and conclude by coding the Inventory System menu and additions modules.

You may see some small changes in the final design as presented in this section of the book and in the appendices when you compare it to the design shown in the first two sections. These changes allow a more comprehensive presentation of the commands that are used in dBASE III.

CREATING THE DATABASES

Fred wants to test his programs just as quickly as he writes them. He knows that you can't test the programs without the databases. The first thing Fred wants to do is to create his databases. He can add data to them after he creates the programs that will enable the operator to add data to each module. The databases should be created in *native* dBASE III and not from a command procedure (program).

Fred begins with the customer system. He knows that the customer system is designed to print the mailing labels for his circulars and produce a customer directory so he can look up data such as phone numbers or discounts. The customer database will also be one of the files needed by his order system, which he will code after he finishes the customer system. The customer system seems the most logical place for Fred to start.

Actually the real reason is Fred's brother Frank. After Fred went out and bought a book on how to program and design databases using dBase III, Frank was very upset. Fred spent most of the day reading and writing these strange charts. Instead of cutting through the paperwork each day, Fred was creating this huge computer design. Now Fred wants to go and spend six months' profit on a computer. Frank says, "Fred, since you bought that book, Elsa and Fred Jr. haven't seen you; I haven't seen you; and the lobsters are beginning to wonder. If you can really save us six hours a day, then go buy the machine. But if we don't save that time, you and that computer are going into the ocean." Fred has heard enough. He is already on his way to the bus stop.

Fred quickly sets his machine up and is ready to go. He has been practicing on his friend Myron's computer and is all set to start with the databases. Fred begins by reviewing his customer file design, getting dBASE III working on his machine, and creating his customer database:

```
                CUSTOMER DATABASE
    Fieldname        Data Type          Length

    CUSTNO           N                     5
    COMPANY          C                    20
    FNAME            C                    20
    LNAME            C                    20
    ADDRESS          C                    25
    CITY             C                    15
    STATE            C                     2
    ZIP              N                     9
    PHONE            C                    13
    DISCOUNT         N                     2
```

Fred's customer database is ready to be typed in. All the fields he has defined in his reports and those needed by other programs, such as the discount field, which is used by the order program, are there. Fred starts dBASE III and creates the customer database.

After creating the customer file, Fred uses the DISPLAY STRUCTURE command to check his database. Fred uses the abbreviation DISP STRU to save time:

```
. DISP STRU
Structure for database: CUSTOMER
Number of data records:        0
Date of last update: 08/13/84
```

```
Field    Field name    Type          Width    DEC
  1      CUSTN         Numeric          5
  2      COMP          Character       20
  3      FNAME         Character       20
  4      LNAME         Character       20
  5      ADDR          Character       25
  6      CITY          Character       15
  7      ST            Character        2
  8      ZIP           Character       10
  9      PHONE         Character       13
 10      DIS           Numeric          2
** Total **                           133
```

Fred notices the total number of characters is 133. He counts his fields again. "133, this is strange!" says Fred. "I know there are only 132 characters, I guess dBASE III doesn't know how to count." Actually the character counter always counts an extra character when responding to the DISPLAY STRUCTURE command. dBASE III keeps an extra character to tell when a record has been deleted. Note that the creation data and the number of records are also shown. When a database is created, it will have 0 records.

Fred decides to define the rest of his databases now. He will create the order databases next. He looks up his design for the order databases:

```
                ORDER DATABASE

    ORDER NUMBER         N                5
    CUSTOMER NUMBER      N                5
    DATE ORDERED         C                8
```

```
              ORDER ITEMS DATABASE

    ORDER NUMBER         N                5
    ITEM NUMBER          N                5
    QUANTITY             N                3
    PRICE                N              5.2
```

These are Fred's databases for the order program. Just because the order-items database will contain multiple records for each order number does not mean that anything in the creation of the databases is different. They will be created and displayed in exactly the same way as the customer databases:

```
. USE ORDER
. DISP STRU
Structure for database: ORDER
Number of data records:        0
Date of last update: 08/13/84
```

```
Field  Field name  Type          Width  DEC
  1    ORDRN       Numeric         5
  2    CUSTN       Numeric         5
  3    DATE        Character       8
** Total **                       19

. USE OREDRITM
. DISP STRU
Structure for database: ORDERITM
Number of data records:        0
Date of last update: 08/13/84
Field  Field name  Type          Width  DEC
  1    ORDRN       Numeric         5
  2    ITEMN       Numeric         5
  3    QTY         Numeric         3
  4    PRICE       Numeric         5      2
** Total **                       19
```

Fred has created the two-order databases. He has called the main database ORDER and the order-items database ORDERITM. He decides to create just one more database at this time. The item database is needed by the order program. Even though he doesn't plan to write the inventory program now, he will need the item database in order to test the order program.

The design for the item database looked like this:

ITEM DATABASE

```
ITEM NUMBER       C         5
ITEM DESC         C        25
PRICE             N         5.2
ON HAND           N         5
STOCK LEVEL       N         5
ORDER AMOUNT      N         5
ORDER FLAG        L         1
```

Fred decides to create only the fields he needs now. He can modify the database later. He creates and displays the following:

```
. USE ITEM
. DISP STRU
Structure for database: ITEM
Number of data records:        0
Date of last update: 08/13/84
Field  Field name  Type          Width  DEC
  1    ITEMN       Numeric         5
  2    DESC        Character      25
  3    PRICE       Numeric         5      2
** Total **                       36
```

INDEXING THE DATABASES

The last thing to do for these databases is to set up the index pointers. There will be one index field in each database. The customer number field will be used in the customer database, the order number field in the order and order-items databases, and the item number field in the item database. Fred decides to give the index the same name as the database. If there is only going to be one index, it is usually a good idea to give the index the same name as the database. Otherwise you may want to give the index the same name as the index field. The index field in the customer database is called CUSTN, in the order and order-item databases, it is called ORDRN, and in the ITEM database, it is called ITEMN. Fred creates the indicies with the following dBASE III commands:

```
. USE CUSTOMER
. INDEX ON CUSTN TO CUSTOMER

. USE ORDER
. INDEX ON ORDRN TO ORDER

. USE ORDERITM
. INDEX ON ORDRN TO ORDERITM

. USE ITEM
. INDEX ON ITEMN TO ITEM
```

That's all there is to it. Whenever a record is added to the databases, it will automatically be indexed according to the index field as long as the database was USEd with the index. It doesn't matter that there are no records in the database yet, dBASE III only sets up the initial pointers.

The command to use the customer index with the customer database looks like this:

. USE CUSTOMER INDEX CUSTOMER

The same type of command would be used with the other databases. If they are indexed, you will almost always want to USE them with the index. If you don't, errors may occur, especially when you are adding records or PACKing the database after using the DELETE command.

If Fred were to look on his storage media (disk, or tape) he would see eight files:

```
CUSTOMER.DBF
CUSTOMER.NDX
ORDER.DBF
ORDER.NDX
ORDERITM.DBF
ORDERITM.NDX
ITEM.DBF
ITEM.NDX
```

Remember all database files have the extension .DBF, while all indicies will have the extension .NDX.

MODIFYING DATABASES

Fred's friend Myron walks in and looks at the design. "Fred why is your design different from what you created for the item file?" Fred explained that he was only going to use the item file to retrieve the description and price. Fred also tells Myron that he didn't want to have to put data in all the other fields such as ONHAND, STKLVL, ORDRAMT, and ORDRFLAG. Myron tells Fred, "Fred you don't have to put data in any field you don't want to

unless you are using the field as an index field. You should always create the database as it will be. You can always go back and add data later. dBASE III can store blanks without any problem."

That costs Fred another lobster and Fred modifies the database:

Fred checks the new ITEM structure:

```
. USE ITEM
. DISP STRU
Structure for database: ITEM
Number of data records:        0
Date of last update: 08/13/84
Field  Field name  Type       Width    DEC
  1    ITEMN       Numeric      5
  2    DESC        Character   25
  3    PRICE       Numeric      5       2
  4    ONHAND      Numeric      5
  5    STKLVL      Numeric      5
  6    ORDAMT      Numeric      5
  7    ORDFLG      Logical      1

** Total **                    52
```

He decided that it is satisfactory.

Chapter 18

dBase III
Programming Commands

Fred has finished creating the database structures. He is now ready to begin programming. Fred will review his design to remind himself what there is to program. This is where his design techniques are put to the test. How long it will take to code and test the programs will depend on how good his screen designs and pseudocode are.

There are many new commands that you will need contained in the programs in the following chapters. In order to make the explanations easier, this section will briefly review the commands, mostly out of context. You will see them put to the ultimate test in the programs themselves.

ASSIGNMENT STATEMENTS

The only command used in the following examples to assign values to variables will be the STORE command. The statements using the STORE command simply allow the "storage" of the values of literals, variables, or expressions in another variable:

```
STORE 25 TO QTY
STORE 'JOE SMITH' TO NAME
STORE QTY TO NEWQTY
STORE QTY*100/NEWQTY TO PCTCHNG
```

In the first example you can see the number 25 being put into the variable QTY. The second example shows the character literal "JOE SMITH" being placed in the variable NAME. The third shows the value of one variable being assigned to another variable. Here whatever is in the variable QTY is put into NEWQTY. QTY stays the same. It doesn't matter if QTY is a character string or a number; dBASE III adjusts for either. The final example shows an expression QTY*100/NEWQTY being calculated and the value placed into the new variable PCTCHNG.

dBASE III also allows direct assignment statements. The above statements could have been written:

```
QTY = 25
NAME = 'JOE SMITH'
```

```
NEQTY = QTY
PCTCHNG = QTY * 100
```

SCREEN AND PRINTER OUTPUT COMMANDS

The following set of commands enable you to display material on the screen and to print it on paper. By using the various commands you can precisely determine how the material will look.

This command is used to write literals and variables to the screen or printer. Remember, literals are constants such as titles, while variables are those fields that receive data:

Order Number: 203

In this example, Order Number: is a literal, and 203 is a value that has been assigned to a variable.

The ? command is used at the beginning of a line and writes the line to the device previously specified (more about that later). The ? command that produced the example shown above looked like this:

```
? '          Order Number: ' + ORDRN
```

The phrase Order Number: is enclosed in single quotes to show that it is a literal. Because the ORDRN field is a variable, it is not enclosed in quotes. The value of ORDRN is printed as shown above.

The line is printed wherever the screen cursor or printer head is at that moment. Subsequent lines are printed following the original line.

You will notice a + between the literal and the variable in the command. The + is a connector between literals and variables that allows them to be *concatenated*. Concatenation is a term that means putting strings together. In math, 1+1=2, in concatenation 1+1=11. There is also another symbol for concatenation. The − concatenates fields but eliminates any blanks between the fields. The following example shows the difference:

```
? 'Order Number: ' + ORDRN

    yields  Order Number:  231

? 'Order Number: ' − ORDRN

    yields  Order Number:231
```

There is no limit to the number of concatenations on a line. You can combine many variables and literals:

```
? 'Dear ' + NAME

? 'On ' + DATE + ' You bought ' + AMT +
'Widgets'
```

Set Print On, Set Print Off

The SET PRINT ON command must be used before the ? command if you want the output to go to the printer. The SET PRINT OFF command follows the printing.

You can use the ? command to control the printer. Any printer code you might wish to send can be sent with the ? command. For example

```
SET PRINT ON
SET PRINT OFF

. SET PRINT ON
. ? CHR(15)
. ? 'This would be compressed print'

. ? CHR(27) + CHR(69)
. ? 'This would be emphasized print'

. SET PRINT OFF
```

@ row, column SAY xxxxxxxxx

This command allows literals or variables to be positioned at a precise spot on the screen or paper. The @ command signals that the literal or variable following the SAY should be displayed on the screen or printed at the exact location indicated by the values for the line and the column. The "row" and "column" can be numbers or variables. The "row" can be a number from 1 to 23 for screens or 1 to the maximum number of lines per page allowed by your printer. The "column" can be 1 to 79 for eighty column screens, and 1 to the maximum number of columns allowed by your printer. Row and column 0 are reserved for dBASE III.

Programmers depend on this command because of its ability to put any output at any location of the screen or paper. Whether you are programming menus or screens of any kind, or printed reports you will need to use the @ SAY command.

Some examples of the use of this command follow:

```
@ 5,15 SAY 'Dear'
@ 5,20 SAY NAME
@ 6,15 SAY 'On'
@ 6,18 SAY DATE
@ 6,27 SAY 'You bought'
@ 6,37 SAY AMT
@ 6,42 SAY 'Widgets'
```

Though this command requires more effort than the ? command, there are times when the ? cannot precisely position your output for you. You can also use the two together if you wish:

```
@ 5,15 SAY 'Dear'
@ 5,20 SAY NAME
? 'On ' + DATE + ' You bought ' + AMT +
   'Widgets'
```

The commands above allow the exact positioning of the first two words. The first line of the text follows them because the ? command is used.

There is also an advanced form of the @ SAY command called the @ SAY PICTURE command. It allows you to determine what the value of a variable will look like when it is output. This form of the command is usually used with numeric variables to form an *edit mask*. Special *digit selectors* or *edit mask characters* are used to determine the form in which the values will be printed.

Some of the edit mask characters and their functions are as follows.

```
$ - Displays dollar signs instead of
    leading zeros
* - Displays asterisks instead of
    leading zeros
! - Displays characters as capital
    letters
9 - Displays only digits and signs
# - Displays only digits, signs, and
    blanks
A - Displays only letters
X - Displays any character
```

The #, 9, $, and ₁ are used for numbers while the X, !, and A are used for characters. Any other characters in the "edit mask" such as (,), - or any others also will appear but not be counted as "digit selectors"

```
STORE 12345 TO XYZ

1.  @ 5,10 SAY XYZ PICTURE  '99999'
2.  @ 5,10 SAY XYZ PICTURE  '$$$,$$$.99'
3.  @ 5,10 SAY XYZ * 50 PICTURE
    '**$,$$$,$99'
4.  @ 5,10 SAY XYZ * 50 PICTURE  '999'

5.  STORE 2035557463 TO PHONE
    @ 1,5 SAY PHONE PICTURE
    '(999)999-9999

1.          12345
2.          $12,345.00
3.          **$617,250
4.          250
5.          (203)555-7463
```

As indicated in examples 3 and 4, you can use expressions in the @ SAY command. Any mathematical expression may appear here.

As can be seen the same number looks very different when different edit masks are used. Be very careful not to specify an edit mask that does not contain enough digit selectors such as #,9,X,A,$,!, or ₁. If there are not enough, the number will be shortened from left to right as in example number 4.

Set Device To Print,
Set Device to Screen

The SET FORMAT TO PRINT command comes before the @ SAY command if you want your output to go to the printer. The SET DEVICE TO SCREEN redirects all @ SAY command to the screen after you are done printing. The initial default is to the screen, if no SET DEVICE TO command is used.

Remember the Last Line

When using any type of output command be very, very careful to remember the last line. When you print a line in dBASE III, you actually only send it to an internal buffer or storage area. Only when the next line is output, is the preceding line printed out. In order to print the last line, you should always print one extra blank line. With the ? commands, this means printing a line such as ? '   '. With the @SAY command, you would print:

@LINE+1, 1 SAY ' '

CLEAR

The CLEAR command will clear the screen and reposition the cursor at position 0,0.

EJECT

The EJECT command will advance the paper to the top of the form on the printer and set the line and column count to 1,1.

SCREEN INPUT COMMANDS

The following commands allow you to enter information into the system.

@line,column GET variable and READ

These commands allows input to be read from the screen directly into the named variable. The screen location for the input may be exactly determined with the @line, column GET command. The @GET command signals that there should be an area set up and defined by a reverse video block with a length equal to the variable length. The variable can be predefined as a new variable or it can be a field from a database. If the field name exists as a memory variable, that is, as a variable created with a STORE command outside of a database, and also exists as a field in an open database, the length from the database field will be used. Normally the area of the reverse video block will be blank unless the variable presently has data in it. If the memory variable or database field has data in it, the data will be displayed in the block. The cursor will be positioned to the beginning of the field ready to receive input. If there are more than one field to be input, the cursor will be positioned at the first one.

dBASE III will not stop to "read" all the GETS until a READ command is issued. This causes dBASE III to stop and look for all pending GETS. If there is no READ command, there will be no input from the screen.

The exact location of the inverse block depends on the line and column. The line and column values can be numbers or variables. The line value can be a number from 0 to 23 while column can be 0 to 79 for eighty column screens.

Generally the @GET command is preceded by

a @ SAY command.

An example of this is the following:

```
STORE '              ' TO NAME
@ 5,15 SAY 'Enter Your Name:
@ 5,31 GET NAME
READ
```

> Enter Your Name: :

In Fig. 18-1, you can see multiple @SAY and @GET commands. The first four fields already have data in them and new data can now be entered. The last field is blank as no data is present. Notice the @SAY and @GET are on the same line. You will also notice there is no line and column specification for the @GET command. If they are on the same line the @GET is assumed to be one character to the right of where the @ SAY ends.

There is also an advanced form of the @GET command called the @GET PICTURE command. Here we can determine what a variable will look like when it is INPUT. This is used with numeric variables to form an *edit mask*. For the input just as the SAY PICTURE command can be used to form a mask for the output.

Figure 18-2 shows how the edit masks specified in the GETs commands allow special characters to be inserted in the fields. The quantity field is straight forward and allows up to three numbers to be inserted. The birthdate field will accept six numbers with each set of two being separated by slashes. The part number field uses some of the more interesting digit selectors for GET commands; it is an eight character field. The first three places can contain alphabetic characters only (A-Z); the next two places can contain any character or number; and the last three must contain numbers (0-9). The phone number field is a ten character field in which all characters must be numeric. Parentheses and a dash are included in the field.

When these fields are saved, they will be saved with the special characters. The birthdate field will grow to eight characters, the part number field to ten, and the phone number field to thirteen. All these fields, except the quantity field, must be defined as character fields because of the use of special characters. You may enter — sign in front of quantity

```
        STORE 'CAROL ZARSKY        ' TO NAME
        STORE '212 Auburn Rd.      'TO ADDR
        STORE 'Springfield, MA     ' TO LOCATION
        STORE '05774' TO ZIP
        STORE '            ' TO BIRTH
        @  5,15 SAY 'Enter Your Changes:'
        @  7,10 SAY 'NAME        'GET NAME
        @  8,10 SAY 'ADDRESS     'GET ADDR
        @  9,10 SAY 'LOCATION    'GET LOCATION
        @ 10,10 SAY 'ZIP CODE    'GET ZIP
        @ 11,10 SAY 'BIRTHDATE   'GET BIRTH
        READ


              Enter Your Changes

           NAME        :CAROL ZARSKY        :
           ADDRESS     :212 Auburn Rd.      :
           LOCATION    :Springfield, MA     :
           ZIP CODE    :05774:
           BIRTHDATE   :                    :
```

Fig. 18-1. Example of the multiple @ GET Command.

to show a negative value or a . to show decimal places. These characters will also take up room. If decimals are to be stored, the database field must be defined as having decimals.

The final two examples in Fig. 18-2 show the @ SAY and GET on separate lines. This is allowed as long as the @ SAY line ends with a semicolon, (;).

A final note about inputting numbers: when you enter numbers into the system they will sometimes not look correct. This is because the system stores numbers right-justified but you are entering them left-justified:

QUANTITY: 0: (before anything is typed)
QUANTITY:23 0: (after 23 is typed)
QUANTITY: 23: (after the enter key is
                 pressed)
QUANTITY: 205: (before anything is typed)
QUANTITY:2135: (after 213 is typed)
QUANTITY: 213: (after the enter key is
                 pressed)

When you specify a certain number of characters in your edit mask, make sure that the field itself is set up for at least the same number of characters. Though the edit mask will decrease the number of spaces allowed for input, it will not lengthen the input field itself. A three character input field with a few digit mask will still only accept three characters.

CLEAR GETS

The CLEAR GETS command is a seldom understood or used command, but it has great potential as a shortcut. You usually hear about this command only because of a limitation in dBASE III. When using GET commands you must either ERASE the screen or CLEAR GETS after every 128 GETS. Normally this never needs to be done as a good program erases the screen constantly. If you have a lot of input fields on a screen and will execute them a number of times without using the ERASE command, then you should have a CLEAR GETS after each READ.

```
      STORE 0 TO QTY
      STORE '          ' TO BIRTH
      STORE '            ' TO PARTNO
      STORE '             ' TO PHONE
      @  5,15 SAY 'Enter Your Changes:'
      @  7,10 SAY 'QUANTITY  'GET QTY PICTURE '999'
      @  8,10 SAY 'BIRTHDATE 'GET BIRTH PICTURE '99/99/99'
      @  9,10 SAY 'PARTNO    ' ;
         GET PARTNO PICTURE 'AAA-XX-999'
      @ 10,10 SAY 'PHONE NO. ' ;
         GET PHONE PICTURE '(999)999-9999'
      READ

              Enter Your Changes

          QUANTITY  :     :
          BIRTHDATE :   /  /  :
          PARTNO    :     -  -     :
          PHONE NO. :(    )   -     :
```

Fig. 18-2. Examples of Input Edit Masks.

The CLEAR GETS command can also be used when data is to be retrieved from a database for the purposes of display only. Consider the following examples; the first one does not use the CLEAR GETS command. The second one does.

```
@ 5,10 SAY 'Persons Name:'
@ 5,25 SAY NAME
@ 7,10 SAY 'Address:'
@ 7,25 SAY ADDR
@ 8,10 SAY 'City:'
@ 8,25 SAY CITY
@ 9,10 SAY 'Zipcode:'
@ 9,25 SAY ZIP



@ 5,10 SAY 'Persons Name:  ' GET NAME
@ 7,10 SAY 'Address:       ' GET ADDR
@ 8,10 SAY 'City:          ' GET CITY
@ 9,10 SAY 'Zipcode:       ' GET ZIP
CLEAR GETS
```

Since the @ SAY command cannot display both literals and variables at the same time, you must use many @SAY commands, as shown in the first example. In the second example, there are fewer statements. Notice the absence of the READ command and the inclusion of the CLEAR GETS command. These two examples are equivalent.

CHARACTER, STRING, AND NUMERIC COMMANDS

There are many commands that allow the use of character strings as numbers and numbers as character strings. There are also commands to put characters in the uppercase, trim blanks from the end of a field, and use only part of a field. There are also several numeric commands that should be known.

STR

The STR command allows a numeric value to

be used as a character string. Normally numbers are defined as numeric. There are many times you will want to use a number and place it in a field that has been defined a character field. To do this you must use the STR command:

```
STORE 765 TO X
STORE STR(X,3) TO CHARX

STORE STR(633*265,4) TO CHARX
```

The first example changes the number 765 to the character string 765. The ,3 indicates the number of characters to be transferred to the variable CHARX. The second example calculates the value of the expression 633×265 as 167745, and then transfers only first four characters to the variable CHARX, which now has the character value 1677. The variable CHARX can now be used in any character string expression.

VAL

The opposite of the STR function is the VAL function. This translates character strings that contain legitimate numerical characters into numbers of any length. The only characters that are considered legitimate are the digits 0-9, one decimal point, and a negative (−) sign at the beginning of the number. A legitimate use of the VAL command is

```
STORE '765' TO X
STORE VAL(X) TO NUMX
```

TRIM

The TRIM command removes final blanks from character fields. This is especially useful when you are concatenating fields with ? commands. The TRIM command works on character fields only. This is how the TRIM command functions:

```
STORE 'BILL          ' TO FIRST
STORE 'SMITH         ' TO LAST

? FIRST + LAST
? FIRST - LAST
? TRIM(FIRST) + ' ' + LAST
```

```
BILL          SMITH
BILLSMITH
BILL SMITH
```

SUBSTR

The SUBSTR command is called the substring command. It allows you to use only part of a character string. To use the substring function, you must specify the variable or literal, the starting character, and the length.

```
STORE 'BILL          ' TO FIRST
STORE 'SMITH         ' TO LAST

? FIRST + LAST
? SUBSTR(FIRST,1,1) + '. ' + LAST
? SUBSTR('ABCDEFG',3,4)

BILL          SMITH
B. SMITH
CDEF
```

```
STORE 123.456 TO NUMBER
STORE 75.6 TO ROUNDTST
STORE 56 TO DIVTEST1
STORE 66 TO DIVTEST2

1)   ? NUMBER
     ? INT(NUMBER)

2)   ? INT(NUMBER+.5)
     ? INT(ROUNDTST+.5)

3)   ? DIVTEST1/7-INT(DIVTEST1/7)
     ? DIVTEST2/7-INT(DIVTEST2/7)

1)   123.456
     123

2)   123
     76

3)   0
     .42857
```

INT

The INT command is the integer command. It allows you to take only the whole number part of a numeric field. It eliminates all decimals. It is especially useful for rounding numbers and for determining common dividers. Three uses of the command are illustrated below.

The first example simply shows the number 123.456 before and after the use of the INT command. The INT command simply removes the decimal portion of the number.

The second example shows the use of INT command as part of the rounding procedure. If there were no row function in dBASE III, you could round numbers using the INT function. This is done by taking one-half of the value that you wish to round to, adding that to the original value, and taking the integer of the total. Simply put, to round to a whole number, add .5 to the original value and take the integer. To round to two decimal places add .005, multiply by 100, take the integer, and divide by 100. To round to five decimal places, add .000005, multiply by 100000, take the integer, and divide by 100000.

The final example shows how you can determine whether or not two numbers can be divided evenly by the same number. Does seven go into fifty-six evenly? Yes. Does it go into sixty-six evenly? No, when the integer of the result of the division is subtracted from the complete result, the answer is greater than zero. Therefore 66 cannot be evenly divided by 7.

ROUND

The ROUND function in dBASE III lets you round a number to a specified number of decimal places.

```
        STORE 123.447 TO NUM1
        STORE 123.457 TO NUM2
        STORE 13456 TO NUM3

  1)    ? ROUND(NUM1,1)
        ? ROUND(NUM1,2)

  2)    ? ROUND(NUM2,1)
        ? ROUND(NUM2,2)

  3)    ? ROUND(NUM3,0)
        ? ROUND(NUM3,-1)
        ? ROUND(NUM3,-2)
        ? ROUND(NUM3,-3)
        ? ROUND(NUM3,-4)


  1)    123.4
        123.45
```

```
2)   123.5
     123.46

3)   13456    (0 places  - ones)
     13460    (-1 places - tens)
     13500    (-2 places - hundreds)
     14000    (-3 places - thousands)
     10000    (-4 places - ten thousands)
```

The first two examples show the rounding of the numbers 123.447 and 123.457 to one and two places. Rounding always occurs by looking one digit to the right of the number of decimal places you are rounding to. If the number on the right is 5 through 9 the number is rounded up—that is, the digit in the number of decimal places you are rounding to is increased by 1. If this number is a 9, it is changed to 0 and the digit to the left is increased by 1. The first example shows no rounding up for one place, but a rounding up for two places. The second example shows a rounding up in both cases.

The third example shows the effect on large numbers being rouned not to a number of decimal places, but to a number of digits. This is accomplished with the digits to the left of the decimal. The rounding is handled in a way opposite to the way normal rounding is handled. The digit to the left of the number of places being rounded is checked. If it is 5 or more the number to the left of that number is increased by one, and the rest of the digits to the right are set to 0. If it is 4 or less the number to the left of it is left untouched, and the rest of the numbers to the right are set to 0.

UPPER

The UPPER is the uppercase function. This translates a value into uppercase or evaluates a value in uppercase.

```
        STORE 'abcde' TO X
        STORE UPPER(X) TO Y
        STORE 'y' TO CHECK

  1) ? 'X = ' X
     ? 'Y = ' Y
  2) IF UPPER(X) = 'ABCDE'
          ? 'OK'
       ELSE
          ? 'NOT OK'
```

```
ENDIF
? 'X = ' X

1)  X = abcde
    Y = ABCDE

2)  OK
    X = abcde
```

In the first example, the upper command is used to physically change the characters abcde to the characters ABCDE. The upper in the second example allows you to check to see if the uppercase version of the variable is the same as a given literal, in this case, its uppercase equivalent—and it is.

The LOWER command does just the opposite.

COMPARISON OPERATORS AND LOGICAL CONNECTORS

There are several groups of comparison operators and logical operators that are used in dBASE III. The major groups are *arithmetic operators, comparison operators,* and *logical connectors.*

The arithmetic operators are

```
    +           Addition
    -           Subtraction
    *           Multiplication
    /           Division
    ** or ^     Exponentiation
```

The comparison operators are

```
    =           Equal
    #           Not Equal
    <           Less Than
    >           Greater Than
    <=          Less Than or Equal
    >=          Greater Than or Equal
```

The logical connectors are

```
    .AND.
    .OR.
    .NOT.
    .T.
    .F.
```

LOGICAL CONSTRUCTS USED IN dBASE III

The logical constructs explained in detail in Section I are written according to various rules of *syntax* (computer grammar) in dBASE III. The basic constructs, which are the IF-THEN-ELSE statement, the loop construction, the subroutines call, and the CASE statement are shown here.

IF-THEN-ELSE . . . ENDIF

The IF-THEN-ELSE logical construct allows a decision between two courses of action to be made. The action following the IF clause is followed if the expression in the IF clause is true. If it is not, and there is an ELSE clause, control passes to the ELSE clause.

There is no actual THEN clause in dBASE III. It is implied that everything after the IF clause is part of the THEN clause until the ELSE clause is reached. Notice that all IF-THEN-ELSE statements end with an ENDIF.

```
1)  STORE 'DEF' TO X
    IF X = 'ABC'
        ? 'THEN CLAUSE'
    ENDIF


    NO OUTPUT


2)  STORE 'ABC' TO X
    IF X = 'ABC'
        ? 'THEN CLAUSE'
      ELSE
        ? 'ELSE CLAUSE'
    ENDIF

    THEN CLAUSE


3)  STORE 'DEF' TO X
    IF X = 'ABC'
        ? 'THEN CLAUSE'
      ELSE
        ? 'ELSE CLAUSE'
    ENDIF

    ELSE CLAUSE
```

In the first example, there is only an IF-THEN clause. Since the condition X="ABC" is false, there is no output and control passes out of the IF-THEN construct.

The condition in the second example is true and the then clause is executed. The condition in the final example is false and control passes to the ELSE clause.

DO WHILE . . . ENDDO

Looping is accomplished through a command known as DO WHILE. The DO WHILE loop is performed over and over again until the condition is no longer true.

```
STORE 1 TO COUNTER
DO WHILE COUNTER <= 5
  @ COUNTER,COUNTER SAY COUNTER
  STORE COUNTER + 1 TO COUNTER
ENDDO


1
 2
  3
   4
    5
```

In this example, a variable COUNTER is set to one. The loop is entered, and the condition COUNTER < = 5 is checked to see if it is true. Since it is true, the loop continues. Each pass through the loop adds one to the variable COUNTER and outputs the value of counter at screen location COUNTER,COUNTER. The first pass puts it at 1,1, the next at 2,2, the third pass at 3,3 and so on all the way to 5,5. Notice the diagonal pattern that is created.

Any expression can be put in a DO WHILE loop. It can be a simple nomparison or a complex conditional expression. You can even make the loop last forever (an *infinite loop*) if you never make the condition being tested false. Each DO WHILE ends with an ENDDO.

A complex loop is shown below. The SKIP command shows that you are moving through an indexed database.

```
DO WHILE CUSTNO='00001' .AND. DATE =
  '05/45/83'
  @ 5,10 SAY AMOUNT
  SKIP
ENDDO
```

An infinite loop caused by not incrementing the variable X is shown below.

```
STORE 1 TO X
DO WHILE X < 5
  @ 1,1 SAY 'HELLO'
ENDDO
```

LOOP

The LOOP command is used to exit a DO WHILE construct regardless of what is between the LOOP and the ENDDO. For example

```
WITHOUT "LOOP"

STORE 1 TO X
DO WHILE X <= 5
  STORE X+6 TO Y
  @ X,X SAY 'HELLO'
  @ X,Y SAY 'THERE
ENDDO
@ X,20 SAY X



HELLO THERE
 HELLO THERE
  HELLO THERE
   HELLO THERE
    HELLO THERE      5

WITH "LOOP"

STORE 1 TO X
  DO WHILE X <= 5
  STORE X+6 TO Y
  @ X,X SAY 'HELLO'
  IF X = 3
    LOOP
  ENDIF
  @ X,Y SAY 'THERE'
ENDDO
@ X,20 SAY X


HELLO THERE
 HELLO THERE
  HELLO          3
```

In the first example, the DO WHILE construct is performed five times as specified in the DO WHILE condition. The phrase HELLO and THERE are repeated 5 times. The second example contains a LOOP command. This tells the program that when X = 3, it should go immediately to the statement following the ENDDO without performing any of the other statements in the DO WHILE. As you can see, the statement following the ENDDO prints the value of X. In the second example X is 3. The LOOP command caused a premature and immediate end to the DO WHILE loop.

The main use for the LOOP command is as a

quick way out when an error condition occurs. If you are performing a series of IF statements and an error condition occurs, it is usually faster to use a LOOP statement than a series of ELSE statements. The LOOP statement should be used sparingly, however, as it is not the most stable statement, and has been known to cause the loss of the end of a loop.

DO . . . RETURN

The subroutine call procedure is another form of the DO command. It requires no ENDDO. Instead of performing a series of statements over and over again, it calls another program.

```
MAIN.PRG

HOUSEKEEPING
READ COMMANDS
DO SUB1
DO SUB2

SUB1.PRG

SOME STATEMENTS
MORE STATEMENTS
RETURN

SUB2.PRG

SOME STATEMENTS
MORE STATEMENTS
RETURN
```

In the example above, the command procedure (program) MAIN.PRG calls the subprocedures SUB1.PRG and SUB2.PRG. These subprocedures can be programs by themselves, but it is likely that they share options and data with the main program. A subprocedure can call another subprocedure. The RETURN statement is dBASE IIIs way of keeping track of where it is. The RETURN statement immediately returns control to the statement that follows the DO statement that called the subprocedure. In the case of the RETURN statement in SUB1.PRG, control is returned to the DO SUB2 command. The RETURN in SUB2.PRG returns control to the statement after the DO SUB2 in the main program.

QUIT

The QUIT command causes an immediate exit from dBASE III and a return to the operating system. All loops are ended; all files are closed; no further statements are processed.

DO CASE . . . ENDCASE

The last logical construct is the CASE statement. This statement is used when an IF-THEN-ELSE statement is not sufficient to handle the situation. The IF-THEN-ELSE condition allows only two paths—one for true and one for false. The CASE construct allows an infinite number of paths along with an OTHERWISE clause:

```
READ AN ANSWER
DO CASE
  CASE ANS = 1
    DO SOMETHING
  CASE ANS = 2
    DO SOMETHING
  CASE ANS > 2 .AND. ANS <= 10
    DO SOMETHING
  OTHERWISE
    DO SOMETHING
ENDCASE
```

This DO CASE statement allows four different courses of action. If the answer was a 1 the first path is followed; 2 causes something else to be performed; an answer between 2 and 10 causes a third path to be followed, while anything else will follow the instructions in the OTHERWISE clause. These CASE statements are often used in selection menus. All DO CASE statements will end with an ENDCASE statement. If there is no OTHERWISE clause and none of the CASE statements are true, none of the commands within the CASE structure will be performed. The DO CASE construct is not a loop of any kind. It is performed only once unless it is inside a DO WHILE loop. Many IF-THEN-ELSE statements can be used instead of a CASE construct, but the procedure will not be as easy to use or understand.

DATABASE COMMANDS
USED IN PROGRAMMING

There are many database commands that can be used in programming. Some commands have already been talked about and will be reviewed. Others are new and are only used in programming in dBASE III. They would have no value outside of a program.

For the next few commands let's assume a database with the following structure:

```
NAME     Character
AGE      Numeric
SEX      Character
PHONE    Character
```

REPLACE

The REPLACE command is used to add or change fields in a database. For the REPLACE command to be used, the database must be open. When the REPLACE command is issued, the current contents of the specified fields are REPLACEd by the contents for those fields specified in the REPLACE command. If you wish to place a numeric field into character fields or vice-versa the STR or VAL command must also be used. Here are two examples of the REPLACE command.

```
USE DATABASE

STORE 'FRED SMITH' TO MYNAME
STORE 'M' TO GENDER
REPLACE NAME WITH MYNAME,SEX WITH GENDER

STORE '35' TO MYAGE
STORE 2347767 TO PHONENO
STORE 'BILL SMITH TO MYNAME
REPLACE AGE WITH VAL(MYAGE),PHONE WITH
    STR(MYPHONE,7) ;
    NAME WITH MY NAME
```

The first example shows a simple REPLACE on two fields of the database. Usually the values come from screen input, not from a direct assignment statement. The second example shows the method of converting from nameric data to character data using the STR command and from character data to numeric data using the VAL command. These conversions are only necessary when the data types are incompatible.

The ; at the end of the first line of the REPLACE command in the second example is a *continuation* character and is needed by dBASE III to indicate that there is more to the line. All the fields in a database need not be referenced within the REPLACE command; reference only those you wish to change.

APPEND BLANK

While the REPLACE command lets you change existing fields, the APPEND BLANK command is needed to add fields. This command adds a totally blank record to the end of the database. The APPEND BLANK command is usually followed by a REPLACE command as shown below.

```
READ IN A NAME, AGE, SEX, and PHONE
IF NAME # '          '
    APPEND BLANK
    REPLACE NAME WITH NAME, AGE WITH AGE, ;
    SEX WITH SEX, PHONE WITH PHONE
  ELSE @ 5,10 SAY 'ERROR - NO NAME FOUND'
ENDIF
```

The indexes of an indexed database will automatically be updated by either command. If an APPEND BLANK command is performed and no REPLACE command ever follows it, there will be a blank record in the file. Therefore the APPEND BLANK command should not be used unless a REPLACE will immediately follow it. You should do all your error checking first, and then use the APPEND BLANK and REPLACE commands

FIND, RECNO( ), SKIP, EOF( )

These four commands are used together to search databases for records. The FIND command works only on indexed databases. The FIND command allows a database to be searched very quickly. Almost any record can be found in under two seconds. Use of the LOCATE statement should be avoided if at all possible. (See Chapter 13).

The FIND command is used with a *memory variable*. A memory variable is a variable outside of a database. If you have a database field called NAME and you wish to search another database for that name, you must STORE the database variable to a memory variable. This is done with a normal store command. The memory variable is then used with a & preceding it.

```
STORE NAME TO NAME
FIND &NAME
```

Here, the memory variable NAME is stored separately from the database field NAME. The memory variable can now be changed without affecting the database field. When using the FIND command, the memory variable, or macro as it is sometimes called, must be a character variable. If it is a number you can use the STR command to change it as shown below.

FIND STR(&PHONE,7)

The FIND command will search the database for the first occurrence of the *key* being searched for. You can tell if it is found because the *record counter* will be set to the record number in the file. The record counter is represented by RECNO( ). You can check the RECNO( ) function. If it is less than the number of records in the file, the key was found. If it is equal to the number of records in the file, the key may not have been found. The better way to tell whether or not the key was found is to use the EOF( ) function.

End-of-File means that the last record of the file has been retrieved, and an attempt was made to retrieve another record. A variable called EOF is set to true. If EOF is false, the end of the file has not been reached, and the record has been found.

The SKIP command will not continue the search. The SKIP command simply moves to the next record in the database. You must check each record to see if it is still equal to the key. Another item you must check for is end-of-file. If you don't check for EOF, and you continue to use the SKIP command, your record pointer will just sit at the bottom of the file.

```
USE NAMES INDEX NAMES
STORE 'BILL SMITH' TO NAME
FIND &NAME
IF .NOT. EOF()
  DO WHILE NAME='BILL SMITH' .AND.
    .NOT. EOF()
    WRITE A RECORD
    SKIP
  ENDDO
ENDIF
```

This example shows the use of a database called NAMES, and the STORing of the name "BILL SMITH" to a memory variable called NAME. The database is then searched with the search key of BILL SMITH. Remember, the key field is not necessarily the first field on the database. The key

field is determined when the INDEX is initially set up with the INDEX command. If EOF( ) is .F. or .NOT. EOF( ), the record is found. Only if the record is found will the statements inside the IF condition be performed.

If the record is found the DO WHILE loop is performed. As long as the NAME is "BILL SMITH" and the end-of-file has not been reached (".NOT. EOF( )"), the loop will continue. The SKIP command will move the record pointer to the next record in the indexed database.

DELETE, PACK, DELETED( )

The final group of commands are used when records are being deleted or have been deleted. Whenever a record is no longer wanted, the DELETE command is used. This will not physically remove the record but will mark it for removal.

In order to remove the record, you must use the PACK command. The PACK command copies the entire file except for the marked records to a new database and then gives the new database the same name as the old database had. The old database with the marked records is then deleted. If the old file was indexed, the new file is indexed using the same key fields.

One problem you can have is that after you DELETE records, they can still be found when search commands are used. The DELETED( ) command can be used to see if any of the records found are marked for deletion and are just "hanging around" until the PACK command is given. The following is an example of the use of these commands using both pseudocode and dBASE III code:

```
ASK FOR A RECORD TO BE DELETED
DO WHILE MORE RECORDS
  FIND THE RECORD
  IF .NOT. EOF() .AND. .NOT. DELETED()
    DELETE
  ENDIF
ENDDO
PACK
```

The .NOT. DELETED( ) phrase checks to see that the record has not already been deleted. This is especially useful when PACKs are done infrequently and searches of a database yield deleted records. This in effect makes them invisible. This problem can also be avoided with the SET DELETED ON command, which makes deleted records invisible.

The DELETE command marks the current record in the database for deletion. At the end of the DO WHILE loop, after the ENDO command, the database is finally PACKed.

Since PACKing a database means copying all the records, it can take some time. Use a PACK command only when you have to, not every time you delete a single record.

SUMMARY

This chapter has presented the new programming commands in dBASE III. For another look at the database statements that are used outside of the programming system of dBASE III, see Section II. The statements in this chapter are all used in the programs in the next several chapters. You may want to use this chapter for reference as you analyze Fred's coding efforts.

Chapter 19

Coding Selection Menus

The following chapters will show you how Fred went about coding his system. Each program will be built from the middle outward. The body or sequence part of a program will be built first; then any IF conditions and error checking routines will be coded, and finally the loops will be added. As new code is added, the new lines will be set in darker type to make them easier to find.

Fred is now ready to code. He has learned how to use all the dBASE III programming statements that he learned about in the programming section. He now knows some interesting techniques and is ready to code.

SETTING THE ENVIRONMENT

Before Fred starts the coding of the main body of the menu he must set his *environment*. The environment consists of global parameters that will affect the rest of the program. The most important ones are

SET BELL OFF. This turns off the warning bell

that sounds every time the end of a field is reached. In dBASE III, one of the defaults is to sound the alarm each time the last character of a field is entered. It is used as a warning to tell you that you can't type anymore. It is also most annoying if most of your entries will reach the end of the field.

SET CONFIRM OFF. When you are entering fields that fill the entire space allowed for the field, especially in one character spaces of selection menus, this command will automatically enter the input when the end of the field is reached. This keeps the operator from having to hit the enter key every time a field is entered. This only works at the end of a field.

SET DEFAULT to drive. This allows you to specify a drive that contains the files you are working with. This eliminates the need to prefix databases, command procedures, or other files with the letter of the drive they are contained on.

SET DELETED ON. This command makes

recordsthat are deleted but not yet packed invisible to most operations.

SET DELIMITER OFF. If you like seeing the reverse video blocks delimiting the fields where you can type, then this default is correct. If you want some other form of delimiter to the left and right of the field entry, you must SET DELIMITER ON and use SET DELIMITER TO ' ' some set of symbols. The command SET DELIMITER TO '<>', would make a five character field like this: < >.

SET DEVICE TO SCREEN. This is the default for all output from SAY commands. If you wish to direct output to the printer, you must SET DEVICE TO PRINTER.

SET ECHO OFF. This command turns off the display of commands from the command file. If the echo is not set to off, the actual commands themselves will show up on the screen. This display is used only as a testing tool when all else fails.

SET TALK OFF. This command turns off the display of database command results. When a database command is given, such as DELETE, the message "1 record deleted" appears on the screen. The SET TALK OFF command eliminates this unnecessary display.

SET EXACT ON. This will assure that only exact matches are found when searches are performed. Without it, computer will not detect the difference between "BILL SMITH" and "BILL SMITH JONES".

The other major SET commands either are not often used or are defaults that you would want in the programming mode.

The beginning of Fred's program is shown in Fig. 19-1. Notice that Fred has not forgotten to document his program. Each module is clearly marked with the module name and purpose, along with the system name. Fred decides to call his main menu MAIN. It will be MAIN.PRG.

Fred has defined his environment and is now ready to continue coding.

CODING THE SELECTION MENUS

First, Fred looks at the system hierarchy chart shown in Fig. 19-2. He sees that there are four main subsystems: the customer system, the employee system, the order system, and the inventory system.

The Main Menu

Fred looks at the design screen, shown in Fig. 19-3, and pseudocode for the main system menu:

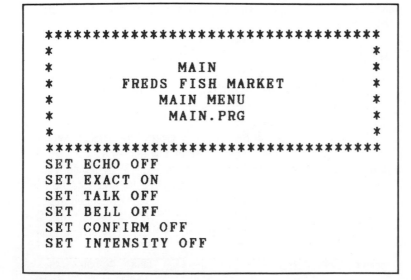

```
*************************************
*                                   *
*                                   *
*              MAIN                 *
*       FREDS FISH MARKET           *
*          MAIN MENU                *
*          MAIN.PRG                 *
*                                   *
*************************************
SET ECHO OFF
SET EXACT ON
SET TALK OFF
SET BELL OFF
SET CONFIRM OFF
SET INTENSITY OFF
```

Fig. 19-1. The main program—setting the environment.

```
MAIN MENU

  SET EXIT TO "N"
  DO WHILE NOT EXIT
    READ SELECTION
    CASE
      WHEN SELECTION = "1"
          PERFORM CUSTOMER SYSTEM
      WHEN SELECTION = "2"
          PERFORM EMPLOYEE SYSTEM
      WHEN SELECTION = "3"
          PERFORM ORDER SYSTEM
      WHEN SELECTION = "4"
          PERFORM INVENTORY SYSTEM
      WHEN SELECTION = "X"
          SET EXIT TO "Y"
      OTHERWISE
          WRITE "INVALID OPTION" ENDCASE
    ENDCASE
  ENDDO
```

He realizes that he forgot to put DISPLAY SCREEN in his pseudocode. It would have gone before the READ SELECTION. "The screen is a good place to start," says Fred. He codes the body of the screen display:

```
@  1,20 SAY 'FREDS FRIENDLY FISH MARKET'
@  3,20 SAY '           MAIN MENU           '
@  7,19 SAY '  ENTER SELECTION  ===>     ';
           GET OPTION
@ 10,22 SAY ' 1 - CUSTOMER SYSTEM        '
@ 11,22 SAY ' 2 - EMPLOYEE SYSTEM        '
@ 12,22 SAY ' 3 - ORDER SYSTEM           '
@ 13,22 SAY ' 4 - INVENTORY SYSTEM       '
@ 15,22 SAY ' X - EXIT SYSTEM            '
```

Fred uses the @ SAY commands. He prefers these commands to the ? commands. If he wants to add changes later, it will just be a matter of changing the line and column specifications. This code

will produce the screen design shown in Fig. 19-3.

The next part of the pseudocode indicates that the ability to get the selection from the screen must be coded. Fred adds the necessary commands to read the input:

```
STORE ' ' TO OPTION
CLEAR
@  1,20 SAY 'FREDS FRIENDLY FISH MARKET'
@  3,20 SAY '           MAIN MENU           '
@  7,19 SAY '  ENTER SELECTION  ===>     ';
           GET OPTION
@ 10,22 SAY ' 1 - CUSTOMER SYSTEM        '
@ 11,22 SAY ' 2 - EMPLOYEE SYSTEM        '
@ 12,22 SAY ' 3 - ORDER SYSTEM           '
@ 13,22 SAY ' 4 - INVENTORY SYSTEM       '
@ 15,22 SAY ' X - EXIT SYSTEM            '
READ
```

He added three lines. First the STORE command was necessary to allow a "field" for the entry of the option. Next he added the ; to the end of the "ENTER SELECTION === >" line to indicate that the line continued. Then he added the GET OPTION command on the next line. The READ at the end will allow the selection to be read into the variable OPTION.

Now the program will display the menu and read the selection. But, what is it to do after it reads the selection? The next step is to process the selection. As shown in the pseudocode on the preceding page, the next step is to code the CASE statement that will process the selection:

```
DO CASE
  CASE OPTION = '1'
    DO CUSTOMER
```

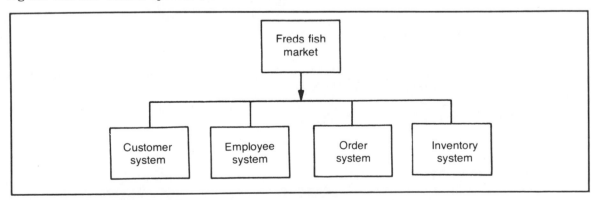

Fig. 19-2. The main system hierarchy.

155

```
CASE OPTION = '2'
  DO EMPLOYEE
CASE OPTION = '3'
  DO ORDER
CASE OPTION = '4'
  DO INVENTRY
CASE UPPER(OPTION) = 'X'
  RETURN
OTHERWISE
  ? CHR(7)
  @ 5,18 SAY '*** INVALID ENTRY-TRY
      AGAIN ***'
```

The CASE statement was easy to code. Each option contains a DO statement, which calls a subroutine. These subroutines are to be written later.

If OPTION = 'X', control will go to the operating system, just as the menu selection says. Notice the UPPER before the option clause. This means that the response should be evaluated as an uppercase letter when it is compared to the literal "X". Without the UPPER, an entry of "x" would not be equated with "X". Any time you use character strings in comparisons, you should translate the response to uppercase letters instead of comparing the response to both the lowercase and the uppercase versions of the expected response.

The OTHERWISE clause displays the error message. If the operator does not type one of the listed responses, the system will write an error message to the screen after issuing an alarm (a beep or a sound from the speaker on hardware so equipped).

This might be the completed menu program, thought Fred. But when he compared it to the pseudocode, he saw he had forgotten the main loop. Without the loop, this menu would only be displayed once. If an improper response was entered, the error message would have been displayed but, the program would not have allowed a reentry of the option. Fred adds the loop and reexamines the complete menu program, which is shown in Fig. 19-4.

The DO WHILE EXIT = 'F' is actually an infinite loop because nowhere will the value of EXIT ever be changed. However there is no need to ever exit the loop in the normal fashion because the QUIT option allows an exit from the loop.

Fred decides it is time to test the code. He starts by typing DBASE MAIN because his program is called MAIN. Immediately the main menu appeared just as it was supposed to. "So far, so good," thought Fred. "Now since I don't have any of the other programs working yet, I'll just try making an incorrect entry." Fred types in a D and observes the results shown in Fig. 19-5.

Now, Fred wonders, "Why is that D still there? Wow! my first bug." It is time for Fred to begin debugging. Some people will spend hours writing great pseudocode, and after typing in their code,

```
-----------------------------------------
:                                         :
:    FRED'S FRIENDLY FISH MARKET          :
:           MAIN MENU                     :
:                                         :
:                                         :
:                                         :
:    ENTER SELECTION ===>  __             :
:                                         :
:       1 - CUSTOMER SYSTEM               :
:       2 - EMPLOYEE SYSTEM               :
:       3 - ORDER SYSTEM                  :
:       4 - INVENTORY SYSTEM              :
:                                         :
:                                         :
:       X - EXIT SYSTEM                   :
:                                         :
-----------------------------------------
```

Fig. 19-3. The main system menu.

156

```
        SET DELIMITER TO '::'
        SET DELIMITER ON
        SET ECHO OFF
        SET EXACT ON
        SET TALK OFF
        SET BELL OFF
        SET CONFIRM OFF
        SET INTENSITY OFF
        STORE 'F' TO EXIT
        STORE ' ' TO OPTION
        CLEAR
        DO WHILE EXIT = 'F'
          @  1,20 SAY 'FREDS FRIENDLY FISH MARKET'
          @  3,20 SAY '         MAIN MENU          '
          @  7,19 SAY '  ENTER SELECTION  ===>   ';
                   GET OPTION
          @ 10,22 SAY ' 1 - CUSTOMER SYSTEM      '
          @ 11,22 SAY ' 2 - EMPLOYEE SYSTEM      '
          @ 12,22 SAY ' 3 - ORDER SYSTEM         '
          @ 13,22 SAY ' 4 - INVENTORY SYSTEM     '
          @ 15,22 SAY ' X - EXIT SYSTEM          '
          READ
          DO CASE
            CASE OPTION = '1'
              DO CUSTOMER
            CASE OPTION = '2'
              DO EMPLOYEE
            CASE OPTION = '3'
              DO ORDER
            CASE OPTION = '4'
              DO INVENTRY
            CASE UPPER(OPTION) = 'X'
              RETURN
            OTHERWISE
              ? CHR(7)
              @ 5,18 SAY '*** INVALID ENTRY-TRY AGAIN ***'
          ENDCASE
        ENDDO
```

Fig. 19-4. The main system dBASE III code.

they will check it for hours before running it. Others will type in what they want, run the program, find one error, and change the program over and over again. Though this takes less thinking time, it will take you hours longer to code the program.

Fred quickly realizes the problem. He is not

clearing out the OPTION field after an error. He adds the line STORE ' ' TO OPTION after the ENDCASE statement, retests the program and voila! It is done! After a final look at the program, Fred is ready to move on.

The Customer System Menu

The next system to code is the customer subsystem. Fred looks at the hierarchy chart, shown in Fig. 19-7, to determine which module to begin with.

Fred realizes that the main customer menu should be first part of the system to be coded. After his success with the main menu, he figures this should be easy. He starts by looking at the menu and pseudocode for the customer system menu shown in Fig. 19-8.

Something immediately strikes Fred as being strange. How do you return to the main menu from the customer menu? There should be a RETURN option in the menu. Fred will remember to add one in.

Fred knows he can use his main menu program over again and just change some words and lines. He makes a copy of the program using his word processor—that's right, his word processor. The MODIFY COMMAND commands (that is, the set of commands used to change program lines) of dBASE III are difficult to use. You are much better off to use a fullscreen word processor to enter and modify your programs.

Fred makes a copy and makes a few changes and produces the code shown in Fig. 19-9.

It is now time to test again. Fred starts up dBASE III enters the main menu and types a "1". What he sees is shown in Fig. 19-10.

Fred tries the error message routine by typing a blank entry. This too works. Great, says Fred. "I plagiarized a whole module; programming is easy! Now I'll make sure the RETURN function works, and I am done."

Fred types an "R" and—Oh-Oh! There seems to be a problem. Part of the customer menu appears at the bottom of the main menu, shown in Fig. 19-11. Fred reviews the code of the main menu. "Nothing wrong here," he thinks. Fred looks again at the customer menu and finds nothing wrong again. Fred has a nice bowl of Elsa's chowder and comes back later.

Now Fred is really wondering. There is nothing wrong with the main menu, and there is nothing wrong with the customer menu, but the program is not working. Maybe something is wrong going between menus. Fred is about to discover that when you redisplay menus it is a good idea to use a

Fig. 19-5. The main system screen with an error code.

```
          FREDS FRIENDLY FISH MARKET

                  MAIN MENU

      *** INVALID ENTRY-TRY AGAIN ***

      ENTER SELECTION  ===>     :D:


            1 - CUSTOMER SYSTEM
            2 - EMPLOYEE SYSTEM
            3 - ORDER SYSTEM
            4 - INVENTORY SYSTEM

            X - EXIT SYSTEM
```

```
      ************************************
      *                                  *
      *             MAIN                 *
      *        FREDS FISH MARKET         *
      *           MAIN MENU              *
      *            MAIN.PRG              *
      *                                  *
      ************************************
      SET DELIMITER TO '::'
      SET DELIMITER ON
      SET ECHO OFF
      SET EXACT ON
      SET TALK OFF
      SET BELL OFF
      SET CONFIRM OFF
      SET INTENSITY OFF
      STORE 'F' TO EXIT
      STORE ' ' TO OPTION
      CLEAR
      DO WHILE EXIT = 'F'
        @  1,20 SAY 'FREDS FRIENDLY FISH MARKET'
        @  3,20 SAY '          MAIN MENU          '
        @  7,19 SAY '  ENTER SELECTION  ===>   ';
                GET OPTION
        @ 10,22 SAY ' 1 - CUSTOMER SYSTEM        '
        @ 11,22 SAY ' 2 - EMPLOYEE SYSTEM        '
        @ 12,22 SAY ' 3 - ORDER SYSTEM           '
        @ 13,22 SAY ' 4 - INVENTORY SYSTEM       '
        @ 15,22 SAY ' X - EXIT SYSTEM            '
        READ
        DO CASE
          CASE OPTION = '1'
            DO CUSTOMER
          CASE OPTION = '2'
            DO EMPLOYEE
          CASE OPTION = '3'
            DO ORDER
          CASE OPTION = '4'
            DO INVENTRY
          CASE UPPER(OPTION) = 'X'
            RETURN
          OTHERWISE
            ? CHR(7)
            @ 5,18 SAY '*** INVALID ENTRY-TRY AGAIN ***'
        ENDCASE
        STORE ' ' TO OPTION
      ENDDO
```

Fig. 19-6. The main system dBase III Code—the final version.

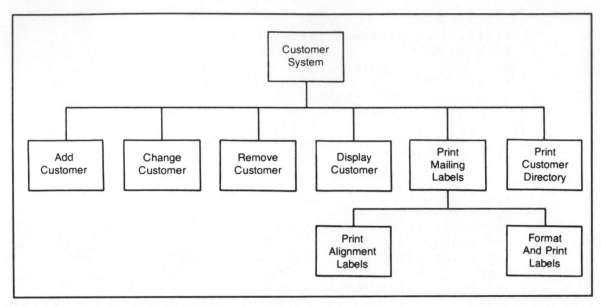

Fig. 19-7. Customer System Hierarchy Chart.

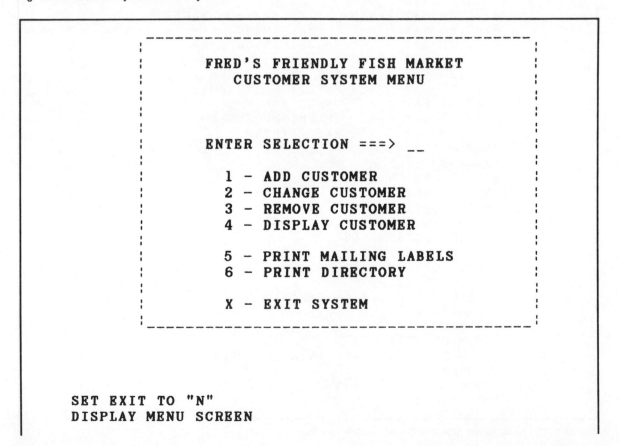

```
          FRED'S FRIENDLY FISH MARKET
            CUSTOMER SYSTEM MENU


       ENTER SELECTION ===> __

           1 - ADD CUSTOMER
           2 - CHANGE CUSTOMER
           3 - REMOVE CUSTOMER
           4 - DISPLAY CUSTOMER

           5 - PRINT MAILING LABELS
           6 - PRINT DIRECTORY

           X - EXIT SYSTEM
```

SET EXIT TO "N"
DISPLAY MENU SCREEN

```
DOWHILE EXIT = "N"
  READ OPTION
  CASE
    WHEN OPTION = 1 PERFORM "ADD CUSTOMER"
    WHEN OPTION = 2 PERFORM "CHANGE CUSTOMER"
    WHEN OPTION = 3 PERFORM "REMOVE CUSTOMER"
    WHEN OPTION = 4 PERFORM "DISPLAY CUSTOMER"
    WHEN OPTION = 5 PERFORM "PRINT MAILING LABELS"
    WHEN OPTION = 6 PERFORM "PRINT DIRECTORY"
    WHEN OPTION = X SET EXIT TO "Y"
    OTHERWISE WRITE "INVALID OPTION"
  ENDCASE
ENDDO
```

Fig. 19-8. The customer system menu screen and pseudocode.

```
STORE 'F' TO CUSTEXIT
STORE ' ' TO OPTION
CLEAR
DO WHILE CUSTEXIT = 'F'
  @  1,20 SAY 'FREDS FRIENDLY FISH MARKET'
  @  3,20 SAY '   CUSTOMER SYSTEM MENU    '
  @  7,19 SAY '  ENTER SELECTION  ===>    ';
          GET OPTION
  @ 10,21 SAY ' 1 - ADD CUSTOMER          '
  @ 11,21 SAY ' 2 - CHANGE CUSTOMER       '
  @ 12,21 SAY ' 3 - REMOVE CUSTOMER       '
  @ 13,21 SAY ' 4 - DISPLAY CUSTOMER      '
  @ 15,21 SAY ' 5 - PRINT MAILING LABELS '
  @ 16,21 SAY ' 6 - PRINT DIRECTORY       '
  @ 18,21 SAY ' R - RETURN TO MAIN MENU   '
  @ 19,21 SAY ' X - EXIT SYSTEM           '
  READ
  DO CASE
    CASE OPTION = '1'
      DO CUSTADD
    CASE OPTION = '2'
      DO CUSTCHG
    CASE OPTION = '3'
      DO CUSTREM
    CASE OPTION = '4'
      DO CUSTDIS
```

```
              CASE OPTION = '5'
                 DO CUSTLBL
              CASE OPTION = '6'
                 DO CUSTDIR
            CASE UPPER(OPTION) = 'R'
                 CLEAR
                 RETURN
             CASE UPPER(OPTION) = 'X'
                 QUIT
             OTHERWISE
                 ? CHR(7)
                 @ 5,20 SAY '*** INVALID ENTRY -TRY AGAIN ***'
         ENDCASE
         STORE ' ' TO OPTION
      ENDDO
```

Fig. 19-9. The customer system menu code.

```
FREDS FRIENDLY FISH MARKET

    CUSTOMER SYSTEM MENU



  ENTER SELECTION  ===>    : :


     1 - ADD CUSTOMER
     2 - CHANGE CUSTOMER
     3 - REMOVE CUSTOMER
     4 - DISPLAY CUSTOMER

     5 - PRINT MAILING LABELS
     6 - PRINT DIRECTORY

     R - RETURN TO MAIN MENU
     X - EXIT SYSTEM
```

Fig. 19-10. The customer system menu screen.

```
         FREDS FRIENDLY FISH MARKET

                MAIN MENU



         ENTER SELECTION   ===>     :  :


              1 - CUSTOMER SYSTEM
              2 - EMPLOYEE SYSTEM
              3 - ORDER SYSTEM
              4 - INVENTORY SYSTEM

              X - EXIT SYSTEM
              6 - PRINT DIRECTORY

              R - RETURN TO MAIN MENU
              X - EXIT SYSTEM
```

Fig. 19-11. The main menu and the customer menu shown overlaid together.

```
       ************************************
       *                                  *
       *               1                  *
       *        FREDS FISH MARKET         *
       *         CUSTOMER MENU            *
       *          CUSTOMER.PRG            *
       *                                  *
       ************************************
       STORE 'F' TO CUSTEXIT
       STORE ' ' TO OPTION
       CLEAR
       DO WHILE CUSTEXIT = 'F'
          @  1,20 SAY 'FREDS FRIENDLY FISH MARKET'
          @  3,20 SAY '   CUSTOMER SYSTEM MENU   '
          @  7,19 SAY '  ENTER SELECTION  ===>   ';
                  GET OPTION
          @ 10,21 SAY ' 1 - ADD CUSTOMER          '
          @ 11,21 SAY ' 2 - CHANGE CUSTOMER       '
          @ 12,21 SAY ' 3 - REMOVE CUSTOMER       '
          @ 13,21 SAY ' 4 - DISPLAY CUSTOMER      '
          @ 15,21 SAY ' 5 - PRINT MAILING LABELS  '
          @ 16,21 SAY ' 6 - PRINT DIRECTORY       '
          @ 18,21 SAY ' R - RETURN TO MAIN MENU   '
          @ 19,21 SAY ' X - EXIT SYSTEM           '
```

```
READ
DO CASE
   CASE OPTION = '1'
      DO CUSTADD
   CASE OPTION = '2'
      DO CUSTCHG
   CASE OPTION = '3'
      DO CUSTREM
   CASE OPTION = '4'
      DO CUSTDIS
   CASE OPTION = '5'
      DO CUSTLBL
   CASE OPTION = '6'
      DO CUSTDIR
  CASE UPPER(OPTION) = 'R'
     RETURN
  CASE UPPER(OPTION) = 'X'
     QUIT
  OTHERWISE
     ? CHR(7)
     @ 5,20 SAY '*** INVALID ENTRY -TRY AGAIN ***'
  ENDCASE
  STORE ' ' TO OPTION
ENDDO
```

Fig. 19-12. The customer system menu dBASE III code—the final version.

CLEAR command. CLEAR would go before RE-TURN in the customer menu. Fred adds this and his problem is solved. He takes a final look at his program, shown in Fig. 19-12.

SUMMARY

In this chapter, you have seen how to create, test, and debug selection menus. Selection menus are the cornerstones of any interactive system. They play the role of the traffic cop, enabling the operator to determine what road to take and when to return.

Now that the selection menus are coded it is time to move on to the data entry menus.

Chapter 20

Coding Data Entry Screens

The next step is to code the data entry screens for the customer system. The first subsystem to code is the ADD CUSTOMERS module. Fred begins by looking at the screen design and pseudocode for the system, both of which are shown in Fig. 20-1.

Fred decides to approach the problem by creating the screen display first. He starts coding the body of the data entry screen:

```
@  1,20 SAY 'FREDS FRIENDLY FISH MARKET'
@  3,20 SAY '  CUSTOMER ADDITIONS MENU  '
@  7,18 SAY 'CUSTOMER NUMBER: '
@  9,15 SAY 'COMPANY:       '
@ 10,15 SAY 'LAST NAME:   '
@ 11,15 SAY 'FIRST NAME:  '
@ 13,15 SAY 'ADDRESS: '
@ 14,15 SAY 'CITY:        '
@ 16,15 SAY 'STATE:     '
@ 16,30 SAY 'ZIP: '
@ 18,15 SAY 'PHONE NUMBER:  '
@ 20,15 SAY 'DISCOUNT: '
```

That was easy, thought Fred, "Now to add the commands to get the data from the screen." Fred remembers to use the initialization commands for the fields that are used in the GET commands. Figure 20-2 shows the results of his efforts.

Fred has defined the input section of his customer additions screen. He began by listing the field names needed for the GET and defining their lengths with a series of blanks. The lengths of the fields correspond to the lengths of the matching fields in the database.

As explained earlier in this section, it is better to initialize these variables in this manner than by using the APPEND BLANK command and then reading the lengths of the fields from the database. If you use the fields from the database, and you decide not to use the blank record, you must then take the extra step of deleting the blank record and packing the database.

In his last three fields, Fred has used the PICTURE clause to change how the input data will look. The special characters such as the dashes and parentheses will be stored along with the data in the database. Fred also used the PICTURE clause in the first field to make sure that no data other than

```
-------------------------------------------------
:                                               :
:          FRED'S FRIENDLY FISH MARKET          :
:              CUSTOMER ADDITIONS               :
:                                               :
:                                               :
:    CUSTOMER NUMBER: CUSTN                      :
:                                               :
:    COMPANY:      COMPANY-------------X         :
:    LAST NAME:    LNAME--------------X          :
:    FIRST NAME:   FNAME--------------X          :
:                                               :
:    ADDRESS: ADDRESS------------------X         :
:    CITY:       CITY---------X                  :
:                                               :
:    STATE: ST     ZIP: ZIP-----X                :
:                                               :
:    PHONE NUMBER: PHONE-------X                 :
:                                               :
:    DISCOUNT: DS                                :
:                                               :
-------------------------------------------------


     ADD A CUSTOMER

          ACCESS CUSTOMER FILE
          SET CUSTOMER NUMBER TO NOT BLANK
          DO WHILE CUSTOMER NUMBER NOT BLANK
             DISPLAY SCREEN
             ENTER DATA
             VERIFY CUSTOMER NUMBER
             IF NEW NUMBER
                THEN
                   ADD CUSTOMER DATA
                   CLEAR DATA FIELDS
                ELSE
                   WRITE "NUMBER ALREADY ON FILE"
             ENDIF
          ENDDO
```

Fig. 20-1. The customer additions screen and pseudocode.

numbers could be entered into that field. In dBASE III the PICTURE clause is used a lot when data is entered into fields. It provides an easy way to re-format the data as you read it into the program.

Notice that the @ SAY clause and the @ GET clause are on the same line. As explained earlier in

```
STORE '      ' TO CSN
STORE '                    ' TO CMP
STORE '                    ' TO LNM
STORE '                    ' TO FNM
STORE '                      ' TO ADR
STORE '                ' TO CTY
STORE '   ' TO STT
STORE '        ' TO ZP
STORE '              ' TO PHN
STORE 0 TO DS
   @  1,20 SAY 'FREDS FRIENDLY FISH MARKET'
   @  3,20 SAY '  CUSTOMER ADDITIONS MENU   '
   @  7,18 SAY 'CUSTOMER NUMBER: ' GET CSN      PICTURE '#####'
   @  9,15 SAY 'COMPANY:        '  GET CMP
   @ 10,15 SAY 'LAST NAME:  '      GET LNM
   @ 11,15 SAY 'FIRST NAME: '      GET FNM
   @ 13,15 SAY 'ADDRESS: '         GET ADR
   @ 14,15 SAY 'CITY:     '        GET CTY
   @ 16,15 SAY 'STATE:    '        GET STT
   @ 16,30 SAY 'ZIP: '             GET ZP       PICTURE '#####-####'
   @ 18,15 SAY 'PHONE NUMBER: '    GET PHN      PICTURE '(###)###-####'
   @ 20,15 SAY 'DISCOUNT: '        GET DS       PICTURE '##'
READ
```

Fig. 20-2. The customer additions program—the main body and GETS.

this section, this is an important way to save some work in coding. The input space will appear one space to the right of the end of the @ SAY line.

The discount input variable, DS, is set to 0, but the PICTURE clause will use two characters. The number is actually assumed to be eight digits long until it is set into the database.

According to the pseudocode, the next step is to verify the customer number to make sure it doesn't already exist and then to add the customer data to the database. The pseudocode also says to clear the data fields if the record is added to the database. An error already exists. Fred writes the code shown in Fig. 20-3.

This section of code would come directly after the READ command in the previous section. Fred begins by using the FIND command to check the open database for the key CSN. This should be the customer number that was typed in. There is a single IF-THEN-ELSE construction that handles the FIND. If the EOF( ) is true, there is no existing

record with the current customer number and the record should be added. The APPEND BLANK command will create a blank record, while the RE-PLACE command will fill the fields of the record. A message is printed on the screen saying that the customer was added. All the fields are then cleared so that when the menu is redisplayed, the data fields will again be empty.

If the result of the FIND was that the current customer number already existed the error message saying CUSTOMER ALREADY ON FILE would be displayed. The fields are not cleared as it is possible that only the customer number need be entered again.

The screen should now be redisplayed so that any new customers can be entered or any errors corrected. Fred needs to add the DO WHILE loop. He also must remember to add a check to see whether or not there are more customers to be added. If the operator does not have any more customers to add, he will press the enter key, with-

```
FIND &CSN
IF EOF()
    APPEND BLANK
    REPLACE CUSTN WITH VAL(CSN),COMP WITH CMP,LNAME WITH LNM;
      FNAME WITH FNM,ADDR WITH ADR,CITY WITH CTY,ST WITH STT;
      ZIP WITH ZP,PHONE WITH PHN,DIS WITH DS
    @ 5,1
    @ 5,15 SAY '        *** CUSTOMER ADDED   *** '
    STORE '        ' TO CSN
    STORE '                            ' TO CMP
    STORE '                       ' TO LNM
    STORE '                       ' TO FNM
    STORE '                          ' TO ADR
    STORE '                    ' TO CTY
    STORE '  ' TO STT
    STORE '          ' TO ZP
    STORE '              ' TO PHN
    STORE 0 TO DS
  ELSE
    ? CHR(7)
    @ 5,15 SAY '*** CUSTOMER NUMBER ALREADY ON FILE ***'
ENDIF
```

Fig. 20-3. The code for adding a new customer.

out typing a customer number, and the CSN field will be blank. Fred adds the appropriate loop to the action section as shown in Fig. 20-4.

To show the loop and the IF condition better the code for the screen has been removed. An IF condition that checked to see if customer number was blank was added. If it is blank, the RETURN statement will cause the system to go to the customer menu so that all the customer functions can be redisplayed. The main part of the action statements were moved under an ELSE condition. This is the process known as *nesting*. You can put as many IF-THEN-ELSE expressions within each other as you wish.

The use of indentation can be seen in this code. The process of indenting your code does nothing for the performance of the computer, but it does everything for you when you are testing and debugging your code. Remember to match each IF with its ENDIF, each DO with its ENDDO, and each CASE

with its ENDCASE. This will save you many hours later on.

Again, as in the selection menus, the loop is actually an infinite loop that you are exiting from with the RETURN statement. Some people would say this is not correct. They would say that instead of having the RETURN where it is, the RETURN should be after the ENDDO, and the current location of the RETURN should contain the condition that makes the loop false—STORE 'F' TO MORECUST. The program will work either way. dBASE III does allow you to leave a loop quickly as Fred did. If the method works, use it.

Fred is ready to add the final touches and test the program. He adds the USE filename command to open the data file at the beginning of the program and the file close command (USE alone) in the RETURN procedure. Fred also adds an ERASE at the beginning to clear the screen. The resulting program is shown in Fig. 20-5.

```
          STORE .T. TO MORECUST
          DO WHILE MORECUST = 'T'
             IF CSN = '         '
                  CLEAR
                  RETURN
                ELSE
                  FIND &CSN
                  IF EOF()
                      APPEND BLANK
                      REPLACE CUSTN WITH VAL(CSN),COMP WITH CMP,LNAME WITH LNM;
                        FNAME WITH FNM,ADDR WITH ADR,CITY WITH CTY,ST WITH STT;
                        ZIP WITH ZP,PHONE WITH PHN,DIS WITH DS
                      @ 5,15 SAY '        *** CUSTOMER ADDED  *** '
                      STORE '        ' TO CSN
                      STORE '                        ' TO CMP
                      STORE '                    ' TO LNM
                      STORE '                    ' TO FNM
                      STORE '                            ' TO ADR
                      STORE '                  ' TO CTY
                      STORE '  ' TO STT
                      STORE '            ' TO ZP
                      STORE '                 ' TO PHN
                      STORE 0 TO DS
                    ELSE
                      ? CHR(7)
                      @ 5,15 SAY '*** CUSTOMER NUMBER ALREADY ON FILE ***'
                  ENDIF
             ENDIF
          ENDDO
```

Fig. 20-4. The customer additions program—the DO WHILE and more customers Loops.

```
               ************************************
               *                                  *
               *              1.1                 *
               *        FREDS FISH MARKET         *
               *     CUSTOMER ADDITIONS PROGRAM   *
               *            CUSTADD.PRG           *
               *                                  *
               ************************************
               CLEAR
               USE CUSTOMER INDEX CUSTOMER
               STORE .T. TO MORECUST
               STORE '        ' TO CSN
               STORE '                        ' TO CMP
               STORE '                    ' TO LNM
               STORE '                    ' TO FNM
               STORE '                            ' TO ADR
               STORE '                  ' TO CTY
               STORE '  ' TO STT
               STORE '            ' TO ZP
               STORE '                 ' TO PHN
               STORE 0 TO DS
               DO WHILE MORECUST = 'T'
```

```
@  1,20 SAY 'FREDS FRIENDLY FISH MARKET'
@  3,20 SAY '   CUSTOMER ADDITIONS MENU   '
@  7,18 SAY 'CUSTOMER NUMBER: ' GET CSN      PICTURE '#####'
@  9,15 SAY 'COMPANY:       '  GET CMP
@ 10,15 SAY 'LAST NAME:   '    GET LNM
@ 11,15 SAY 'FIRST NAME: '     GET FNM
@ 13,15 SAY 'ADDRESS: '        GET ADR
@ 14,15 SAY 'CITY:      '      GET CTY
@ 16,15 SAY 'STATE:     '      GET STT
@ 16,30 SAY 'ZIP: '            GET ZP       PICTURE '#####-####'
@ 18,15 SAY 'PHONE NUMBER: '   GET PHN      PICTURE '(###)###-####'
@ 20,15 SAY 'DISCOUNT: '       GET DS       PICTURE '##'
READ
IF CSN = '       '
    USE
    CLEAR
    RETURN
  ELSE
    FIND &CSN
    IF EOF()
        APPEND BLANK
        REPLACE CUSTN WITH VAL(CSN),COMP WITH CMP,LNAME WITH LNM;
          FNAME WITH FNM,ADDR WITH ADR,CITY WITH CTY,ST WITH STT;
          ZIP WITH ZP,PHONE WITH PHN,DIS WITH DS
        @ 5,1
        @ 5,15 SAY '      *** CUSTOMER ADDED   *** '
        STORE '      ' TO CSN
        STORE '                      ' TO CMP
        STORE '                 ' TO LNM
        STORE '                 ' TO FNM
        STORE '                         ' TO ADR
        STORE '                  ' TO CTY
        STORE '   ' TO STT
        STORE '          ' TO ZP
        STORE '             ' TO PHN
        STORE 0 TO DS
      ELSE
        ? CHR(7)
        @ 5,15 SAY '*** CUSTOMER NUMBER ALREADY ON FILE ***'
    ENDIF
  ENDIF
ENDDO
```

Fig. 20-5. The customer Additions dBase III code—final version.

The USE CUSTOMER INDEX CUSTOMER that has been added to the top of the program illustrates the first step in most programs that deal with data files: the opening of the database. By the same token, one of the last things done is the closing of the file. The USE command with no parameters closes the active file. Since there is only one file open, the customer file is closed.

Realistically, there would probably be some bugs in this code. With good design techniques and previously written *clean* code, you can minimize your errors almost totally. Fred decides to test his screen.

He starts dBASE III. After he gets the main

menu, he types a 1 to get to the customer menu. Again he types a 1 to use the add customer function. This function is known as 1.1, because it was called by typing a one followed by a one. This information appears in the documentation. The main program doesn't really have a name and is called MAIN. The customer menu is called 1 and each function of the customer menu is called 1, choice number. The add customers function is 1.1, the change customer function is 1.2 and so on.

After the pair of ones are typed, the screen in Fig. 20-6 is shown. The operator can now type in the input for any or all fields. The only field that must be filled is the customer number. If this is blank, the program will return to the main customer menu.

Figure 20-7 shows a completed customer record. The screen has been filled in and the record is ready to be entered into the database. When the last field is filled in, the blank data-entry screen is displayed again ready for the information for the next record to be entered. A message indicates that the previous customer record has been successfully added. Figure 20-8 shows the results of attempting to assign an existing customer number to a new customer. Although all the data the operator has entered is different, the customer number has already been used. The operator is alerted by the error message. Only the customer number has to be changed; the rest of the data is good. The operator has two choices: He can change the customer number to a nonexisting one, and the record will be added, or he can blank out the number and return to the customer menu without adding the record. The data fields that were typed in will be lost if the operator chooses the second option. Fred decides to change the customer number and the record is added to the file. Figure 20-9 shows the result.

There seems to be a small problem. Part of the old message is still there. dBASE III doesn't totally clear a display line just because you write to it. It only clears as much of the line as is required for the new text. Since the old message is longer than the new message, the longer portion isn't erased. A solution for this is to code the statement @ 5,1 before

```
            FREDS FRIENDLY FISH MARKET

            CUSTOMER ADDITIONS MENU



      CUSTOMER NUMBER:  :        :

   COMPANY:       :                        :
   LAST NAME:     :                        :
   FIRST NAME:    :                        :

   ADDRESS:  :                              :
   CITY:        :                    :

   STATE:     :   :  ZIP: :        —      :

   PHONE NUMBER:  : (    )     —        :

   DISCOUNT:  :  0:
```

Fig. 20-6. The customer additions screen ready for input.

```
        FREDS FRIENDLY FISH MARKET

        CUSTOMER ADDITIONS MENU


      CUSTOMER NUMBER: :200  :

      COMPANY:      :LEE SIDE FISHERIES  :
      LAST NAME:  :KAY                    :
      FIRST NAME: :LEE JAY                :

      ADDRESS: :151 FARMINGTON AVE        :
      CITY:    :NORTH HAVEN    :

      STATE:   :CA:  ZIP: :88667-2443:

      PHONE NUMBER: :(968)555-1424:

      DISCOUNT: :10:
```

Fig. 20-7. The filled-in customer additions screen.

```
        FREDS FRIENDLY FISH MARKET

        CUSTOMER ADDITIONS MENU

    *** CUSTOMER NUMBER ALREADY ON FILE ***

      CUSTOMER NUMBER: :200  :

    COMPANY:      :SAMS LOX HAVEN    :
    LAST NAME:  :BURTON               :
    FIRST NAME: :SAMUEL               :

    ADDRESS: :18465 TRAIL STREET       :
    CITY:    :BOCA DELRAY    :

    STATE:   :MO:  ZIP: :88673-2227:

    PHONE NUMBER: :(564)555-1525:

    DISCOUNT: : 0:
```

Fig. 20-8. The customer additions screen error message.

```
        FREDS  FRIENDLY  FISH  MARKET

        CUSTOMER  ADDITIONS  MENU

     ***  CUSTOMER  ADDED    ***   FILE  ***

     CUSTOMER  NUMBER:  :          :

     COMPANY:      :                        :
     LAST  NAME:   :                        :
     FIRST  NAME:  :                        :

     ADDRESS:  :                                 :
     CITY:     :                    :

     STATE:    :   :  ZIP:  :       —        :

     PHONE  NUMBER:  :(    )      —        :

     DISCOUNT:  :  0:
```

Fig. 20-9. The customer additions screen message problem.

the CUSTOMER ADDED message. The @ 5,1 command means that line 5 will be totally cleared. This is the only change that has to be made to this module.

Fred's last test is to test the return to the main customer menu. Fred enters a blank line for a customer number and the customer system menu is correctly displayed.

Fred is done with the ADD CUSTOMER function. Next he will turn his sights to the CHANGE CUSTOMER function.

CHANGING RECORDS

To start, Fred looks at the screens and pseudocode for the CHANGE CUSTOMER function. These are shown in Fig. 20-10. He sees remarkable similarities between the add screen and the change screen. The biggest difference is in the looping. First, it appears that there will be two READ statements. The first will get the customer number to be retrieved from the file; the second,

which will be used if the customer number is found, will enter any changes.

There does not need to be any defining and clearing of the variables in this module. Fred notices that the database field names themselves can be used. He begins with the first part of the code, the preliminary screen:

```
@  1,20 SAY 'FREDS FRIENDLY FISH MARKET'
@  3,20 SAY '    CUSTOMER CHANGES         '
@  7,18 SAY 'CUSTOMER NUMBER: ' GET CSN
   PICTURE '#####'
READ
```

This part will display the top part of the screen and allow the input of the customer number for the retrieval process.

Fred than codes the retrieve and display section as shown in Fig. 20-11. This code begins by checking the customer number for a nonblank entry. If it is blank, the usual RETURN is performed, and the system returns to the main customer menu. If there is a customer number entered, the system

```
 ------------------------------------------
|                                          |
|        FRED'S FRIENDLY FISH MARKET       |
|            CUSTOMER CHANGES              |
|                                          |
|                                          |
|     CUSTOMER NUMBER: CUSTN               |
|                                          |
|                                          |
|                                          |
|                                          |
 ------------------------------------------
```

```
 ------------------------------------------
|                                          |
|        FRED'S FRIENDLY FISH MARKET       |
|            CUSTOMER CHANGES              |
|                                          |
|                                          |
|     CUSTOMER NUMBER: CUSTN               |
|                                          |
|     COMPANY:     COMPANY------------X    |
|     LAST NAME:   LNAME--------------X    |
|     FIRST NAME: FNAME---------------X    |
|                                          |
|     ADDRESS: ADDRESS----------------X    |
|     CITY:    CITY----------X             |
|                                          |
|     STATE: ST    ZIP: ZIP-----X          |
|                                          |
|     PHONE NUMBER: PHONE-------X          |
|                                          |
|     DISCOUNT: DS                         |
|                                          |
 ------------------------------------------
```

CHANGE A CUSTOMER

        ACCESS CUSTOMER FILE
        SET CUSTOMER NUMBER TO NOT BLANK
        DO WHILE CUSTOMER NUMBER NOT BLANK
           DISPLAY SCREEN

```
        ENTER CUSTOMER NUMBER
        VERIFY CUSTOMER NUMBER
        IF FOUND
          THEN
             RETRIEVE CUSTOMER DATA
             CHANGE DESIRED FIELDS
             UPDATE RECORD
             CLEAR DATA FIELDS
          ELSE
             WRITE "NUMBER NOT ON FILE"
        ENDIF
     ENDDO
```

Fig. 20-10. The customer change data entry screen, pseudocode and preliminary screen code.

checks to make sure it exists. If the customer number does not exist, an error message is displayed, the preliminary screen is redisplayed, and the opportunity to enter another customer number is given.

After the customer number is found, the record pointer in the database would be pointing at the found record. When the @ GET commands are is-

```
IF CSN = '         '
    USE
    CLEAR
    RETURN
 ELSE
    FIND &CSN
    IF .NOT. EOF()
        @  9,15 SAY 'COMPANY:       '        GET COMP
        @ 10,15 SAY 'LAST NAME:   '          GET LNAME
        @ 11,15 SAY 'FIRST NAME: '           GET FNAME
        @ 13,15 SAY 'ADDRESS: '              GET ADDR
        @ 14,15 SAY 'CITY:       '           GET CITY
        @ 16,15 SAY 'STATE: '                GET ST
        @ 16,30 SAY 'ZIP: '                  GET ZIP    PICTURE '#####-####'
        @ 18,15 SAY 'PHONE NUMBER: '         GET PHONE  PICTURE '(###)###-####'
        @ 20,15 SAY 'DISCOUNT: '             GET DIS    PICTURE '##'
        READ
        CLEAR
        @ 5,1
        @ 5,15 SAY '     *** CUSTOMER CHANGED   ***            '
        STORE '       ' TO CSN
     ELSE
        ? CHR(7)
        CLEAR
        @ 5,15 SAY '*** CUSTOMER NUMBER NOT FOUND ***'
    ENDIF
 ENDIF
```

Fig. 20-11. The customer changes main screen code.

sued and the field names match the field names in the database, the data from the database is automatically put into the fields in the menu program.

The IF .NOT. EOF( ) command is different from the IF EOF( ) command used for the CUSTOMER ADDITIONS screen because opposite outcome is desired. The IF EOF( ) is checking to make sure a record with that customer number does not exist as you wish to add the record with that number. In the CHANGE function, you are hoping the customer number exists. IF .NOT. EOF means that end of file has not been reached and therefore the record has been found.

When the record is found the data is displayed on the screen and any fields except the customer number can be changed. As soon as the cursor

```
**************************************
*                                    *
*              1.2                   *
*        FREDS FISH MARKET           *
*     CUSTOMER CHANGE PROGRAM        *
*           CUSTCHG.PRG              *
*                                    *
**************************************
USE CUSTOMER INDEX CUSTOMER
STORE 'T' TO MORECUST
STORE '       ' TO CSN
CLEAR
DO WHILE MORECUST = 'T'
   @  1,20 SAY 'FREDS FRIENDLY FISH MARKET'
   @  3,20 SAY '      CUSTOMER CHANGES      '
   @  7,18 SAY 'CUSTOMER NUMBER: ' GET CSN PICTURE '#####'
   READ
   IF CSN = '      '
      USE
      CLEAR
      RETURN
   ELSE
      FIND &CSN
      IF .NOT. EOF()
         @  9,15 SAY 'COMPANY:      '         GET COMP
         @ 10,15 SAY 'LAST NAME:  '           GET LNAME
         @ 11,15 SAY 'FIRST NAME: '           GET FNAME
         @ 13,15 SAY 'ADDRESS: '              GET ADDR
         @ 14,15 SAY 'CITY:        '          GET CITY
         @ 16,15 SAY 'STATE: '                GET ST
         @ 16,30 SAY 'ZIP: '                  GET ZIP   PICTURE '#####-####'
         @ 18,15 SAY 'PHONE NUMBER: '         GET PHONE PICTURE '(###)###-####'
         @ 20,15 SAY 'DISCOUNT: '             GET DIS   PICTURE '##'
         READ
         CLEAR
         @ 5,1
         @ 5,15 SAY '     *** CUSTOMER CHANGED  ***             '
         STORE '       ' TO CSN
      ELSE
         ? CHR(7)
         CLEAR
         @ 5,15 SAY '*** CUSTOMER NUMBER NOT FOUND ***'
      ENDIF
   ENDIF
ENDDO
```

Fig. 20-12. The customer changes dBase III code—final version.

passes the last field, the record is entered into the file.

Notice that there is no REPLACE command. This is because you are updating the database by the direct method. Since you are using the fields directly, there is no need to use a REPLACE command. The fields are updated when the READ command is performed.

All Fred needs to add now is the USE file command to open the data file and the main loop. These procedures are the same as the ones used in the CUSTOMER screen. Fred adds these statements and looks at the final results as shown in Fig. 20-12.

REMOVING RECORDS

Fred thinks, "It is amazing how similar each program is to the next. All I have to do is code the basic screen layout for one module, and the rest of the modules just fall into place. I think I'll code the other two functions, REMOVE CUSTOMERS and DISPLAY CUSTOMERS before I test the system."

Fred looks at the design for the REMOVE CUSTOMER function, which is shown in Fig. 20-13. He thinks to himself, "I must be getting lazy. I forgot to design the preliminary screen. Oh well, I'm getting good at this. The CUSTOMER REMOVAL screen should be easy. Its the same in the beginning, except there is no READ for the rest of the data, just a retrieve. Then instead of updating the database, I will ask for a confirmation of the removal. If it is confirmed, I'll delete the record; otherwise I'll leave it alone."

Fred should not be getting lazy, a good and complete design is important no matter what. Fred codes the program as shown in Fig. 20-14.

There are a few things that are different in this program than they are in the CUSTOMER CHANGE program. The first difference is in the display section. After the @ GETs, there is a new command called CLEAR GETS. This makes the GETs useless. This is a programming shortcut to quickly display fields from a database. The CLEAR GETS simply makes it so the cursor will not go to the fields and therefore no changes can be made.

There are differences in the display portion of the data fields. There are no PICTURE phrases associated with the GETs because there will be no input taking place.

As you can see, following the CLEAR GETS command is the section of code for the DELETE CONFIRMATION. This portion starts with the display of the confirmation message. Notice the same line is always used for error messages, informational messages, and input. Prior to the display of the confirmation message is a line of code that sets up a one character field called DELCON. You must always set up a field and space for an entry before using a field name. The READ will allow the entering of the confirmation. The uppercase command is used in case the operator types a lowercase d. If the delete is confirmed, the record is deleted. If the operator types anything other than a D, the record is not deleted. Either way a message is output telling what happened.

The final difference is found in the line of code before the RETURN command. It is the PACK command. As explained earlier, the PACK command physically deletes the records after they are marked for deletion by the DELETE command.

DISPLAYING RECORDS

The next step is to code the CUSTOMER DISPLAY module. There are very few differences between the CUSTOMER REMOVAL module and the CUSTOMER DISPLAY module. Instead of the delete confirmation message, there is an opportunity to pause before the display clears itself and gets ready for the next customer record to be displayed.

Fred looks at the design and makes the necessary changes: the screen design and pseudocode are in Fig. 20-15. The final code is shown in Fig. 20-16.

There are only two differences between the two modules. The first is the line SET DELIMITER OFF at the top of the display lines. This command turns off the display of the colons (: :) that Fred has displayed around his input data. This is used for two reasons. First, because Fred is using the GET, there are colons around the data even though the data is only being displayed. There is no need to have these field size delimiters if no data is being

```
  ----------------------------------------------------
  !                                                  !
  !           FRED'S FRIENDLY FISH MARKET            !
  !                CUSTOMER DELETION                 !
  !                                                  !
  !    ENTER "D" TO CONFIRM DELETE ===>  __          !
  !                                                  !
  !      CUSTOMER NUMBER: CUSTN                       !
  !                                                  !
  !      COMPANY:     COMPANY------------X           !
  !      LAST NAME:   LNAME--------------X           !
  !      FIRST NAME:  FNAME--------------X           !
  !                                                  !
  !      ADDRESS: ADDRESS-----------------X          !
  !      CITY:     CITY----------X                   !
  !                                                  !
  !      STATE: ST    ZIP: ZIP-----X                 !
  !                                                  !
  !      PHONE NUMBER: PHONE-------X                 !
  !                                                  !
  !      DISCOUNT: DS                                 !
  !                                                  !
  ----------------------------------------------------

          ACCESS CUSTOMER FILE
          SET CUSTOMER NUMBER TO NOT BLANK
          DO WHILE CUSTOMER NUMBER NOT BLANK
            DISPLAY SCREEN
            ENTER CUSTOMER NUMBER
            VERIFY CUSTOMER NUMBER
            IF FOUND
              THEN
                RETRIEVE CUSTOMER DATA
                ENTER DELETE CONFIRMATION
                IF CONFIRM = "D"
                  THEN
                    DELETE RECORD
                    CLEAR DATA FIELDS
                ENDIF
              ELSE
                WRITE "NUMBER NOT ON FILE"
            ENDIF
          ENDDO
```

Fig. 20-13. The customer removal screen and pseudocode.

```
**************************************
*                                    *
*              1.3                   *
*        FREDS FISH MARKET           *
*    CUSTOMER REMOVAL PROGRAM        *
*           CUSTREM.PRG              *
*                                    *
**************************************
USE CUSTOMER INDEX CUSTOMER
STORE 'T' TO MORECUST
STORE '     ' TO CSN
CLEAR
DO WHILE MORECUST = 'T'
  @ 1,20 SAY 'FREDS FRIENDLY FISH MARKET'
  @ 3,20 SAY '     CUSTOMER REMOVAL      '
  @ 7,18 SAY 'CUSTOMER NUMBER: ' GET CSN PICTURE '#####'
  READ
  IF CSN = '     '
      PACK
      USE
      CLEAR
      RETURN
    ELSE
      FIND &CSN
      IF .NOT. (EOF() .OR. BOF())
          @  9,15 SAY 'COMPANY:        '    GET COMP
          @ 10,15 SAY 'LAST NAME:      '    GET LNAME
          @ 11,15 SAY 'FIRST NAME:     '    GET FNAME
          @ 13,15 SAY 'ADDRESS:        '    GET ADDR
          @ 14,15 SAY 'CITY:           '    GET CITY
          @ 16,15 SAY 'STATE:          '    GET ST
          @ 16,35 SAY 'ZIP:   '             GET ZIP
          @ 18,15 SAY 'PHONE NUMBER: '      GET PHONE
          @ 20,15 SAY 'DISCOUNT:       '    GET DIS
          CLEAR GETS
          STORE ' ' TO DELCON
          @ 5,15 SAY 'ENTER "D" TO CONFIRM DELETE ===> ' GET DELCON
          READ
          IF UPPER(DELCON) = 'D'
              DELETE
              CLEAR
              @ 5,15 SAY '     *** CUSTOMER DELETED ***          '
            ELSE
              CLEAR
              @ 5,15 SAY '   *** CUSTOMER NOT DELETED ***        '
          ENDIF
          STORE '     ' TO CSN
        ELSE
          ? CHR(7)
          CLEAR
          @ 5,15 SAY '*** CUSTOMER NUMBER NOT FOUND ***'
      ENDIF
  ENDIF
ENDDO
```

Fig. 20-14. The customer removal dBase III code—final version.

```
----------------------------------------
|                                        |
|       FRED'S FRIENDLY FISH MARKET       |
|            CUSTOMER DISPLAY             |
|                                        |
|                                        |
|   CUSTOMER NUMBER: CUSTN                |
|                                        |
|   COMPANY:      COMPANY-------------X   |
|   LAST NAME:    LNAME---------------X   |
|   FIRST NAME:   FNAME---------------X   |
|                                        |
|   ADDRESS:  ADDRESS-----------------X  |
|   CITY:     CITY----------X             |
|                                        |
|   STATE: ST     ZIP: ZIP------X         |
|                                        |
|   PHONE NUMBER: PHONE--------X          |
|                                        |
|   DISCOUNT: DS                          |
|                                        |
----------------------------------------
```

```
ACCESS CUSTOMER FILE
SET CUSTOMER NUMBER TO NOT BLANK
DO WHILE CUSTOMER NUMBER NOT BLANK
   DISPLAY SCREEN
   ENTER CUSTOMER NUMBER
   VERIFY CUSTOMER NUMBER
   IF FOUND
     THEN
        RETRIEVE CUSTOMER DATA
        DISPLAY INFORMATION
     ELSE
        WRITE "CUSTOMER NUMBER NOT ON FILE
   ENDIF
ENDDO
```

Fig. 20-15. The customer display screen and pseudocode.

```
    **************************************
    *                                    *
    *              1.4                   *
    *        FREDS FISH MARKET           *
    *    CUSTOMER DISPLAY PROGRAM        *
    *          CUSTDIS.PRG               *
    *                                    *
    **************************************
    USE CUSTOMER INDEX CUSTOMER
    STORE 'T' TO MORECUST
    STORE '     ' TO CSN
    CLEAR
    DO WHILE MORECUST = 'T'
       @  1,20 SAY 'FREDS FRIENDLY FISH MARKET'
       @  3,20 SAY '     CUSTOMER DISPLAY       '
       @  7,18 SAY 'CUSTOMER NUMBER: ' GET CSN PICTURE '#####'
       READ
       @ 5,1
       IF CSN = '       '
           USE
           CLEAR
           RETURN
       ELSE
          FIND &CSN
          IF .NOT. EOF()
              SET DELIMITER OFF
              @  9,15 SAY 'COMPANY:        '  GET COMP
              @ 10,15 SAY 'LAST NAME:      '  GET LNAME
              @ 11,15 SAY 'FIRST NAME:     '  GET FNAME
              @ 13,15 SAY 'ADDRESS:        '  GET ADDR
              @ 14,15 SAY 'CITY:           '  GET CITY
              @ 16,15 SAY 'STATE:          '  GET ST
              @ 16,35 SAY 'ZIP: '            GET ZIP
              @ 18,15 SAY 'PHONE NUMBER: '    GET PHONE
              @ 20,15 SAY 'DISCOUNT:       '  GET DIS
              STORE ' ' TO RESP
              CLEAR GETS
              @ 5,20 SAY 'ENTER ANY KEY TO CONTINUE'  GET RESP
              READ
              SET DELIMITER ON
              STORE '     ' TO CSN
              CLEAR
          ELSE
              ? CHR(7)
              CLEAR
              @ 5,15 SAY '*** CUSTOMER NUMBER NOT FOUND ***'
          ENDIF
       ENDIF
    ENDDO
```

Fig. 20-16. The customer display dBase code—final version.

read into the file.

The second reason for using the SET DELIMITER OFF command involves the lines of code following the CLEAR GETS command. These lines form an example of the use of a *pause code*. Because the colon has been set to off, there is no entry line shown—just the words ENTER ANY KEY TO CONTINUE. The display appears to pause until the operator presses any key. The READ command enables the program to continue, and then the SET DELIMITER ON command is given so that when the next customer number is input, it will be surrounded by colons.

It is now time for Fred to test the modules he has built. Usually you should test the module as it is completed, but Fred has put off testing the CHANGE CUSTOMER module until now. Fred first displays the CUSTOMER CHANGE screen.

```
          FREDS FRIENDLY FISH MARKET

               CUSTOMER CHANGES



     CUSTOMER NUMBER:  :        :
```

He can then enter the customer number for the record he wishes to change. He enters customer number 100 and presses the enter key. Figure 20-17 shows the display that he sees. He can now make any changes he wants. So far, the system is working. He makes his changes and the screen changes to:

```
        FREDS FRIENDLY FISH MARKET

             CUSTOMER CHANGES

        ***  CUSTOMER CHANGED   ***

        CUSTOMER NUMBER:  :        :
```

To test the error condition, Fred tries to enter a customer number that does not exist:

```
        FREDS FRIENDLY FISH MARKET

             CUSTOMER CHANGES

   ***  CUSTOMER NUMBER NOT FOUND  ***

        CUSTOMER NUMBER:  :5000 :
```

So far, so good—no errors so far. After Fred

```
         FREDS FRIENDLY FISH MARKET

              CUSTOMER CHANGES



     CUSTOMER NUMBER:  :100   :

   COMPANY:        :KARENS CHOWDER POT   :
   LAST NAME:     :HAYDEN                :
   FIRST NAME:  :KAREN                   :

   ADDRESS:  :46 OBERLAND PARK           :
   CITY:        :WHEAT FIELD      :

   STATE:  :KY:     ZIP:  :35546-2223:

   PHONE NUMBER:   :(454)555-1626:

   DISCOUNT:  :15:
```

Fig. 20-17. The customer change screen.

enters a blank customer number, the system returns to the main customer menu screen. Fred enters a 3 to test the CUSTOMER REMOVAL program.

FREDS FRIENDLY FISH MARKET

CUSTOMER REMOVAL

CUSTOMER NUMBER: :   :

He enters customer number 300 and presses the enter key. The resulting display is shown in Fig. 20-18. Fred can now see the record to make sure it is the one he wishes to delete. Fred decides to leave it on the file. He just presses the enter key, and the next screen appears.

FREDS FRIENDLY FISH MARKET

CUSTOMER REMOVAL

*** CUSTOMER NOT DELETED ***

CUSTOMER NUMBER: :   :

The final module to be tested is the CUSTOMER DISPLAY program. Fred returns to the main customer menu and enters a 4 for the customer display. He decides to display customer number 200. The resulting display is shown in Fig. 20-19.

Fred once again has had a clean test. Actually these screens and programs took Fred over two days to develop. Considering it was his first experience, it wasn't bad. With the exception of the initial additions program, Fred has had very little trouble

FREDS FRIENDLY FISH MARKET

CUSTOMER REMOVAL

ENTER "D" TO CONFIRM DELETE ===> : :

CUSTOMER NUMBER: :300   :

COMPANY: :SAMS LOX HAVEN   :
LAST NAME: :BURTON   :
FIRST NAME: :SAMUEL   :

ADDRESS: :18465 TRAIL STREET
CITY: :BOCA DELRAY   :

STATE: :MO: ZIP: :35546-2223:

PHONE NUMBER: :(564)555-1525:

DISCOUNT: : 0:

Fig. 20-18. The customer removal screen with a confirmation message.

```
┌─────────────────────────────────────────────────────────────────┐
│                                                                   │
│            FREDS  FRIENDLY  FISH  MARKET                           │
│                                                                   │
│                 CUSTOMER  DISPLAY                                  │
│                                                                   │
│            ENTER  ANY  KEY  TO  CONTINUE                           │
│                                                                   │
│          CUSTOMER  NUMBER:  :200   :                               │
│                                                                   │
│         COMPANY:        LEE  SIDE  FISHERIES                       │
│         LAST  NAME:     KAY                                        │
│         FIRST  NAME:    LEE  JAY                                   │
│                                                                   │
│       : ADDRESS:        151  FARMINGTON  AVE                       │
│         CITY:           NORTH  HAVEN                               │
│                                                                   │
│         STATE:          CA      ZIP:   88667-2443                  │
│                                                                   │
│         PHONE  NUMBER:  (968)555-1424                              │
│                                                                   │
│         DISCOUNT:       10                                         │
│                                                                   │
└─────────────────────────────────────────────────────────────────┘
```

Fig. 20-19. The preliminary customer display screen.

with the programs so far. Once he learned to test his pseudocode over and over again, he was able to program much more effectively.

As Fred has seen, the most important part of coding the programs is the correct coding of the original module. When using standard add, change, remove, and display record modules, most of the code can be revised.

Chapter 21

Customizing and Printing Reports

There are two programs left for Fred to write in the customer system. Both involve printing reports. Fred decides to start with the customer label program.

A MAILING LABEL PROGRAM

When coding reports, there is usually very little screen work and a lot of printer work. This program is no different. Fred decides to tackle the mailing label program by breaking it into several smaller modules. He first examines the screen he must code, along with the mailing label format, and the pseudocode for the main part of the printing routine, as shown in Fig. 21-1.

Fred decides that since this is a new type of module for him, he will start with the main part of the screen.

```
STORE ' ' TO OPTION
    @ 1,20 SAY 'FREDS FRIENDLY FISH MARKET'
    @ 3,20 SAY ' CUSTOMER MAILING LABELS'
    @ 7,18 SAY 'ENTER "A" FOR ALIGNMENT
        PRINT,'
    @ 8,18 SAY '        "X" TO EXIT PRINT,'
```

```
    @  9,18 SAY '    OR <cr> TO BEGIN PRINT'
    @ 11,18 SAY '        ====> ' GET OPTION
READ
```

This code is straight forward. The first six lines simply set up the option field and display the body of the menu. The next line contains the GET command, which will allow the entry of the option field.

The next step is to put in the loop and IF condition. For some reason Fred has used multiple IF statements instead of a CASE statement. Either way the program will work. The resulting code is shown in Fig. 21-2.

You will notice two new commands here—the PUBLIC and the RELEASE commands. When using subroutines, you may want to share information with the called modules. dBASE III does not automatically do this for you. The PUBLIC command lets you specify memory variables that are to be shared between modules. Sometimes you may use this command in a main or menu module. Other times you will use it in a calling module so the called module can use the memory variables.

The RELEASE command releases the vari-

```
-------------------------------------------------
:                                               :
:          FRED'S FRIENDLY FISH MARKET          :
:             MAILING LABEL PRINT               :
:                                               :
:                                               :
:                                               :
:          ENTER "A" FOR ALIGNMENT PRINT,       :
:               "X" TO EXIT PRINT,              :
:            OR <cr> TO BEGIN PRINT             :
:                                               :
:                ====>  ___                     :
:                                               :
:                                               :
:                                               :
:                                               :
:                                               :
:                                               :
-------------------------------------------------

    X-----COMPANY------X
    X------FNAME-------X X------LNAME-------X
    X------ADDRESS----------X
    X----CITY-----X, ST X--ZIP--X

PRINT MAILING LABELS

    STORE " " TO CHOICE
    DO WHILE CHOICE NOT "X"
      DISPLAY SCREEN
      READ CHOICE
      IF CHOICE = "X"
        THEN EXIT
      ENDIF
      IF CHOICE = "A"
        THEN PERFORM "ALIGNMENT PRINT"
      ENDIF
      IF CHOICE = "<cr>"
        ACCESS CUSTOMER FILE
        READ A CUSTOMER RECORD
        INITIALIZE RECORD COUNTER
        DOWHILE MORE RECORDS
          PERFORM "FORMAT FOR PRINT"
          IF LABEL COUNTER = 3
            THEN
                PRINT A ROW OF LABELS
                RESET LABEL COUNTER
```

```
            ENDIF
            READ NEXT RECORD
         ENDDO
         IF LABEL COUNTER # 0
            THEN PRINT PARTIAL ROW
         ENDIF
      ENDIF
   ENDDO
```

Fig. 21-1. The customer mailing label print screen, layout, and pseudocode.

ables when the module is finished with them. This is sometimes needed to keep from exceeding the limit of 256 memory variables or 6000 total memory variable characters.

This code forms the basis for the coding of the options. The first option is X, to exit the program. Fred uses the usual commands in this routine: USE, ERASE, and RETURN. The A command will call another subroutine. Fred codes the subroutine call. Fred looks over his new code which is shown in Fig. 21-3.

Fred is now ready to land the big one. He will code the routine to print the labels. He has coded the beginning of this routine using the compound expression IF OPTION # "A" . AND. OPTION # "X". This means that anything other than an A or X will cause the labels to be printed. The A routine is used only if Fred wishes to have some dummy labels printed so he can make sure that the printer is printing on the labels and not between them.

The pseudocode can be followed almost literally. The pseudocode directs Fred to ACCESS

```
STORE 'T' TO MOREANS
STORE ' ' TO OPTION
PUBLIC A1,A2,A3,B1,B2,B3,C1,C2,C3,D1,D2,D3
DO WHILE MOREANS = 'T'
   CLEAR
   @  1,20 SAY 'FREDS FRIENDLY FISH MARKET'
   @  3,20 SAY ' CUSTOMER MAILING LABELS'
   @  7,18 SAY 'ENTER "A" FOR ALIGNMENT PRINT,'
   @  8,18 SAY '        "X" TO EXIT PRINT,'
   @  9,18 SAY '    OR <cr> TO BEGIN PRINT'
   @ 11,18 SAY '            ====> ' GET OPTION
   READ
   IF UPPER(OPTION) = 'X'
   ENDIF
   IF UPPER(OPTION) = 'A'
   ENDIF
   IF UPPER(OPTION) # 'A' .AND. UPPER(OPTION) # 'X'
   ENDIF
   STORE ' ' TO OPTION
ENDDO
```

Fig. 21-2. The customer mailing label program main body code and subroutine stubs.

187

```
STORE 'T' TO MOREANS
STORE ' ' TO OPTION
PUBLIC A1,A2,A3,B1,B2,B3,C1,C2,C3,D1,D2,D3
DO WHILE MOREANS = 'T'
  CLEAR
  @ 1,20 SAY 'FREDS FRIENDLY FISH MARKET'
  @ 3,20 SAY ' CUSTOMER MAILING LABELS'
  @ 7,18 SAY 'ENTER "A" FOR ALIGNMENT PRINT,'
  @ 8,18 SAY '         "X" TO EXIT PRINT,'
  @ 9,18 SAY '      OR <cr> TO BEGIN PRINT'
  @ 11,18 SAY '             ====> ' GET OPTION
  READ
  IF UPPER(OPTION) = 'X'
    USE
    RELEASE A1,A2,A3,B1,B2,B3,C1,C2,C3,D1,D2,D3
    CLEAR
    RETURN
  ENDIF
  IF UPPER(OPTION) = 'A'
    DO CUSTLBLA
  ENDIF
  IF UPPER(OPTION) # 'A' .AND. UPPER(OPTION) # 'X'
  ENDIF
  STORE ' ' TO OPTION
ENDDO
```

Fig. 21-3. The customer mailing label program main body code.

CUSTOMER FILE, which Fred translates into the USE CUSTOMER INDEX CUSTOMER command. Since Fred must read all the customer records, he must start another loop. Fred develops the following program:

```
USE CUSTOMER INDEX CUSTOMER
DO WHILE .NOT. EOF ()
  STORE 0 TO LBLCNT
  DO CUSTLBLF
  SKIP
ENDDO
```

The CUSTLBLF is a subroutine of the CUSTOMER LABEL PRINT subroutine. On the hierarchy chart, this subroutine is shown on the third level. Before Fred can code any more in the main program, he must code this subroutine.

The point of the subroutine is to take a record and format it on the label. It takes three records to fill the width of the label sheet because there are three labels across. The format subroutine will store the required fields until there are three labels. Fred writes the codes shown in Fig. 21-4.

Fred divides the labels into labels one, two, and three. He also divides the fields into A through D. Depending upon which label is being formatted, the appropriate code will be used.

Notice the use of the different concatenation symbols. The labels will be in the form of

```
X-----COMPANY------X
I. X------LNAME-------X
X------ADDRESS----------X
X----CITY-----X ST XZIPX
```

188

Fred will use only the first initial of the first name. He will use only the first five characters of the zip code because he discovered he couldn't fit any more on the labels. The same reasoning explains his use of the first initial. Even though he had designed his program for the full name, when he went to look at his labels, he realized he could not get forty characters (the maximum length of two twenty-character fields) on a label.

Knowing how the labels will be formatted allows Fred to start to finish the print label routine as shown in Fig. 21-5.

The SET PRINT ON phrase redirects the output from the ? commands to the printer. At the end of the printing, the SET PRINT OFF phrase directs the output back to the screen.

The DO WHILE .NOT. EOF( ) loop will read records and process them from the first record to the last. After each set of three records the formatting will be complete, and a set of labels can be printed. After counting the spaces Fred decided it was easier to use the ? commands than the @ SAY commands. The code inside the IF statement prints a full set of labels. The label counter is reset to 0 to get ready for the next set. When the end-of-file is reached, there may be only one or two records left

```
*****************************************
*                                       *
*           1.5.CUSTLBLF                 *
*         FREDS FISH MARKET              *
*   CUSTOMER MAILING LABEL FORMAT        *
*           CUSTLBLF.PRG                 *
*                                       *
*****************************************
STORE LBLCNT + 1 TO LBLCNT
IF LBLCNT = 1
   STORE COMP TO A1
   STORE SUBSTR(FNAME,1,1)-'. '+LNAME TO B1
   STORE ADDR TO C1
   STORE CITY+'  '+ST+' '+SUBSTR(ZIP,1,5) TO D1
ENDIF
IF LBLCNT = 2
   STORE COMP TO A2
   STORE SUBSTR(FNAME,1,1)-'. '+LNAME TO B2
   STORE ADDR TO C2
   STORE CITY+'  '+ST+' '+SUBSTR(ZIP,1,5) TO D2
ENDIF
IF LBLCNT = 3
   STORE COMP TO A3
   STORE SUBSTR(FNAME,1,1)-'. '+LNAME TO B3
   STORE ADDR TO C3
   STORE CITY+'  '+ST+' '+SUBSTR(ZIP,1,5) TO D3
ENDIF
RETURN
```

Fig. 21-4. The customer mailing label format-labels code.

```
IF UPPER(OPTION) # 'A' .AND. UPPER(OPTION) # 'X'
   USE CUSTOMER INDEX CUSTOMER
   STORE 0 TO LBLCNT
   DO WHILE .NOT. EOF()
      DO CUSTLBLF
      IF LBLCNT = 3
         SET PRINT ON
         ? A1,'          ',A2,'          ',A3
         ? B1,'     ',B2,'     ',B3
         ? C1,' ',C2,' ',C3
         ? D1,' ',D2,' ',D3
         ?
         STORE 0 TO LBLCNT
      ENDIF
      SKIP
   ENDDO
   SET PRINT OFF
ENDIF
```

Fig. 21-5. The customer mailing label print code.

to print. After the ENDDO, some code must be added to account for this. Fred adds the following code:

```
IF LBLCNT = 1
   ? A1
   ? B1
   ? C1
   ? D1
   ?
ENDIF
IF LBLCNT = 2
   ? A1,'          ',A2
   ? B1,'     ',B2
   ? C1,' ',C2
   ? D1,' ',D2
   ?
ENDIF
```

This takes care of any labels left over at the end of the program if there were not a number exactly divisible by three. There is a different routine used for one remaining label than for two remaining labels. When there is one label, there will be two empty labels, while when there are two labels to be printed, there will be only one empty label.

Fred has now coded everything but the alignment routine. He has the program shown in Fig. 21-6.

The final coding for this module is the label alignment program. This code is shown in Fig. 21-7.

This code will print three sets of dummy labels with Xs where the fields normally go. This is done using a simple DO WHILE loop and a few ? commands.

Did you notice the extra ? ' ' at the end of the printing routine? This is to prevent the last line from remaining in the internal print buffer. In the main program, the extra ? ' ' is there for the same reason. In this program, the extra line also serves to separate the labels from each other.

A DIRECTORY PROGRAM

The final program Fred must code for the customer system is the CUSTOMER DIRECTORY program. Fred again starts by looking at the design, which is shown in Fig. 21-8.

Fred decides to try to use the same rough skeleton from his last printing module. After all, if it works for add, change, and delete, it may work for printing too. Red plagiarizes the code shown in Fig. 21-9.

```
*****************************************
*                                       *
*               1.5                     *
*          FREDS FISH MARKET            *
*      CUSTOMER MAILING LABEL PRINT     *
*             CUSTLBL.PRG               *
*                                       *
*****************************************
USE CUSTOMER INDEX CUSTOMER
STORE 'T' TO MOREANS
STORE ' ' TO OPTION
PUBLIC A1,A2,A3,B1,B2,B3,C1,C2,C3,D1,D2,D3
DO WHILE MOREANS = 'T'
  CLEAR
  @  1,20 SAY 'FREDS FRIENDLY FISH MARKET'
  @  3,20 SAY ' CUSTOMER MAILING LABELS'
  @  7,18 SAY 'ENTER "A" FOR ALIGNMENT PRINT,'
  @  8,18 SAY '        "X" TO EXIT PRINT,'
  @  9,18 SAY '     OR <cr> TO BEGIN PRINT'
  @ 11,18 SAY '           ====> ' GET OPTION
  READ
  IF UPPER(OPTION) = 'X'
    USE
    RELEASE A1,A2,A3,B1,B2,B3,C1,C2,C3,D1,D2,D3
    CLEAR
    RETURN
  ENDIF
  IF UPPER(OPTION) = 'A'
    DO CUSTLBLA
  ENDIF
  IF UPPER(OPTION) # 'A' .AND. UPPER(OPTION) # '>'
    USE CUSTOMER INDEX CUSTOMER
    STORE 0 TO LBLCNT
    DO WHILE .NOT. EOF()
          DO CUSTLBLF
          IF LBLCNT = 3
            SET PRINT ON
            ? A1,'        ',A2,'           ',A3
            ? B1,'    ',B2,'    ',B3
            ? C1,' ',C2,' ',C3
            ? D1,' ',D2,' ',D3
            ?
            STORE 0 TO LBLCNT
          ENDIF
          SKIP
```

```
                    ENDDO
                    IF LBLCNT = 1
                        ? A1
                        ? B1
                        ? C1
                        ? D1
                        ?
                    ENDIF
                    IF LBLCNT = 2
                        ? A1,'          ',A2
                        ? B1,'      ',B2
                        ? C1,' ',C2
                        ? D1,' ',D2
                        ?
                    ENDIF
                    SET PRINT OFF
                ENDIF
                STORE ' ' TO OPTION
            ENDDO
```

Fig. 21-6. The customer mailing label print code—final version.

```
    ************************************
    *                                  *
    *          1.5.CUSTLBLA            *
    *        FREDS FISH MARKET         *
    *     CUSTOMER LABEL ALIGNMENT     *
    *          CUSTLBLA.PRG            *
    *                                  *
    ************************************
    SET COLON OFF
    STORE ' ' TO ANS
    @ 7,13 SAY 'ALIGN PRINTER AND HIT ANY KEY TO CONTINUE' GET ANS
    @ 8,1
    @ 9,8  SAY 'THIS WILL PRINT THREE ROWS OF LABEL ALIGNMENT DATA'
    @ 11,1
    READ
    SET PRINT ON
    STORE 1 TO COUNT
    DO WHILE COUNT <= 3
     STORE COUNT + 1 TO COUNT
     ? 'XXXXXXXXXXXXXXXXXX        XXXXXXXXXXXXXXXXXX        XXXXXXXXXXXXXXXXXX'
     ? 'X. XXXXXXXXXXXXXXXXXX   X. XXXXXXXXXXXXXXXXXX   X. XXXXXXXXXXXXXXXXXX'
     ? 'XXXXXXXXXXXXXXXXXXXXXX XXXXXXXXXXXXXXXXXXXXXX XXXXXXXXXXXXXXXXXXXXXX'
     ? 'XXXXXXXXXXXXXX, XX XXXXX XXXXXXXXXXXXXX, XX XXXXX XXXXXXXXXXXXXX, XX XXXXX'
     ? ' '
    ENDDO
    SET PRINT OFF
    RETURN
```

Fig. 21-7. The customer label alignment code—final version.

```
+-------------------------------------------------+
:  - - - - - - - - - - - - - - - - - - - - - - -  :
:                                                 :
:         FRED'S FRIENDLY FISH MARKET             :
:         CUSTOMER DIRECTORY PRINT                :
:                                                 :
:                                                 :
:                                                 :
:         ENTER <cr> TO BEGIN PRINT               :
:         OR "X" TO EXIT PRINT                    :
:                                                 :
:             ====>  ___                          :
:                                                 :
:                                                 :
:                                                 :
:                                                 :
:                                                 :
:  - - - - - - - - - - - - - - - - - - - - - - -  :
+-------------------------------------------------+
```

Customer Number: CUSTN

```
X------COMPANY------X
X------LNAME-------X,  X------FNAME------X
                       X------ADDRESS---------X
                       X----CITY-----X, ST X--ZIP--X

                       Phone: (AAA)NNN-NNNN

                       Discount: XX%
```

PRINT MAILING LIST

```
    READ CHOICE
    IF CHOICE = 'X'
      THEN EXIT
    ENDIF
    IF CHOICE = "<cr>"
      THEN
        ACCESS CUSTOMER FILE
        READ CUSTOMER RECORD
        SET LINECOUNT TO 1
        DO WHILE MORE RECORDS
          IF LINECOUNT = 1 OR = 56
            THEN
              PRINT HEADER
```

193

```
            SET LINECOUNT TO 4
        ENDIF
        PRINT DIRECTORY ENTRY
        UPDATE LINECOUNT
        READ NEXT RECORD
      ENDDO
    ENDIF
```

Fig. 21-8. The customer directory print screen, layout, and pseudocode.

"Not bad," decides Fred. All that's left is the actual printing format commands and some type of paging routine. Everything will come between the DO WHILE and ENDDO. Fred adds the appropriate code, and his program, shown in Fig. 21-10, is complete.

Fred decided to use all @SAY commands. He has used a line counter variable called LINECNT instead of directly specifying the vertical placement of each line. This was necessary in order to print multiple records on the same page. Within each record, the line counter is updated several times. Fred has found that he can fit only four records on a page. Each time he prints a line, he updates the line counter. At the bottom of the loop Fred used the SKIP command to read another record and continue processing.

Fred used another new command in his output,

```
USE CUSTOMER INDEX CUSTOMER
STORE 'T' TO MOREANS
STORE ' ' TO OPTION
DO WHILE MOREANS = 'T'
  CLEAR
  @  1,20 SAY 'FREDS FRIENDLY FISH MARKET'
  @  3,20 SAY ' CUSTOMER DIRECTORY PRINT '
  @  7,20 SAY 'ENTER "X" TO EXIT PRINT,'
  @  8,18 SAY '    OR <cr> TO BEGIN PRINT'
  @ 10,18 SAY '         ====> ' GET OPTION
  READ
  IF UPPER(OPTION) = 'X'
    USE
    STORE ' ' TO OPTION
    CLEAR
    RETURN
  ENDIF
  USE CUSTOMER INDEX CUSTOMER
  DO WHILE .NOT. EOF()
    SKIP
  ENDDO
  STORE ' ' TO OPTION
ENDDO
```

Fig. 21-9. The beginnings of the customer directory program.

```
    ***********************************
    *                                 *
    *              1.6                *
    *        FREDS FISH MARKET        *
    *     CUSTOMER DIRECTORY PRINT    *
    *           CUSTDIR.PRG           *
    *                                 *
    ***********************************
    USE CUSTOMER INDEX CUSTOMER
    STORE 'T' TO MOREANS
    STORE ' ' TO OPTION
    DO WHILE MOREANS = 'T'
      CLEAR
      @  1,20 SAY 'FREDS FRIENDLY FISH MARKET'
      @  3,20 SAY ' CUSTOMER DIRECTORY PRINT '
      @  7,20 SAY 'ENTER "X" TO EXIT PRINT,'
      @  8,18 SAY '    OR <cr> TO BEGIN PRINT'
      @ 10,18 SAY '            ====> ' GET OPTION
      READ
      IF UPPER(OPTION) = 'X'
        USE
        STORE ' ' TO OPTION
        CLEAR
        RETURN
      ENDIF
      USE CUSTOMER INDEX CUSTOMER
      STORE 1 TO LINECNT
      SET DEVICE TO PRINT
      DO WHILE .NOT. EOF()
        IF LINECNT = 1 .OR. LINECNT = 56
          @ 1,30 SAY '   FREDS FISH MARKET'
          @ 2,30 SAY 'CUSTOMER DIRECTORY PRINT'
          STORE 4 TO LINECNT
        ENDIF
        STORE LINECNT + 4 TO LINECNT
        @ LINECNT,1 SAY 'Customer Number:'
        @ LINECNT,18 SAY CUSTN
        STORE LINECNT + 2 TO LINECNT
        @ LINECNT,1 SAY COMP
        STORE LINECNT + 1 TO LINECNT
        @ LINECNT,1 SAY TRIM(LNAME)+', '+FNAME
        STORE LINECNT + 1 TO LINECNT
        @ LINECNT,15 SAY ADDR
        STORE LINECNT + 1 TO LINECNT
        @ LINECNT,15 SAY TRIM(CITY)+', '+ST+' '+ZIP
```

195

```
        STORE LINECNT + 2 TO LINECNT
        @ LINECNT,15 SAY 'Phone: '+PHONE
        STORE LINECNT + 2 TO LINECNT
        @ LINECNT,15 SAY 'Discount: '
        @ LINECNT,25 SAY DIS
        @ LINECNT,27 SAY '%'
        SKIP
     ENDDO
     @ LINECNT+1,1 SAY ' '
     SET DEVICE TO SCREEN
     STORE ' ' TO OPTION
ENDDO
```

Fig. 21-10. The customer directory program code—final version.

the TRIM command. This is used to eliminate trailing blanks from the end of a field. This command is necessary when you are concatenating two fields in which the value does not fill the full size of the first field. In this case, the LNAME must be trimmed so that it will be followed immediately by a comma and the first name.

At the beginning of the DO WHILE loop Fred has added a *header* routine:

```
IF LINECNT = 1 .OR. LINECNT = 56
  @ 1,30 SAY '    FREDS FISH MARKET'
  @ 2,30 SAY 'CUSTOMER DIRECTORY PRINT'
  STORE 4 TO LINECNT
ENDIF
```

A header routine is a block of code that should only be performed at the top of a page. In this program, the routine will be performed at the top of the first page, because that is the only time LINECNT will be 1 and whenever LINECNT reaches 56 (after the printing of the fourth customer record on a page). The line count of 56 was determined by counting printed lines. When LINECNT is 56 and there are more customers, LINECNT is set back to 4, so the topmost customer record will always start in the same spot on each page.

There is a SET DEVICE TO PRINT in this code. When it is time to direct all output to the printer, you will use this code. When printing is through, you will use the SET DEVICE TO SCREEN command to redirect output to the screen. Fred has remembered the last line. He has added the command @ LINECNT+1,1. This will release the last line in the print buffer. Remember, dBASE III is always one line behind—if you print only one line, you will never see it. The blank line at the end of a program will print the last line of output.

SUMMARY

Printing routines are simple but time consuming to write. Many a program has been written in just thirty minutes to produce a report that then took three hours to format correctly on the page. The best way to work fast is to use graph paper. There is special paper for computers that is 60 rows by 132 columns, the size of large computer paper. You can use any part of that to layout your output design. This is also very handy for screen design. You can usually buy a version that is 24 rows by 80 columns. The use of this technique can save you a lot of time at the keyboard.

Chapter 22

Adding Records in a Two-File System

Fred is really moving now. In the last two chapters of this book you will see Fred code two different type of modules. This chapter will explain how Fred coded the additions module of the order program. The final chapter will discuss a report that Fred did that does some calculating and totaling. The complete design for all programs in Fred's system can be found in Appendix A. The dBASE III code for the customer and order systems, in their entirety are found in Appendix B.

THE MAIN RECORD

Fred designed his order system using a two-file approach. As explained before, the order file is actually made up of two files, the main records file, and the item records file. In the main file there will only be one record for each order number. In the order-item file there will be as many records for each order as there are items.

This is very typical of relational database systems. Each record in the order-item file represents one item in the total order. This way there are no limits to the number of items that can appear on an order.

Fred starts by coding the main order program. This is a simple program that closely follows Fred's work in the customer system. Figure 22-1 shows the screen displays.

Fred designed this program in two parts. First he would read in the order number and customer number. Then he would verify both—the order number to make sure it didn't already exist, and the customer number to make sure that it did exist. If either field had no error, the error was to be displayed. If the data was correct, the customer name was to be displayed to show the operator which customer the number belonged to, just in case he had made a mistake. The operator could then enter the date of the order.

Once the order is created, the items can be entered. This program will use the two-file system. The SELECT A, and SELECT B commands enable Fred to use two files at once. He will use one file as the A or primary file, and use the B or secondary file

```
        FRED'S FRIENDLY FISH MARKET
             ORDER ADDITIONS


    ORDER NUMBER:        ORDRN

    CUSTOMER NUMBER:    CUSTN
```

```
        FRED'S FRIENDLY FISH MARKET
             ORDER ADDITIONS


    ORDER NUMBER:        ORDRN

    CUSTOMER NUMBER:    CUSTN

    COMPANY:        COMPANY-------------X
    LAST   NAME:    LNAME---------------X
    FIRST NAME:     FNAME---------------X



    DATE ORDERED: MM/DD/YY
```

Fig. 22-1. The order additions screens.

to access any other needed records. The primary file is sometimes the anchor file. While the secondary file is often changed, the primary file is usually set to the file being written to. Although in dBASE III you can have up to 10 files open at one time, Fred will only use two.

Fred looks at the pseudocode that he developed earlier, which is shown in Fig. 22-2. He starts his coding with the first entry screen.

The result is shown in Fig. 22-3. This is easy so far, thought Fred. Nothing new to be seen here. The screen is presented, and the operator can enter an order number and a customer number.

The next step is to add the error checks. The resulting code is shown in Fig. 22-4.

The first section Fred coded were the two IF-THEN-ELSE conditions. The first one checks to see if there was an order number entered. If not, control is passed to the main order menu. Before the RETURN statement are the commands that close the open files. In the two-file system, you should close both the A and B files. Notice the file is selected and then the USE command performed. The last "select" is to the primary file. Always make sure the primary file is selected last. If you do not, the next time you open a file, the system will think it is a secondary file, and you will have problems.

If there is a valid order number entered, the

```
ADD AN ORDER

   ACCESS ORDER FILE
   SET ORDER NUMBER TO NOT BLANK
   DO WHILE ORDER NUMBER NOT BLANK
      DISPLAY SCREEN
      ENTER ORDER NUMBER AND CUSTOMER NUMBER
      IF ORDER NUMBER NOT BLANK
         VERIFY ORDER NUMBER
         IF NEW NUMBER
            THEN
               ACCESS CUSTOMER FILE
               VERIFY CUSTOMER NUMBER
               IF FOUND
                  THEN
                     DISPLAY CUSTOMER DATA
                     ENTER DATE FIELD
                     ADD TO ORDER FILE
                     PERFORM "ADD ITEMS"
                  ELSE
                     WRITE "CUSTOMER NUMBER NOT FOUND"
               ENDIF
            ELSE
               WRITE "ORDER NUMBER ALREADY ON FILE"
         ENDIF
      ENDIF
   ENDDO
```

Fig. 22-2. The order additions pseudocode.

order number is checked to see that it does not exist. If it does, an error message is generated and the preliminary screen is redisplayed. The customer file is then searched for the customer number. An error is produced if the customer number cannot be found.

```
STORE '     ' TO ORN
STORE '     ' TO CSN
STORE '       ' TO DTO
   @ 1,20 SAY 'FREDS FRIENDLY FISH MARKET'
   @ 3,20 SAY '  ORDER ADDITIONS MENU  '
   @ 7,15 SAY 'ORDER NUMBER:     ' GET ORN     PICTURE '#####'
   @ 9,15 SAY 'CUSTOMER NUMBER: ' GET CSN     PICTURE '#####'
   READ
```

Fig. 22-3. The code for the order additions system preliminary screen.

```
STORE '     '  TO ORN
STORE '     '  TO CSN
STORE '        '  TO DTO
  @  1,20 SAY 'FREDS FRIENDLY FISH MARKET'
  @  3,20 SAY '  ORDER ADDITIONS MENU  '
  @  7,15 SAY 'ORDER NUMBER:    ' GET ORN     PICTURE '#####'
  @  9,15 SAY 'CUSTOMER NUMBER: ' GET CSN     PICTURE '#####'
  READ
  IF ORN = '     '
      SELECT A
      USE
      SELECT B
      USE
      CLEAR
      RETURN
    ELSE
      SELECT A
      FIND &ORN
      IF EOF()
          SELECT B
          USE CUSTOMER INDEX CUSTOMER
          FIND &CSN
          IF .NOT. EOF()

            ELSE
              ? CHR(7)
              CLEAR
              @ 5,15 SAY '   *** CUSTOMER NUMBER NOT ON FILE   ***'
          ENDIF
        ELSE
          ? CHR(7)
          CLEAR
          @ 5,15 SAY '*** ORDER NUMBER ALREADY ON FILE ***'
      ENDIF
  ENDIF
ENDIF
```

Fig. 22-4. The order additions system display screen code.

The customer file becomes the secondary file. This is so the main order file can remain open. By selecting the primary and secondary files, you can switch between any two files.

Once the data is found, the customer information should be displayed so the operator can be sure that the right customer will get the order. The date can then be entered, and the record can be written to the main order file.

The final step is the call to the order-items program to add the items. The resulting code is shown in Fig. 22-5.

Unlike other modules you have seen in this book, most of the work is done after the order number and customer number are verified. The customer information is displayed, and then the date is entered. After the READ statement for the date, the customer information is saved in memory variables. This is so the customer information can be displayed on the order-items screen without having

```
*************************************
*                                   *
*             3.1                   *
*        FREDS FISH MARKET          *
*     ORDER ADDITIONS PROGRAM       *
*           ORDRADD.PRG             *
*                                   *
*************************************
CLEAR
USE ORDER INDEX ORDER
STORE .T. TO MOREORDR
STORE '     ' TO ORN
STORE '     ' TO CSN
STORE '       ' TO DTO
DO WHILE MOREORDR = 'T'
  @  1,20 SAY 'FREDS FRIENDLY FISH MARKET'
  @  3,20 SAY '  ORDER ADDITIONS MENU  '
  @  7,15 SAY 'ORDER NUMBER:     ' GET ORN     PICTURE '#####'
  @  9,15 SAY 'CUSTOMER NUMBER: ' GET CSN     PICTURE '#####'
  READ
  @ 5,1
  IF ORN = '      '
      SELECT A
      USE
      SELECT B
      USE
      CLEAR
      RETURN
    ELSE
      SELECT A
      FIND &ORN
      IF EOF()
          SELECT B
          USE CUSTOMER INDEX CUSTOMER
          FIND &CSN
          IF .NOT. EOF()
              @ 11,15 SAY 'COMPANY: '
              @ 11,32 SAY COMP
              @ 12,15 SAY 'LAST NAME:'
              @ 12,32 SAY LNAME
              @ 13,15 SAY 'FIRST NAME: '
              @ 13,32 SAY FNAME
              @ 15,15 SAY 'DATE ORDERED: ' GET DTO PICTURE '##/##/##'
              READ
              STORE COMP TO COMP
              STORE LNAME TO LNAME
              STORE FNAME TO FNAME
              SELECT A
              APPEND BLANK
              REPLACE ORDRN WITH VAL(ORN),CUSTN WITH VAL(CSN),DATE WITH DTO
              DO ORDRADIT
              CLEAR
              @ 5,20 SAY '  *** ORDER ADDED  *** '
              SELECT A
              USE ORDER INDEX ORDER
```

```
                STORE '        ' TO ORN
                STORE '        ' TO CSN
                STORE '          ' TO DTO
            ELSE
            ? CHR(7)
            CLEAR
            @ 5,15 SAY '  *** CUSTOMER NUMBER NOT ON FILE  ***'
        ENDIF
      ELSE
        ? CHR(7)
        CLEAR
        @ 5,15 SAY '*** ORDER NUMBER ALREADY ON FILE ***'
      ENDIF
    ENDIF
  ENDDO
ENDDO
```

Fig. 22-5. The order additions system main module code.

to be retrieved again.

After the date is read, the file is set back to primary and the data is entered into the main file. Fred remembered that both order number and customer number are really numbers and had to be converted to numerics data with the VAL statement before they could be added to the file.

The main file is updated and the order-items program is called. The items can then be entered,

and then control returns to the main module. The primary file is then restored to the main order file. (In the order-item program, the order-item file became the primary file.)

THE SUBSIDIARY RECORDS

The next program to code is the order-items module. Fred first looks over his design, which is

```
----------------------------------------------------
    FRED'S FRIENDLY FISH MARKET
        ORDER ITEM ADDITIONS


    ORDER NUMBER:       ORDRN

    COMPANY:       COMPANY------------X
    LAST   NAME: LNAME--------------X
    FIRST  NAME: FNAME--------------X

       #   QUANTITY   ITEM NUMBER

       1     QTY         ITEMN
       2     QTY         ITEMN
       3     QTY         ITEMN
      ...    QTY         ITEMN
      10     QTY         ITEMN
----------------------------------------------------
```

202

```
ADD ITEMS

    ACCESS ORDER FILE
    ACCESS ORDER ITEM FILE
    SET ITEMCOUNT TO 1
    SET QUANTITY TO NOT BLANK
    DO WHILE QUANTITY NOT BLANK
       DISPLAY SCREEN AND EXISTING ITEM NUMBERS
       ENTER QUANTITY AND ITEM NUMBER
       IF QUANTITY NOT BLANK
          VERIFY ITEM NUMBER
          IF FOUND
             THEN
                RETRIEVE PRICE
                WRITE RECORD TO ORDER ITEM FILE
                INCREMENT ITEMCOUNT BY 1
             ELSE
                WRITE "ITEM NUMBER NOT ON FILE"
          ENDIF
       ENDIF
       IF ITEMCOUNT IS A MULTIPLE OF 10
          THEN REDISPLAY ITEM SCREEN
       ENDIF
    ENDDO
```

Fig. 22-6. The order items additions screen and pseudocode.

shown in Fig. 22-6. The screen displays a lot, but only one line at a time is active for input. Fred codes the basic display section of the program:

```
CLEAR
@  1,20 SAY 'FREDS FRIENDLY FISH MARKET'
@  3,20 SAY 'ORDER ITEM ADDITIONS MENU'
@  7,20 SAY 'ORDER NUMBER:      '
@  7,37 SAY ORN
@  9,20 SAY 'COMPANY:'
@  9,37 SAY COMP
@ 10,20 SAY 'LAST NAME:'
@ 10,37 SAY LNAME
@ 11,20 SAY 'FIRST NAME:'
@ 11,37 SAY FNAME
@ 13,15 SAY '#'
@ 13,20 SAY 'QUANTITY'
@ 13,35 SAY 'ITEM NUMBER'
```

This section simply displays the main part of the screen. The @ SAY commands produce the screen and set up the headers for the record number, quantity, and item-number fields.

The next section to add is the section that allows entry of the quantity and the item number. Fred writes the following codes:

```
STORE 15 TO LINECNT
STORE 1 TO CNT
STORE '   ' TO QT
STORE '     ' TO ITN
DO WHILE MOREORDI = 'T'
   @ LINECNT,14 SAY CNT PICTURE '99'
   @ LINECNT,22 GET QT PICTURE '###'
   @ LINECNT,38 GET ITN PICTURE '#####'
   READ
```

This section will permit the entry of each quantity and item number. The CNT field is just a number from one to ten that tells you how many records have been entered on each screen.

Next Fred adds the error loops and the verification of the item number, and produces the code shown in Fig. 22-7.

```
SELECT A
USE ORDERITM INDEX ORDERITM
SELECT B
USE ITEM INDEX ITEM
STORE .T. TO MOREORDI
CLEAR
@  1,20 SAY 'FREDS FRIENDLY FISH MARKET'
@  3,20 SAY 'ORDER ITEM ADDITIONS MENU'
@  7,20 SAY 'ORDER NUMBER:    '
@  7,37 SAY ORN
@  9,20 SAY 'COMPANY:'
@  9,37 SAY COMP
@ 10,20 SAY 'LAST NAME:'
@ 10,37 SAY LNAME
@ 11,20 SAY 'FIRST NAME:'
@ 11,37 SAY FNAME
@ 13,15 SAY '#'
@ 13,20 SAY 'QUANTITY'
@ 13,35 SAY 'ITEM NUMBER'
STORE 15 TO LINECNT
STORE 1 TO CNT
STORE '    ' TO QT
STORE '     ' TO ITN
DO WHILE MOREORDI = 'T'
  @ LINECNT,14 SAY CNT PICTURE '99'
  @ LINECNT,22 GET QT PICTURE '###'
  @ LINECNT,38 GET ITN PICTURE '#####'
  READ
  @ 5,1
  IF QT = '    '
      RETURN
    ELSE
      SELECT B
      FIND &ITN
      IF .NOT. EOF()
        ELSE
          ? CHR(7)
          @ 5,15 SAY '*** ITEM NUMBER NOT ON FILE ***'
      ENDIF
  ENDIF
ENDDO
```

Fig. 22-7. The order additions code.

"There is nothing hard here," said Fred. Fred is right, so far. The last section is the toughest. Fred has to code the section to retrieve the price from the item file, and add the record to the order-item file.

a field called PRICE. After retrieving the price from the item file, the program switches back to the primary file so the data can be entered into the order-item file.

```
STORE B->PRICE TO PRI
SELECT A
APPEND BLANK
REPLACE ORDRN WITH VAL(ORN),QTY WITH VAL(QT) ;
   ITEMN WITH VAL(ITN),PRICE WITH PRI
@ 5,20 SAY '  *** ORDER ADDED  *** '
STORE '   ' TO QT
STORE '     ' TO ITN
STORE CNT + 1 TO CNT
STORE LINECNT + 1 TO LINECNT
IF LINECNT = 25
   STORE 15 TO LINECNT
   STORE 15 TO ERASER
   DO WHILE ERASER < 25
     @ ERASER,1
     STORE ERASER + 1 TO ERASER
   ENDDO
ENDIF
```

Fig. 22-8. The order additions code.

Fred must also code the section to clear the screen after each set of 10 records. Figure 22-8 shows the resulting code. This section completes the code for the order-items section. After the item file is accessed and the item number is found, the price must be retrieved. It is retrieved as S.PRICE because both the primary and secondary files have

The order is added, and the fields are cleared for another entry. The DO WHILE loop that uses a field called ERASER is used when ten records have been entered. This loop simply clears lines fifteen through twenty-four.

Fred redisplays the final program as shown in Fig. 22-9.

```
*****************************************
*                                       *
*            3.1.ORDRADIT               *
*          FREDS FISH MARKET            *
*   ORDER ITEM ADDITIONS PROGRAM        *
*             ORDRADIT.PRG              *
*                                       *
*****************************************
SELECT A
USE ORDERITM INDEX ORDERITM
```

```
SELECT B
USE ITEM INDEX ITEM
STORE .T. TO MOREORDI
CLEAR
@  1,20 SAY 'FREDS FRIENDLY FISH MARKET'
@  3,20 SAY 'ORDER ITEM ADDITIONS MENU'
@  7,20 SAY 'ORDER NUMBER:      '
@  7,37 SAY ORN
@  9,20 SAY 'COMPANY:'
@  9,37 SAY COMP
@ 10,20 SAY 'LAST NAME:'
@ 10,37 SAY LNAME
@ 11,20 SAY 'FIRST NAME:'
@ 11,37 SAY FNAME
@ 13,15 SAY '#'
@ 13,20 SAY 'QUANTITY'
@ 13,35 SAY 'ITEM NUMBER'
STORE 15 TO LINECNT
STORE 1 TO CNT
STORE '   ' TO QT
STORE '     ' TO ITN
DO WHILE MOREORDI = 'T'
  @ LINECNT,14 SAY CNT PICTURE '99'
  @ LINECNT,22 GET QT PICTURE '###'
  @ LINECNT,38 GET ITN PICTURE '#####'
  READ
  @ 5,1
  IF QT = '   '
      RETURN
    ELSE
      SELECT B
      FIND &ITN
      IF .NOT. EOF()
          STORE B->PRICE TO PRI
          SELECT A
          APPEND BLANK
          REPLACE ORDRN WITH VAL(ORN),QTY WITH VAL(QT) ;
            ITEMN WITH VAL(ITN),PRICE WITH PRI
          @ 5,20 SAY '  *** ORDER ADDED  *** '
          STORE '   ' TO QT
          STORE '     ' TO ITN
          STORE CNT + 1 TO CNT
          STORE LINECNT + 1 TO LINECNT
          IF LINECNT = 25
             STORE 15 TO LINECNT
             STORE 15 TO ERASER
```

```
                    DO WHILE ERASER < 25
                       @ ERASER,1
                       STORE ERASER + 1 TO ERASER
                    ENDDO
                 ENDIF
              ELSE
                 ? CHR(7)
                 @ 5,15 SAY '*** ITEM NUMBER NOT ON FILE ***'
           ENDIF
      ENDIF
   ENDDO
```

Fig. 22-9. The order item additions code—final version.

Chapter 23

Producing Reports in a Multifile System

The final chapter in this book will show how Fred produces a report using the order file, the order-item file, the customer file, and the item file. Not all the files are used at once, but in order to produce this report, data is needed from all four files. The program is a good example of the use of multiple files. The complete report is shown in Fig. 23-1.

MULTIPLE FILES

Data comes from all four files to make up this report. The order file is the main driver for this report. It is accessed for a specific order number. This order-record will contain the customer number through which the customer information is retrieved. The order number then will point to the order-item file records where the quantity, item numbers, and prices are found. The descriptions for the items are found in the item file.

A report of this type is actually made up of four separate parts. The first part is the screen that simply allows the alignment of the paper and the confirmation to print. The second part prints the

customer information on the top of the report. Part three prints the item records, while the last part prints the total amount and discount.

Fred uses his pseudocode shown in Fig. 23-2 and begins with the first part of the report. The code is shown in Fig. 23-3. This code forms the basis of the program. Fred starts by clearing the screen and opening the order database. Since that is the main file that will drive the other files, it becomes the primary file.

The main loop is set up, as well as the preliminary screen which will read and search for the order number, and if it is found, will begin the print. Since the ENTER <cr> TO CONTINUE is only a confirmation request, the colons are turned off.

The next section of code, shown in Fig. 23-4, turns on the print and prints everything up to the items themselves:

This code contains no loops or IF conditions. It retrieves and prints the customer information, main order information, and headers for the items.

First the output is directed to the printer with

```
      Order Number: ORDRN

      X------FNAME-------X  X------LNAME-------X
      X-----COMPANY------X
      X--------ADDRESS--------X
      X-----CITY----X, ST
      X--ZIP--X

      Order Date: MM/DD/YY

Quantity            Description              Price Each         Amount

   QTN       X---------DESC----------X        999.99       $99,999.99
   QTN       X---------DESC----------X        999.99       $99,999.99
   QTN       X---------DESC----------X        999.99       $99,999.99
   QTN       X---------DESC----------X        999.99       $99,999.99
   QTN       X---------DESC----------X        999.99       $99,999.99
   QTN       X---------DESC----------X        999.99       $99,999.99
   QTN       X---------DESC----------X        999.99       $99,999.99
   QTN       X---------DESC----------X        999.99       $99,999.99
                                                           ----------
                                          Total Amount:    $999,999.99

                                          Discount: (xx%)  ($ 99,999.99)
                                                           ----------
                                          Amount Due:      $999,999.99
                                                           ===========
```

Fig. 23-1. The shipping form print layout.

the SET DEVICE TO PRINT commands. There is only one other file needed in this section, the customer file. The SELECT B command is given, and the customer file opened.

Since the customer number is stored on the order file as a numeric field, and to use it in the FIND command requires it to be a character field, the STR command is used for conversion purposes.

Next the customer number is found. Notice that there is no way to verify the number. How can this be? Good programming will generate good data. There is no way that an illegal customer number can get into the order file because the customer file is checked before the customer number is added to the order file. The customer number has already been verified and there is no reason to verify it again.

With the two necessary files open, you can see that the code simply prints each line after retrieving any information needed from the open customer and order files. After the customer information is retrieved, the primary order file is selected to retrieve the date.

The last print command in this part produces the headers for the item information. Four @SAY commands take care of these.

The next portion of code, shown in Fig. 23-5, prints any and all items.

This section begins by defining the files needed for this section of the report. The two files needed are the order-item file and the item file. It doesn't matter which files is the primary or secondary file, as long as you reference them correctly.

The next step is to retrieve the first order-item record with the appropriate order number and set the total amount owed bucket, TOTAL, to zero. As long as the value of the original order number you entered is the same as the order number in the order-item file, this loop will be processed for more items. The end-of-file marker is also checked in case the order number is the last one in the file. Another check inside the loop is IF .NOT. DELETED(). If the record has been marked for deletion and the file has not yet been packed, you don't want the record to appear.

Inside the loop, the quantity and the item number are printed, the item file is searched for the item; and the description is printed. Finally the price is printed, and the amount owed is calculated using B->QTY*B->PRICE printed, and then added to the total for the order. The line STORE TOTAL + B->QTY*B->PRICE TO TOTAL means to take the previous total, add the new amount to it, and

```
PRINT SHIPPING FORMS

    STORE BLANK TO ORDER NUMBER
    DO WHILE ORDER NUMBER NOT BLANK
       DISPLAY SCREEN
       ENTER ORDER NUMBER
       IF ORDER NUMBER NOT BLANK
          ACCESS ORDER FILE
          VERIFY ORDER NUMBER
          IF FOUND
             THEN
                PRINT HEADER OF ORDER
                ACCESS CUSTOMER FILE
                RETRIEVE CUSTOMER INFORMATION
                PRINT ORDER INFORMATION
                ACCESS ORDER ITEM FILE
                SET TOTAL TO 0
                DO WHILE MORE RECORDS
                   RETRIEVE QUANTITY AND ITEM NUMBER
                   ACCESS ITEM FILE
                   RETRIEVE DESCRIPTION AND PRICE
                   AMOUNT = QUANTITY X PRICE
                   ADD AMOUNT TO TOTAL
                   PRINT RECORD
                ENDDO
                WRITE TOTAL
                DISCOUNT AMOUNT = DISCOUNT/100 X TOTAL
                WRITE DISCOUNT
                SUBTRACT DISCOUNT FROM TOTAL
                WRITE AMOUNT DUE
             ELSE
                WRITE "ORDER NUMBER NOT ON FILE"
          ENDIF
       ENDIF
    ENDDO
```

Fig. 23-2. The order shipping forms pseudocode.

210

```
CLEAR
USE ORDER INDEX ORDER
STORE .T. TO MOREORDR
STORE '      ' TO ORN
DO WHILE MOREORDR = 'T'
  @ 1,20 SAY 'FREDS FRIENDLY FISH MARKET'
  @ 3,20 SAY 'SHIPPING FORMS PRINT MENU '
  @ 7,19 SAY 'ORDER NUMBER:      ' GET ORN     PICTURE '#####'
  READ
  @ 5,1
  IF ORN = '      '
      CLEAR
      SELECT B
      USE
      SELECT A
      USE
      RETURN
    ELSE
      SELECT A
      FIND &ORN
      IF .NOT. EOF() .AND. .NOT. DELETED()
          SET DELIMITER OFF
          STORE ' ' TO ANS
          @ 5,1
          @ 5,23 SAY 'ENTER <cr> TO PRINT' GET ANS
          READ
          SET DELIMITER ON
```

Fig. 23-3. The order shipping forms code, part one.

store it back in the total bucket. Finally the linecount is increased by one so the next line prints below the present one.

At the end of the loop is the SKIP command, which is used to advance to the next record.

CALCULATING AND TOTALING

The final section will print the total, calculate and print the discount, and print the total amount due. The code is shown in Fig. 23-6.

Fred is almost done. He has been coding this procedure for almost a week. He starts by under-

lining the last column. "Just like the accounts," he mumbles. He has already calculated the total. He prints it with the PICTURE specification and adds dollar signs and commas to the number. Fred then prints the discount line using the formula DISCOUNT /100. This is used because the discount is stored as a whole number. Twelve really means twelve percent or .12. The number twelve must be divided by one-hundred before it is multiplied by the amount.

Finally the discount is subtracted from the total to yield the amount due. Fred even remembers the last line and adds the "@LINECNT+7,1" command.

```
            SET DEVICE TO PRINT
            SELECT B
            USE CUSTOMER INDEX CUSTOMER
            STORE STR(CUSTN,5) TO CSN
            FIND &CSN
            @ 1,25 SAY 'FREDS FRIENDLY FISH MARKET'
            @ 3,25 SAY '          SHIPPING FORM         '
            @ 6,15 SAY 'Order Number: '
            @ 6,29 SAY ORN PICTURE '99999'
            @ 8,15 SAY TRIM(FNAME)+' '+LNAME
            @ 9,15 SAY COMP
            @ 10,15 SAY ADDR
            @ 11,15 SAY TRIM(CITY)+', '+ST
            @ 12,15 SAY ZIP
            STORE DIS TO DISCOUNT
            SELECT A
            @ 14,15 SAY 'Order Date: '
            @ 14,28 SAY DATE
            @ 16,10 SAY 'Quantity'
            @ 16,30 SAY 'Description'
            @ 16,50 SAY 'Price Each'
            @ 16,70 SAY 'Amount'
```

Fig. 23-4. The order shipping forms code, part two.

```
    PRINTING FROM SEVERAL FILES

      STORE 18 TO LINECNT
      SELECT B
      USE ORDERITM INDEX ORDERITM
      SELECT A
      USE ITEM INDEX ITEM
      SELECT B
      FIND &ORN
      STORE 0 TO TOTAL
      DO WHILE VAL(ORN)=B->ORDRN .AND. .NOT. EOF()
        IF .NOT. DELETED()
          @ LINECNT,13 SAY B->QTY PICTURE '999'
          STORE STR(B->ITEMN,5) TO ITN
          SELECT A
          FIND &ITN
          @ LINECNT,25 SAY DESC
          SELECT B
          @ LINECNT,52 SAY B->PRICE PICTURE '99.99'
```

212

```
      @ LINECNT,67 SAY B->QTY*B->PRICE PICTURE   '$99,999.99'
      STORE TOTAL + B->QTY*B->PRICE TO TOTAL
      STORE LINECNT+1 TO LINECNT
   ENDIF
   SKIP
ENDDO
```

Fig. 23-5. The order shipping forms code, part three.

Fred now puts it all together and looks at the final program, which is shown in Fig. 23-7.

SUMMARY

In this book, you have been given the tools to produce basic programs using dBASE III. (That's basic as in simple, not the language BASIC.) Whether you are a novice or a seasoned professional, this book has shown you tricks and techniques for contemporary program design for the eighties.

You may wish to review each section as you begin to code in dBASE III. A complete list of the designs for the CUSTOMER and ORDER systems are found in Appendix A. Complete listings of the programs can be found in Appendix B. Good luck in all your data processing endeavors, and . . . may the Fred be with you.

```
   @ LINECNT,68 SAY '----------'
   @ LINECNT+1,50 SAY 'Total Amount:'
   @ LINECNT+1,66 SAY TOTAL PICTURE  '$999,999.99'
   @ LINECNT+3,50 SAY 'Discount:('
   @ LINECNT+3,60 SAY DISCOUNT PICTURE '99'
   @ LINECNT+3,62 SAY '%)'
   @ LINECNT+3,65 SAY '('
STORE TOTAL*(DISCOUNT/100) TO DISC
   @ LINECNT+3,66 SAY DISC PICTURE  '$999,999.99'
   @ LINECNT+3,77 SAY ')'
   @ LINECNT+4,66 SAY '------------'
   @ LINECNT+5,50 SAY 'Amount Due: '
   @ LINECNT+5,66 SAY TOTAL-DISC PICTURE  '$999,999.99'
   @ LINECNT+6,66 SAY '==========='
   @ LINECNT+7,1  SAY ' '
SELECT A
USE ORDER INDEX ORDER
SET DEVICE TO SCREEN
CLEAR
STORE '       ' TO ORN
```

Fig. 23-6. The order shipping forms code, part four.

```
**************************************
*                                    *
*              3.6                   *
*         FREDS FISH MARKET          *
*     ORDER SHIPPING FORMS PRINT     *
*            ORDRSHP.PRG             *
*                                    *
**************************************
CLEAR
USE ORDER INDEX ORDER
STORE .T. TO MOREORDR
STORE '     ' TO ORN
DO WHILE MOREORDR = 'T'
   @ 1,20 SAY 'FREDS FRIENDLY FISH MARKET'
   @ 3,20 SAY 'SHIPPING FORMS PRINT MENU '
   @ 7,19 SAY 'ORDER NUMBER:    ' GET ORN    PICTURE '#####'
   READ
   @ 5,1
   IF ORN = '        '
       CLEAR
       SELECT B
       USE
       SELECT A
       USE
       RETURN
   ELSE
       SELECT A
       FIND &ORN
       IF .NOT. EOF() .AND. .NOT. DELETED()
           SET DELIMITER OFF
           STORE ' ' TO ANS
           @ 5,1
           @ 5,23 SAY 'ENTER <cr> TO PRINT' GET ANS
           READ
           SET DELIMITER ON
           SET DEVICE TO PRINT
           SELECT B
           USE CUSTOMER INDEX CUSTOMER
           STORE STR(CUSTN,5) TO CSN
           FIND &CSN
           @ 1,25 SAY 'FREDS FRIENDLY FISH MARKET'
           @ 3,25 SAY '      SHIPPING FORM         '
           @ 6,15 SAY 'Order Number: '
           @ 6,29 SAY ORN PICTURE '99999'
           @ 8,15 SAY TRIM(FNAME)+' '+LNAME
           @ 9,15 SAY COMP
           @ 10,15 SAY ADDR
           @ 11,15 SAY TRIM(CITY)+', '+ST
           @ 12,15 SAY ZIP
           STORE DIS TO DISCOUNT
           SELECT A
           @ 14,15 SAY 'Order Date: '
           @ 14,28 SAY DATE
           @ 16,10 SAY 'Quantity'
           @ 16,30 SAY 'Description'
           @ 16,50 SAY 'Price Each'
```

```
                    @ 16,70 SAY 'Amount'
                    STORE 18 TO LINECNT
                    SELECT B
                    USE ORDERITM INDEX ORDERITM
                    SELECT A
                    USE ITEM INDEX ITEM
                    SELECT B
                    FIND &ORN
                    STORE 0 TO TOTAL
                DO WHILE VAL(ORN)=B->ORDRN .AND. .NOT. EOF()
                   IF .NOT. DELETED()
                      @ LINECNT,13 SAY B->QTY PICTURE '999'
                      STORE STR(B->ITEMN,5) TO ITN
                      SELECT A
                      FIND &ITN
                      @ LINECNT,25 SAY DESC
                      SELECT B
                      @ LINECNT,52 SAY B->PRICE PICTURE '99.99'
                      @ LINECNT,67 SAY B->QTY*B->PRICE PICTURE  '$99,999.99'
                      STORE TOTAL + B->QTY*B->PRICE TO TOTAL
                      STORE LINECNT+1 TO LINECNT
                   ENDIF
                   SKIP
                ENDDO
                @ LINECNT,68 SAY '----------'
                @ LINECNT+1,50 SAY 'Total Amount:'
                @ LINECNT+1,66 SAY TOTAL PICTURE  '$999,999.99'
                @ LINECNT+3,50 SAY 'Discount:('
                @ LINECNT+3,60 SAY DISCOUNT PICTURE '99'
                @ LINECNT+3,62 SAY '%)'
                @ LINECNT+3,65 SAY '('
                STORE TOTAL*(DISCOUNT/100) TO DISC
                @ LINECNT+3,66 SAY DISC PICTURE  '$999,999.99'
                @ LINECNT+3,77 SAY ')'
                @ LINECNT+4,66 SAY '------------'
                @ LINECNT+5,50 SAY 'Amount Due: '
                @ LINECNT+5,66 SAY TOTAL-DISC PICTURE  '$999,999.99'
                @ LINECNT+6,66 SAY '============'
                @ LINECNT+7,1  SAY ' '
                SELECT A
                USE ORDER INDEX ORDER
                SET DEVICE TO SCREEN
                CLEAR
                STORE '       ' TO ORN
             ELSE
                ? CHR(7)
                CLEAR
                @ 5,17 SAY '*** ORDER NUMBER NOT FOUND ***'
          ENDIF
       ENDIF
ENDDO
```

Fig. 23-7. The order shipping forms code, final version.

Appendices

Appendix A
The System Design

This appendix shows all the steps Fred followed in designing his system.

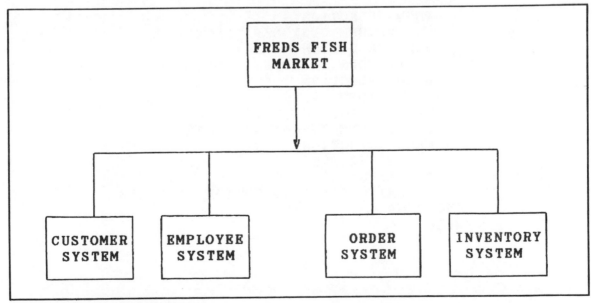

Fig. A-1. The main system hierarchy.

```
          ---------------------------------------------------
          :                                                 :
          :            FRED'S FRIENDLY FISH MARKET          :
          :                  MAIN MENU                      :
          :                                                 :
          :                                                 :
          :           ENTER SELECTION ===>  __              :
          :                                                 :
          :              1 - CUSTOMER SYSTEM                :
          :              2 - EMPLOYEE SYSTEM                :
          :              3 - ORDER SYSTEM                   :
          :              4 - INVENTORY SYSTEM               :
          :                                                 :
          :                                                 :
          :              X - EXIT SYSTEM                    :
          :                                                 :
          ---------------------------------------------------
```

Fig. A-2. The main system menu.

```
     MAIN MENU

       SET EXIT TO "N"
       DO WHILE NOT EXIT
         READ SELECTION
         CASE
           WHEN SELECTION = "1"
               PERFORM CUSTOMER SYSTEM
           WHEN SELECTION = "2"
               PERFORM EMPLOYEE SYSTEM
           WHEN SELECTION = "3"
               PERFORM ORDER SYSTEM
           WHEN SELECTION = "4"
               PERFORM INVENTORY SYSTEM
           WHEN SELECTION = "X"
               SET EXIT TO "Y"
           OTHERWISE
               WRITE "INVALID OPTION" ENDCASE
         ENDCASE
       ENDDO
```

Fig. A-3. The main system pseudocode.

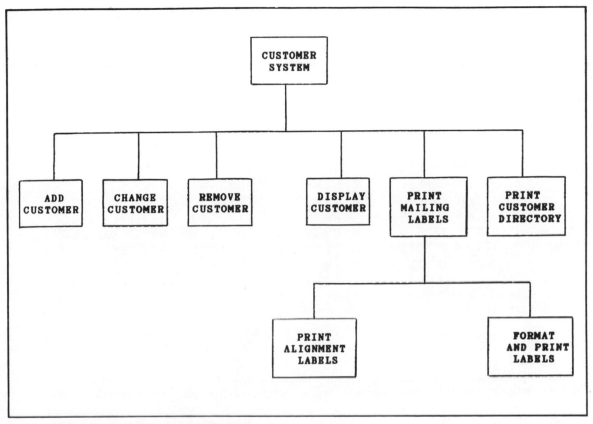

Fig. A-4. The customer system hierarchy chart.

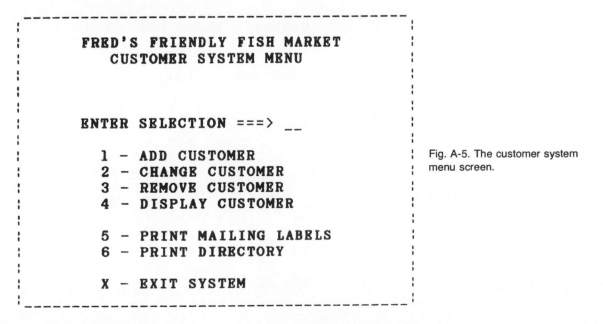

Fig. A-5. The customer system menu screen.

```
SET EXIT TO "N"
DISPLAY MENU SCREEN
DOWHILE EXIT = "N"
  READ OPTION
  CASE
    WHEN OPTION = 1 PERFORM "ADD CUSTOMER"
    WHEN OPTION = 2 PERFORM "CHANGE CUSTOMER"
    WHEN OPTION = 3 PERFORM "REMOVE CUSTOMER"
    WHEN OPTION = 4 PERFORM "DISPLAY CUSTOMER"
    WHEN OPTION = 5 PERFORM "PRINT MAILING LABELS"
    WHEN OPTION = 6 PERFORM "PRINT DIRECTORY"
    WHEN OPTION = X SET EXIT TO "Y"
    OTHERWISE WRITE "INVALID OPTION"
  ENDCASE
ENDDO
```

Fig. A-6. The customer system menu pseudocode.

Fig. A-7. The customer additions screen.

```
    FRED'S FRIENDLY FISH MARKET
          CUSTOMER ADDITIONS


  CUSTOMER NUMBER: CUSTN

  COMPANY:      COMPANY-------------X
  LAST NAME:    LNAME---------------X
  FIRST NAME:   FNAME---------------X

  ADDRESS:  ADDRESS-----------------X
  CITY:     CITY----------X

  STATE: ST    ZIP: ZIP-----X

  PHONE NUMBER: PHONE-------X

  DISCOUNT: DS
```

```
ADD A CUSTOMER

    ACCESS CUSTOMER FILE
    SET CUSTOMER NUMBER TO NOT BLANK
    DO WHILE CUSTOMER NUMBER NOT BLANK
       DISPLAY SCREEN
       ENTER DATA
       VERIFY CUSTOMER NUMBER
       IF NEW NUMBER
          THEN
             ADD CUSTOMER DATA
             CLEAR DATA FIELDS
          ELSE
             WRITE "NUMBER ALREADY ON FILE"
       ENDIF
    ENDDO
```

Fig. A-8. The customer additions pseudocode.

```
          FRED'S FRIENDLY FISH MARKET
                CUSTOMER CHANGES



          CUSTOMER NUMBER: CUSTN
```

Fig. A-9. The customer change preliminary screen.

```
          FRED'S FRIENDLY FISH MARKET
                CUSTOMER CHANGES


      CUSTOMER NUMBER: CUSTN

      COMPANY:      COMPANY------------X
      LAST NAME:    LNAME--------------X
      FIRST NAME:   FNAME--------------X

      ADDRESS: ADDRESS------------------X
      CITY:    CITY----------X

      STATE: ST    ZIP: ZIP-----X

      PHONE NUMBER: PHONE-------X

      DISCOUNT: DS
```

Fig. A-10. The customer change data entry screen.

```
CHANGE A CUSTOMER

        ACCESS CUSTOMER FILE
        SET CUSTOMER NUMBER TO NOT BLANK
        DO WHILE CUSTOMER NUMBER NOT BLANK
           DISPLAY SCREEN
           ENTER CUSTOMER NUMBER
           VERIFY CUSTOMER NUMBER
           IF FOUND
              THEN
                 RETRIEVE CUSTOMER DATA
                 CHANGE DESIRED FIELDS
                 UPDATE RECORD
                 CLEAR DATA FIELDS
              ELSE
                 WRITE "NUMBER NOT ON FILE"
           ENDIF
        ENDDO
```

Fig. A-11. The customer changes pseudocode.

```
FRED'S FRIENDLY FISH MARKET
        CUSTOMER DELETION

ENTER "D" TO CONFIRM DELETE ===>  __

   CUSTOMER NUMBER: CUSTN

   COMPANY:      COMPANY------------X
   LAST NAME:    LNAME--------------X
   FIRST NAME:   FNAME--------------X

   ADDRESS: ADDRESS-----------------X
   CITY:    CITY----------X

   STATE: ST    ZIP: ZIP-----X

   PHONE NUMBER: PHONE-------X

   DISCOUNT: DS
```

Fig. A-12. The customer removal screen.

```
ACCESS CUSTOMER FILE
SET CUSTOMER NUMBER TO NOT BLANK
DO WHILE CUSTOMER NUMBER NOT BLANK
   DISPLAY SCREEN
   ENTER CUSTOMER NUMBER
   VERIFY CUSTOMER NUMBER
   IF FOUND
     THEN
        RETRIEVE CUSTOMER DATA
        ENTER DELETE CONFIRMATION
        IF CONFIRM = "D"
          THEN
             DELETE RECORD
             CLEAR DATA FIELDS
        ENDIF
     ELSE
        WRITE "NUMBER NOT ON FILE"
   ENDIF
ENDDO
```

Fig. A-13. The customer removal pseudocode.

Fig. A-14. The customer display screen.

```
---------------------------------------------------
:                                                  :
:           FRED'S FRIENDLY FISH MARKET            :
:                 CUSTOMER DISPLAY                 :
:                                                  :
:                                                  :
:           CUSTOMER NUMBER: CUSTN                 :
:                                                  :
:           COMPANY:     COMPANY-------------X     :
:           LAST NAME:   LNAME---------------X     :
:           FIRST NAME:  FNAME---------------X     :
:                                                  :
:           ADDRESS: ADDRESS-------------------X   :
:           CITY:     CITY----------X              :
:                                                  :
:           STATE: ST    ZIP: ZIP-----X            :
:                                                  :
:           PHONE NUMBER: PHONE-------X            :
:                                                  :
:           DISCOUNT: DS                           :
:                                                  :
---------------------------------------------------
```

```
ACCESS CUSTOMER FILE
SET CUSTOMER NUMBER TO NOT BLANK
DO WHILE CUSTOMER NUMBER NOT BLANK
   DISPLAY SCREEN
   ENTER CUSTOMER NUMBER
   VERIFY CUSTOMER NUMBER
   IF FOUND
     THEN
        RETRIEVE CUSTOMER DATA
        DISPLAY INFORMATION
     ELSE
        WRITE "CUSTOMER NUMBER NOT ON FILE"
   ENDIF
ENDDO
```

Fig. A-15. The customer display pseudocode.

```
FRED'S FRIENDLY FISH MARKET
     MAILING LABEL PRINT



ENTER "A" FOR ALIGNMENT PRINT,
    "X" TO EXIT PRINT,
 OR <cr> TO BEGIN PRINT

      ====> ___
```

Fig. A-16. The customer mailing label print.

```
X-----COMPANY------X
X------FNAME-------X X------LNAME-------X
X------ADDRESS----------X
X----CITY-----X, ST X--ZIP--X
```

Fig. A-17. The customer mailing label print layout.

```
            PRINT MAILING LABELS

                STORE " " TO CHOICE
                DO WHILE CHOICE NOT "X"
                  DISPLAY SCREEN
                  READ CHOICE
                  IF CHOICE = "X"
                     THEN EXIT
                  ENDIF
                  IF CHOICE = "A"
                     THEN PERFORM "ALIGNMENT PRINT"
                  ENDIF
                  IF CHOICE = "<cr>"
                     ACCESS CUSTOMER FILE
                     READ A CUSTOMER RECORD
                     INITIALIZE RECORD COUNTER
                     DOWHILE MORE RECORDS
                       PERFORM "FORMAT FOR PRINT"
                       IF LABEL COUNTER = 3
                          THEN
                             PRINT A ROW OF LABELS
                             RESET LABEL COUNTER
                       ENDIF
                       READ NEXT RECORD
                     ENDDO
                     IF LABEL COUNTER # 0
                        THEN PRINT PARTIAL ROW
                     ENDIF
                  ENDIF
                ENDDO
```

Fig. A-18. The customer mailing label print pseudocode.

```
 ALIGNMENT PRINT

     PRINT ONE ROW OF LABELS WITH X'S FILLING EVERY FIELD
     ADVANCE TO NEXT LABEL
```

Fig. A-19. The customer mailing label alignment pseudocode.

```
         FORMAT FOR LABELS

     ADD 1 TO LABEL COUNTER
     MOVE CUSTOMER FIELDS TO LABEL 1, 2, OR 3,
          DEPENDING ON LABEL COUNTER
```

Fig. A-20. The customer mailing label format pseudocode.

```
--------------------------------------------------------------
|                                                            |
|       FRED'S FRIENDLY FISH MARKET                          |
|       CUSTOMER DIRECTORY PRINT                             |
|                                                            |
|                                                            |
|       ENTER <cr> TO BEGIN PRINT                            |
|         OR "X" TO EXIT PRINT                               |
|                                                            |
|            ====>  ___                                      |
|                                                            |
--------------------------------------------------------------
```

Fig. A-21. The customer directory print screen.

```
Customer Number: CUSTN

X------COMPANY------X
X------LNAME-------X, X------FNAME-------X
                       X------ADDRESS----------X
                       X----CITY-----X, ST X--ZIP--X

                    Phone: (AAA)NNN-NNNN

                    Discount: XX%
```

Fig. A-22. The customer directory print layout.

```
PRINT MAILING LIST

    READ CHOICE
    IF CHOICE = 'X'
      THEN EXIT
    ENDIF
    IF CHOICE = "<cr>"
      THEN
        ACCESS CUSTOMER FILE
        READ CUSTOMER RECORD
        SET LINECOUNT TO 1
        DO WHILE MORE RECORDS
          IF LINECOUNT = 1 OR = 56
            THEN
              PRINT HEADER
              SET LINECOUNT TO 4
          ENDIF
          PRINT DIRECTORY ENTRY
          UPDATE LINECOUNT
          READ NEXT RECORD
        ENDDO
    ENDIF
```

Fig. A-23. The customer directory print pseudocode.

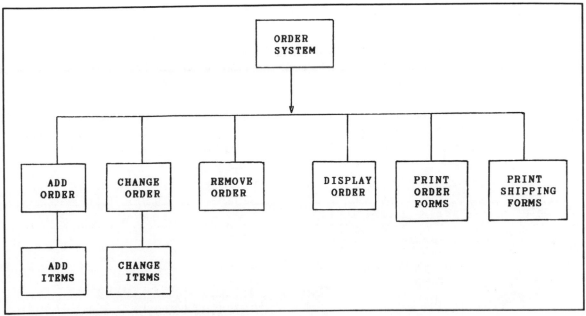

Fig. A-24. The order system hierarchy chart.

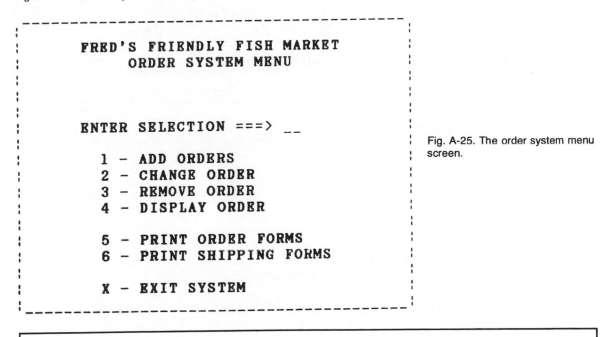

Fig. A-25. The order system menu screen.

```
SET EXIT TO "N"
DISPLAY MENU SCREEN
DOWHILE EXIT = "N"
   READ OPTION
```

```
    CASE
      WHEN OPTION = 1 PERFORM "ADD ORDERS"
      WHEN OPTION = 2 PERFORM "CHANGE ORDER"
      WHEN OPTION = 3 PERFORM "REMOVE ORDER"
      WHEN OPTION = 4 PERFORM "DISPLAY ORDER"
      WHEN OPTION = 5 PERFORM "PRINT ORDER FORMS"
      WHEN OPTION = 6 PERFORM "PRINT SHIPPING FORMS"
      WHEN OPTION = X SET EXIT TO "Y"
      OTHERWISE WRITE "INVALID OPTION"
    ENDCASE
  ENDDO
```

Fig. A-26. The order system menu pseudocode.

Fig. A-27. The order additions preliminary screen.

```
-----------------------------------------
:                                         :
:        FRED'S FRIENDLY FISH MARKET      :
:              ORDER ADDITIONS            :
:                                         :
:                                         :
:     ORDER NUMBER:        ORDRN          :
:                                         :
:     CUSTOMER NUMBER:     CUSTN          :
:                                         :
:                                         :
-----------------------------------------
```

Fig. A-28. The order additions screen.

```
-----------------------------------------
:                                         :
:        FRED'S FRIENDLY FISH MARKET      :
:              ORDER ADDITIONS            :
:                                         :
:                                         :
:     ORDER NUMBER:        ORDRN          :
:                                         :
:     CUSTOMER NUMBER:     CUSTN          :
:                                         :
:     COMPANY:       COMPANY------------X :
:     LAST  NAME: LNAME---------------X   :
:     FIRST NAME: FNAME---------------X   :
:                                         :
:                                         :
:     DATE ORDERED: MM/DD/YY              :
-----------------------------------------
```

```
┌─────────────────────────────────────────────────────┐
│                                                     │
│        FRED'S FRIENDLY FISH MARKET                  │
│           ORDER ITEM ADDITIONS                      │
│     ORDER NUMBER:      ORDRN                         │
│                                                     │
│     COMPANY:      COMPANY------------X              │
│     LAST  NAME:   LNAME--------------X              │
│     FIRST NAME:   FNAME--------------X              │
│                                                     │
│       #   QUANTITY   ITEM NUMBER                    │
│                                                     │
│       1     QTY         ITEMN                       │
│       2     QTY         ITEMN                       │
│       3     QTY         ITEMN                       │
│      ...    QTY         ITEMN                       │
│      10     QTY         ITEMN                       │
│                                                     │
└─────────────────────────────────────────────────────┘
```

Fig. A-29. The order items additions screen.

```
ADD AN ORDER

    ACCESS ORDER FILE
    SET ORDER NUMBER TO NOT BLANK
    DO WHILE ORDER NUMBER NOT BLANK
       DISPLAY SCREEN
       ENTER ORDER NUMBER AND CUSTOMER NUMBER
       IF ORDER NUMBER NOT BLANK
         VERIFY ORDER NUMBER
         IF NEW NUMBER
           THEN
              ACCESS CUSTOMER FILE
              VERIFY CUSTOMER NUMBER
              IF FOUND
                THEN
                   DISPLAY CUSTOMER DATA
                   ENTER DATE FIELD
                   ADD TO ORDER FILE
                   PERFORM "ADD ITEMS"
                ELSE
                   WRITE "CUSTOMER NUMBER NOT FOUND"
              ENDIF
           ELSE
              WRITE "ORDER NUMBER ALREADY ON FILE"
         ENDIF
       ENDIF
    ENDDO
```

Fig. A-30. The order additions pseudocode.

```
ADD ITEMS

    ACCESS ORDER FILE
    ACCESS ORDER ITEM FILE
    SET ITEMCOUNT TO 1
    SET QUANTITY TO NOT BLANK
    DO WHILE QUANTITY NOT BLANK
       DISPLAY SCREEN AND EXISTING ITEM NUMBERS
       ENTER QUANTITY AND ITEM NUMBER
       IF QUANTITY NOT BLANK
         VERIFY ITEM NUMBER
         IF FOUND
            THEN
                RETRIEVE PRICE
                WRITE RECORD TO ORDER ITEM FILE
                INCREMENT ITEMCOUNT BY 1
            ELSE
                WRITE "ITEM NUMBER NOT ON FILE"
         ENDIF
       ENDIF
       IF ITEMCOUNT IS A MULTIPLE OF 10
         THEN REDISPLAY ITEM SCREEN
       ENDIF
    ENDDO
```

Fig. A-31. The order item additions pseudocode.

Fig. A-32. The order changes preliminary screen.

```
------------------------------------------------
|           FRED'S FRIENDLY FISH MARKET          |
|                 ORDER CHANGES                  |
|                                                |
|                                                |
|        ORDER NUMBER:       ORDRN               |
|                                                |
|                                                |
------------------------------------------------
```

```
-------------------------------------------------
|                                               |
|         FRED'S FRIENDLY FISH MARKET           |
|              ORDER CHANGES                    |
|                                               |
|      CHANGE ITEMS? ===> __                    |
|    ENTER <cr> TO CONTINUE, X TO ABORT         |
|                                               |
|    ORDER NUMBER:       ORDRN                  |
|                                               |
|    CUSTOMER NUMBER:   CUSTN                    |
|                                               |
|    COMPANY:      COMPANY-------------X         |
|    LAST  NAME:  LNAME--------------X           |
|    FIRST NAME:  FNAME--------------X           |
|                                               |
|    DATE ORDERED: MM/DD/YY                      |
|                                               |
-------------------------------------------------
```

Fig. A-33. The order changes screen.

```
CHANGE AN ORDER

    ACCESS ORDER FILE
    SET ORDER NUMBER TO NOT BLANK
    DO WHILE ORDER NUMBER NOT BLANK
       DISPLAY SCREEN
       ENTER ORDER NUMBER
       IF ORDER NUMBER NOT BLANK
          VERIFY ORDER NUMBER
          IF FOUND
             THEN
                ACCESS CUSTOMER FILE
                RETRIEVE CUSTOMER INFORMATION
                DISPLAY "CHANGE ITEMS" MESSAGE
                READ CHOICE
                IF CHOICE NOT X
                   THEN PERFORM "CHANGE ITEMS MENU"
                ENDIF
             ELSE WRITE "ORDER NUMBER NOT FOUND"
          ENDIF
       ENDIF
    ENDDO
```

Fig. A-34. The order changes pseudocode.

```
----------------------------------------------------
|                                                  |
|         FRED'S FRIENDLY FISH MARKET              |
|              ORDER ITEM CHANGES                  |
|                                                  |
|          ENTER SELECTION ===>  __                |
|          C/CHANGE,S/SCROLL,X/EXIT                |
|                                                  |
|      ORDER NUMBER:        ORDRN                   |
|                                                  |
|      COMPANY:      COMPANY-------------X          |
|      LAST  NAME:   LNAME---------------X          |
|      FIRST NAME:   FNAME---------------X          |
|                                                  |
|         #   QUANTITY   ITEM NUMBER                |
|                                                  |
|         1     QTY        ITEMN                    |
|         2     QTY        ITEMN                    |
|         3     QTY        ITEMN                    |
|        ...    QTY        ITEMN                    |
|        10     QTY        ITEMN                    |
|                                                  |
----------------------------------------------------
```

Fig. A-35. The order items change screen.

```
----------------------------------------------------
|                                                  |
|       FRED'S FRIENDLY FISH MARKET                |
|            ORDER ITEM CHANGES                    |
|                                                  |
|       RECORD NUMBER ==>  __                      |
|     ENTER RECORD NUMBER TO BE CHANGED            |
|                                                  |
|      ORDER NUMBER:        ORDRN                   |
|                                                  |
|      COMPANY:      COMPANY-------------X          |
|      LAST  NAME:   LNAME---------------X          |
|      FIRST NAME:   FNAME---------------X          |
|                                                  |
|         #   QUANTITY   ITEM NUMBER                |
|                                                  |
|         1     QTY        ITEMN                    |
|         2     QTY        ITEMN                    |
|         3     QTY        ITEMN                    |
|        ...    QTY        ITEMN                    |
|        10     QTY        ITEMN                    |
|                                                  |
----------------------------------------------------
```

Fig. A-36. The second order items change screen.

```
----------------------------------------
|                                        |
|        FRED'S FRIENDLY FISH MARKET      |
|           ORDER ITEM CHANGES            |
|                                         |
|   QUANTITY: QTY   ITEM NUMBER: ITEMN    |
|            ENTER CHANGES                |
|                                         |
|    ORDER NUMBER:      ORDRN             |
|                                         |
|    COMPANY:      COMPANY------------X    |
|    LAST   NAME: LNAME--------------X     |
|    FIRST  NAME: FNAME--------------X     |
|                                         |
|       #   QUANTITY   ITEM NUMBER        |
|                                         |
|       1    QTY        ITEMN             |
|       2    QTY        ITEMN             |
|       3    QTY        ITEMN             |
|      ...   QTY        ITEMN             |
|      10    QTY        ITEMN             |
|                                         |
----------------------------------------
```

Fig. A-37. The third order items change screen.

```
----------------------------------------
|                                        |
|        FRED'S FRIENDLY FISH MARKET      |
|           ORDER ITEM CHANGES            |
|                                         |
|      RECORD NUMBER ==>  __              |
|   ENTER RECORD NUMBER TO BE CHANGED     |
|                                         |
|    ORDER NUMBER:      ORDRN             |
|                                         |
|    COMPANY:      COMPANY------------X    |
|    LAST   NAME: LNAME--------------X     |
|    FIRST  NAME: FNAME--------------X     |
|                                         |
|       #   QUANTITY   ITEM NUMBER        |
|                                         |
|      11    QTY        ITEMN             |
|      12    QTY        ITEMN             |
|       3    QTY        ITEMN             |
|      ...   QTY        ITEMN             |
|      20    QTY        ITEMN             |
|                                         |
----------------------------------------
```

Fig. A-38. The order items scroll screen.

235

```
CHANGE ITEMS

  SET EXIT TO 'N'
  DISPLAY MENU SCREEN
  DOWHILE EXIT = 'N'
    DISPLAY ITEMS
    DISPLAY SELECTION
    READ SELECTION
    CASE
      WHEN SELECTION = 'X'
        SET EXIT TO 'Y'
      WHEN SELECTION = 'C'
        ACCESS ORDER ITEM FILE
        SET RECORD NUMBER TO NOT BLANK
        SET SCROLL COUNTER TO 10
        DO WHILE RECORD NUMBER NOT BLANK
          DISPLAY SCREEN
          ENTER RECORD NUMBER
          IF RECORD NUMBER NOT BLANK
            THEN
              VERIFY RECORD NUMBER IN THE 10 DISPLAYED
              IF IN THE 10
                THEN
                  RETRIEVE RECORD
                  DISPLAY QTY AND ITEMN
                  IF BLANK
                    THEN
                      DISPLAY ADD MESSAGE
                  ENDIF
                  ENTER CHANGES
                  IF QTY AND ITEMN NOT BLANK
                    THEN                              /* ADD RECORD */
                      IF OLD QUANTITY BLANK
                        THEN
                          VERIFY ITEM NUMBER
                          IF FOUND
                            THEN
                              RETRIEVE PRICE
                              WRITE RECORD TO ORDER ITEM FILE
                            ELSE
                              WRITE "ITEM NUMBER NOT ON FILE"
                          ENDIF
                      ENDIF
```

236

```
                       IF QTY OR ITEM NUMBER DIFFERENT THEN ORIGINAL
                    THEN                        /* DELETE RECORD */
                   IF QTY = 0
                      THEN
                         REMOVE RECORD FROM ORDER ITEM FILE
                      ELSE                      /* CHANGE RECORD */
                         VERIFY ITEM NUMBER
                        IF FOUND
                           THEN
                              RETRIEVE PRICE
                              WRITE RECORD TO ORDER ITEM FILE
                           ELSE
                              WRITE "ITEM NUMBER NOT ON FILE"
                        ENDIF
                   ENDIF
                ENDIF
             ELSE
             WRITE "RECORD NUMBER NOT ON DISPLAY"
          ENDIF
       ENDIF
     ENDDO
   WHEN SELECTION = 'S'
      ADD 10 TO SCROLL COUNTER
  ENDCASE
ENDDO
```

Fig. A-39. The order item changes pseudocode.

Fig. A-40. The preliminary order removal screen.

```
------------------------------------------------
:                                              :
:        FRED'S FRIENDLY FISH MARKET           :
:              ORDER REMOVAL                   :
:                                              :
:                                              :
:     ORDER NUMBER:        ORDRN               :
:                                              :
:                                              :
------------------------------------------------
```

237

```
------------------------------------------------
    FRED'S FRIENDLY FISH MARKET
         ORDER REMOVAL

 ENTER D TO CONFIRM DELETE ==>  __


  ORDER NUMBER:      ORDRN

  COMPANY:     COMPANY------------X
  LAST   NAME: LNAME--------------X
  FIRST  NAME: FNAME--------------X

  DATE ORDERED: MM/DD/YY

     #   QUANTITY  ITEM NUMBER

     1     QTY       ITEMN
     2     QTY       ITEMN
     3     QTY       ITEMN
    ...    QTY       ITEMN
    10     QTY       ITEMN

------------------------------------------------
```

Fig. A-41. The order removal screen.

```
   REMOVE ORDERS

          ACCESS ORDER FILE
          SET ORDER NUMBER TO NOT BLANK
          DO WHILE ORDER NUMBER NOT BLANK
             DISPLAY SCREEN
             ENTER ORDER NUMBER
             IF ORDER NUMBER NOT BLANK
                VERIFY ORDER NUMBER
                IF FOUND
                  THEN
                     RETRIEVE ORDER
                     ACCESS CUSTOMER FILE
                     RETRIEVE CUSTOMER INFORMATION
                     DISPLAY ORDER
                     ACCESS ORDER ITEMS FILE
                     DISPLAY 1ST 10 ITEMS
                     ENTER DELETE CONFITMATION
                     IF CONFIRM = D
                        THEN
```

```
                    DELETE MAIN ORDER RECORD
                    DELETE ALL ITEM RECORDS
              ENDIF
            ELSE
              WRITE "ORDER NOT ON FILE"
          ENDIF
        ENDIF
      ENDDO
```

Fig. A-42. The order removal pseudocode.

Fig. A-43. The preliminary order display screen.

```
---------------------------------------------------
                                                   
         FRED'S FRIENDLY FISH MARKET               
               ORDER DISPLAY                       
                                                   
                                                   
      ORDER NUMBER:        ORDRN                   
                                                   
---------------------------------------------------
```

Fig. A-44. The order display screen.

```
---------------------------------------------------
                                                   
         FRED'S FRIENDLY FISH MARKET               
               ORDER DISPLAY                       
                                                   
           ENTER <cr> TO CONTINUE                  
                                                   
                                                   
      ORDER NUMBER:        ORDRN                   
                                                   
      CUSTOMER NUMBER:  CUSTN                       
                                                   
      COMPANY:      COMPANY-------------X          
      LAST   NAME: LNAME---------------X           
      FIRST NAME: FNAME----------------X           
                                                   
      DATE ORDERED: MM/DD/YY                        
                                                   
                                                   
         #   QUANTITY   ITEM NUMBER                 
                                                   
         1     QTY         ITEMN                    
         2     QTY         ITEMN                    
         3     QTY         ITEMN                    
        ...    QTY         ITEMN                    
        10     QTY         ITEMN                    
                                                   
---------------------------------------------------
```

239

```
DISPLAY ORDERS

    ACCESS ORDER FILE
    SET ORDER NUMBER TO NOT BLANK
    DO WHILE ORDER NUMBER NOT BLANK
       DISPLAY SCREEN
       ENTER ORDER NUMBER
       IF ORDER NUMBER NOT BLANK
          VERIFY ORDER NUMBER
          IF FOUND
             THEN
                RETRIEVE ORDER
                ACCESS CUSTOMER FILE
                RETRIEVE CUSTOMER INFORMATION
                DISPLAY ORDER
                ACCESS ITEM FILE
                DO WHILE MORE RECORDS
                   DISPLAY 10 ITEMS
                   ENTER CONTINUE CONFIRMATION
                ENDIF
             ELSE
                WRITE "ORDER NOT ON FILE"
          ENDIF
       ENDIF
    ENDDO
```

Fig. A-45. The order display pseudocode.

Fig. A-46. The print order forms screen.

```
-------------------------------------------------
                FRED'S FRIENDLY FISH MARKET
                     ORDER FORMS PRINT


             ORDER NUMBER:       ORDRN


-------------------------------------------------
```

```
          Order Number: ORDRN

          X-----COMPANY------X
          X------FNAME-------X X------LNAME-------X

          Order Date: MM/DD/YY

 ITEM #      QUANTITY      ITEM NUMBER         DESCRIPTION

    1          QTN           ITEMN        X----------DESC---------X
    2          QTN           ITEMN        X----------DESC---------X
    3          QTN           ITEMN        X----------DESC---------X
    4          QTN           ITEMN        X----------DESC---------X
    5          QTN           ITEMN        X----------DESC---------X
    6          QTN           ITEMN        X----------DESC---------X
    7          QTN           ITEMN        X----------DESC---------X
    8          QTN           ITEMN        X----------DESC---------X
```

Fig. A-47. The order form print layout.

```
    PRINT ORDER FORM

         STORE BLANK TO ORDER NUMBER
         DO WHILE ORDER NUMBER NOT BLANK
            DISPLAY SCREEN
            ENTER ORDER NUMBER
            IF ORDER NUMBER NOT BLANK
               ACCESS ORDER FILE
               VERIFY ORDER NUMBER
               IF FOUND
                  THEN
                     PRINT HEADER OF ORDER
                     ACCESS CUSTOMER FILE
                     RETRIEVE CUSTOMER INFORMATION
                     DISPLAY ORDER INFORMATION
                     ACCESS ORDER ITEM FILE
                     DO WHILE MORE RECORDS
                        RETRIEVE QUANTITY AND ITEM NUMBER
                        ACCESS ITEM FILE
                        RETRIEVE DESCRIPTION
                        PRINT RECORD
                     ENDDO
                  ELSE
                     WRITE "ORDER NUMBER NOT ON FILE"
               ENDIF
            ENDIF
         ENDDO
```

Fig. A-48. The order form print pseudocode.

Fig. A-49. The print shipping forms screen.

```
-----------------------------------------
|                                         |
|     FRED'S FRIENDLY FISH MARKET         |
|        SHIPPING FORMS PRINT             |
|                                         |
|                                         |
|     ORDER NUMBER:        ORDRN          |
|                                         |
|                                         |
|                                         |
-----------------------------------------
```

Fig. A-49. The print shipping forms screen.

```
        Order Number: ORDRN

        X------FNAME-------X X------LNAME-------X
        X-----COMPANY------X
        X--------ADDRESS--------X
        X-----CITY----X, ST
        X--ZIP--X

        Order Date: MM/DD/YY

Quantity           Description              Price Each          Amount

    QTN        X---------DESC----------X      999.99         $99,999.99
    QTN        X---------DESC----------X      999.99         $99,999.99
    QTN        X---------DESC----------X      999.99         $99,999.99
    QTN        X---------DESC----------X      999.99         $99,999.99
    QTN        X---------DESC----------X      999.99         $99,999.99
    QTN        X---------DESC----------X      999.99         $99,999.99
    QTN        X---------DESC----------X      999.99         $99,999.99
    QTN        X---------DESC----------X      999.99         $99,999.99
                                                            ----------
                                   Total Amount:        $999,999.99

                                   Discount: (xx%) ($ 99,999.99)
                                                            ----------
                                   Amount Due:          $999,999.99
                                                        ============
```

Fig. A-50. The shipping form print layout.

```
PRINT SHIPPING FORM

    STORE BLANK TO ORDER NUMBER
    DO WHILE ORDER NUMBER NOT BLANK
       DISPLAY SCREEN
       ENTER ORDER NUMBER
       IF ORDER NUMBER NOT BLANK
          ACCESS ORDER FILE
          VERIFY ORDER NUMBER
          IF FOUND
             THEN
                PRINT HEADER OF ORDER
                ACCESS CUSTOMER FILE
                RETRIEVE CUSTOMER INFORMATION
                PRINT ORDER INFORMATION
                ACCESS ORDER ITEM FILE
                SET TOTAL TO 0
                DO WHILE MORE RECORDS
                   RETRIEVE QUANTITY AND ITEM NUMBER
                   ACCESS ITEM FILE
                   RETRIEVE DESCRIPTION AND PRICE
                   AMOUNT = QUANTITY X PRICE
                   ADD AMOUNT TO TOTAL
                   PRINT RECORD
                ENDDO
                WRITE TOTAL
                DISCOUNT AMOUNT = DISCOUNT/100 X TOTAL
                WRITE DISCOUNT
                SUBTRACT DISCOUNT FROM TOTAL
                WRITE AMOUNT DUE
             ELSE
                WRITE "ORDER NUMBER NOT ON FILE"
          ENDIF
       ENDIF
    ENDDO
```

Fig. A-51. The order shipping form print pseudocode.

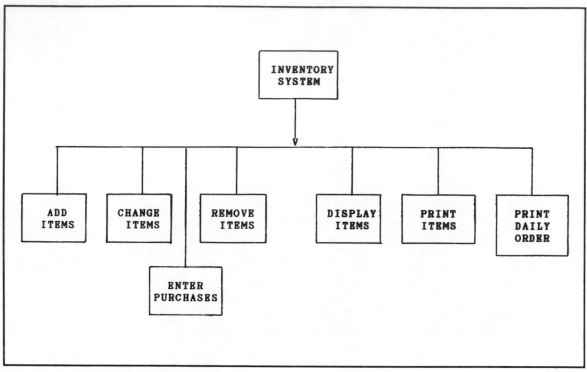

Fig. A-52. The inventory system hierarchy chart.

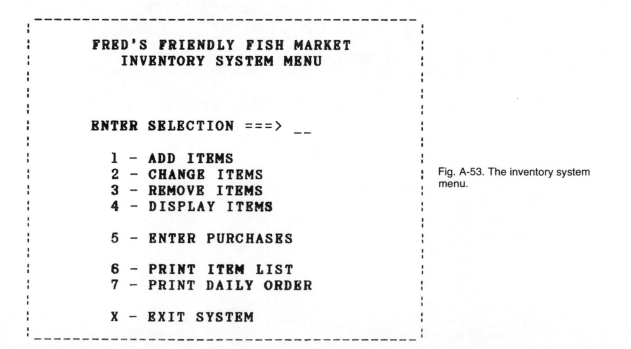

Fig. A-53. The inventory system menu.

```
                SET EXIT TO "N"
                DISPLAY MENU SCREEN
                DOWHILE EXIT = "N"
                  READ OPTION
                  CASE
                    WHEN OPTION = 1 PERFORM "ADD ITEMS"
                    WHEN OPTION = 2 PERFORM "CHANGE ITEMS"
                    WHEN OPTION = 3 PERFORM "REMOVE ITEMS"
                    WHEN OPTION = 4 PERFORM "DISPLAY ITEMS"
                    WHEN OPTION = 5 PERFORM "ENTER PURCHASES"
                    WHEN OPTION = 6 PERFORM "PRINT ITEM LIST"
                    WHEN OPTION = 7 PERFORM "PRINT DAILY ORDER"
                    WHEN OPTION = X SET EXIT TO "Y"
                    OTHERWISE WRITE "INVALID OPTION"
                  ENDCASE
                ENDDO
```

Fig. A-54. The inventory system menu pseudocode.

CUSTOMER DATABASE

Fieldname	Data Type	Length
CUSTNO	N	5
COMPANY	C	20
FNAME	C	20
LNAME	C	20
ADDRESS	C	25
CITY	C	15
STATE	C	2
ZIP	C	10
PHONE	C	13
DISCOUNT	N	2

		131

ITEM DATABASE

ITEM NUMBER	C	5
ITEM DESC	C	25
PRICE	N	5.2
ON HAND	N	5
STOCK LEVEL	N	5
ORDER AMOUNT	N	5

```
ORDER FLAG           L                    1
                                        -----
                                         51


              ORDER DATABASE

ORDER NUMBER         N                    5
CUSTOMER NUMBER      N                    5
DATE ORDERED         C                    8
                                        -----
                                         18
           ORDER ITEMS DATABASE

ORDER NUMBER         N                    5
ITEM NUMBER          N                    5
QUANTITY             N                    3
PRICE                N                    5.2
                                        -----
                                         18
```

Fig. A-55. The fields in the databases.

Appendix B

The Complete Programs

```
*****************************************
*                                       *
*               MAIN                    *
*          FREDS FISH MARKET            *
*             MAIN MENU                 *
*              MAIN.PRG                 *
*                                       *
*****************************************
SET DELIMITER TO '::'
SET DELIMITER ON
SET ECHO OFF
SET EXACT ON
SET TALK OFF
SET BELL OFF
SET CONFIRM OFF
SET INTENSITY OFF
STORE 'F' TO EXIT
STORE ' ' TO OPTION
CLEAR
DO WHILE EXIT = 'F'
   @  1,20 SAY 'FREDS FRIENDLY FISH MARKET'
   @  3,20 SAY '         MAIN MENU            '
```

```
    @  7,19 SAY '   ENTER SELECTION  ===>    ';
            GET OPTION
    @ 10,22 SAY ' 1 - CUSTOMER SYSTEM       '
    @ 11,22 SAY ' 2 - EMPLOYEE SYSTEM       '
    @ 12,22 SAY ' 3 - ORDER SYSTEM          '
    @ 13,22 SAY ' 4 - INVENTORY SYSTEM      '
    @ 15,22 SAY ' X - EXIT SYSTEM           '
    READ
    DO CASE
      CASE OPTION = '1'
        DO CUSTOMER
      CASE OPTION = '2'
        DO EMPLOYEE
      CASE OPTION = '3'
        DO ORDER
      CASE OPTION = '4'
        DO INVENTRY
      CASE UPPER(OPTION) = 'X'
        RETURN
      OTHERWISE
        ? CHR(7)
        @ 5,18 SAY '*** INVALID ENTRY-TRY AGAIN ***'
    ENDCASE
    STORE ' ' TO OPTION
ENDDO
```

```
********************************
*                              *
*              1               *
*      FREDS FISH MARKET       *
*        CUSTOMER MENU         *
*         CUSTOMER.PRG         *
*                              *
********************************


STORE 'F' TO CUSTEXIT
STORE ' ' TO OPTION
CLEAR
DO WHILE CUSTEXIT = 'F'
   @  1,20 SAY 'FREDS FRIENDLY FISH MARKET'
   @  3,20 SAY '   CUSTOMER SYSTEM MENU    '
   @  7,19 SAY '  ENTER SELECTION  ===>    ';
           GET OPTION
   @ 10,21 SAY ' 1 - ADD CUSTOMER          '
   @ 11,21 SAY ' 2 - CHANGE CUSTOMER       '
   @ 12,21 SAY ' 3 - REMOVE CUSTOMER       '
   @ 13,21 SAY ' 4 - DISPLAY CUSTOMER      '
   @ 15,21 SAY ' 5 - PRINT MAILING LABELS '
   @ 16,21 SAY ' 6 - PRINT DIRECTORY       '
   @ 18,21 SAY ' R - RETURN TO MAIN MENU   '
   @ 19,21 SAY ' X - EXIT SYSTEM           '
   READ
   DO CASE
     CASE OPTION = '1'
       DO CUSTADD
     CASE OPTION = '2'
       DO CUSTCHG
     CASE OPTION = '3'
       DO CUSTREM
     CASE OPTION = '4'
       DO CUSTDIS
     CASE OPTION = '5'
       DO CUSTLBL
     CASE OPTION = '6'
       DO CUSTDIR
   CASE UPPER(OPTION) = 'R'
      CLEAR
      RETURN
   CASE UPPER(OPTION) = 'X'
      QUIT
   OTHERWISE
```

```
      ? CHR(7)
      @ 5,20 SAY '*** INVALID ENTRY -TRY AGAIN ***'
   ENDCASE
   STORE ' ' TO OPTION
ENDDO
```

```
***************************************
*                                     *
*          FREDS FISH MARKET          *
*      CUSTOMER ADDITIONS PROGRAM     *
*             CUSTADD.PRG             *
*                                     *
***************************************
CLEAR
USE CUSTOMER INDEX CUSTOMER
STORE .T. TO MORECUST
STORE '        ' TO CSN
STORE '             ' TO CMP
STORE '          ' TO LNM
STORE '          ' TO FNM
STORE '               ' TO ADR
STORE '             ' TO CTY
STORE '   ' TO STT
STORE '          ' TO ZP
STORE '            ' TO PHN
STORE 0 TO DS
DO WHILE MORECUST = 'T'
@ 1,20 SAY 'FREDS FRIENDLY FISH MARKET'
@ 3,20 SAY '  CUSTOMER ADDITIONS MENU  '
@ 7,18 SAY 'CUSTOMER NUMBER: ' GET CSN      PICTURE '*****'
@ 9,15 SAY 'COMPANY: '        GET CMP
@ 10,15 SAY 'LAST NAME: '     GET LNM
@ 11,15 SAY 'FIRST NAME: '    GET FNM
@ 13,15 SAY 'ADDRESS: '       GET ADR
@ 14,15 SAY 'CITY: '          GET CTY
@ 16,15 SAY 'STATE: '         GET STT
@ 16,30 SAY 'ZIP: '           GET ZP       PICTURE '*****-****'
@ 18,15 SAY 'PHONE NUMBER: '  GET PHN      PICTURE '(***)***-****'
@ 20,15 SAY 'DISCOUNT: '      GET DS       PICTURE '**'
READ
IF CSN = '        '
```

```
      USE
    CLEAR
    RETURN
  ELSE
  FIND &CSN
  IF EOF()
      APPEND BLANK
      REPLACE CUSTN WITH VAL(CSN),COMP WITH CMP,LNAME WITH LNM;
          FNAME WITH FNM,ADDR WITH ADR,CITY WITH CTY,ST WITH STT;
          ZIP WITH ZP,PHONE WITH PHN,DIS WITH DS
      @ 5,1
      @ 5,15 SAY '  *** CUSTOMER ADDED  *** '
      STORE '  ' TO CSN
      STORE '  ' TO CMP
      STORE '  ' TO LNM
      STORE '  ' TO FNM
      STORE '  ' TO ADR
      STORE '  ' TO CTY
      STORE '  ' TO STT
      STORE '  ' TO ZP
      STORE '  ' TO PHN
      STORE 0 TO DS
  ELSE
      ? CHR(7)
      @ 5,15 SAY '*** CUSTOMER NUMBER ALREADY ON FILE ***'
  ENDIF
ENDIF
ENDDO
```

```
*********************************
*                               *
*       FREDS FISH MARKET        *
*     CUSTOMER CHANGE PROGRAM     *
*          CUSTCHG.PRG            *
*                               *
*********************************
USE CUSTOMER INDEX CUSTOMER
STORE 'T' TO MORECUST
STORE '   ' TO CSN
CLEAR
DO WHILE MORECUST = 'T'
   @ 1,20 SAY 'FREDS FRIENDLY FISH MARKET'
   @ 3,20 SAY '   CUSTOMER CHANGES   '
   @ 7,18 SAY 'CUSTOMER NUMBER: ' GET CSN PICTURE '#####'
   READ
   IF CSN = '   '
      USE
      CLEAR
      RETURN
   ELSE
      FIND &CSN
      IF .NOT. EOF()
         @  9,15 SAY 'COMPANY:     '     GET COMP
         @ 10,15 SAY 'LAST NAME:   '     GET LNAME
         @ 11,15 SAY 'FIRST NAME:  '     GET FNAME
         @ 13,15 SAY 'ADDRESS:  '        GET ADDR
         @ 14,15 SAY 'CITY:  '           GET CITY
         @ 16,15 SAY 'STATE:  '          GET ST
         @ 16,30 SAY 'ZIP:  '            GET ZIP   PICTURE '#####-####'
         @ 18,15 SAY 'PHONE NUMBER: '    GET PHONE PICTURE '(###)###-####'
         @ 20,15 SAY 'DISCOUNT: '        GET DIS   PICTURE '##'
         READ
         CLEAR
         @ 5,1
```

253

```
          @ 5,15 SAY ' *** CUSTOMER CHANGED ***'
          STORE ' ' TO CSN
        ELSE
          ? CHR(7)
          CLEAR
          @ 5,15 SAY '*** CUSTOMER NUMBER NOT FOUND ***'
        ENDIF
      ENDIF
    ENDDO
```

```
**************************************
*                                    *
*         FREDS FISH MARKET          *
*      CUSTOMER REMOVAL PROGRAM      *
*            CUSTREM.PRG             *
*                                    *
**************************************
USE CUSTOMER INDEX CUSTOMER
STORE 'T' TO MORECUST
STORE ' ' TO CSN
CLEAR
DO WHILE MORECUST = 'T'
  @ 1,20 SAY 'FREDS FRIENDLY FISH MARKET'
  @ 3,20 SAY '    CUSTOMER REMOVAL     '
  @ 7,18 SAY 'CUSTOMER NUMBER:' GET CSN PICTURE '*****'
  READ
  IF CSN = '      '
    PACK
    USE
    CLEAR
    RETURN
  ELSE
    FIND &CSN
    IF .NOT. (EOF() .OR. BOF())
      @ 9,15 SAY 'COMPANY:       ' GET COMP
      @ 10,15 SAY 'LAST NAME:     ' GET LNAME
      @ 11,15 SAY 'FIRST NAME:    ' GET FNAME
      @ 13,15 SAY 'ADDRESS:       ' GET ADDR
      @ 14,15 SAY 'CITY:          ' GET CITY
      @ 16,15 SAY 'STATE:         ' GET ST
      @ 16,35 SAY 'ZIP:     ' GET ZIP
      @ 18,15 SAY 'PHONE NUMBER:  ' GET PHONE
      @ 20,15 SAY 'DISCOUNT:      ' GET DIS
      CLEAR GETS
      STORE ' ' TO DELCON
```

255

```
      @ 5,15 SAY 'ENTER "D" TO CONFIRM DELETE ===> ' GET DELCON
      READ
      IF UPPER(DELCON) = 'D'
         DELETE
         CLEAR
         @ 5,15 SAY '     *** CUSTOMER DELETED ***           '
      ELSE
         CLEAR
         @ 5,15 SAY ' *** CUSTOMER NOT DELETED ***          '
      ENDIF
      STORE '     ' TO CSN
   ELSE
      ? CHR(7)
      CLEAR
      @ 5,15 SAY '*** CUSTOMER NUMBER NOT FOUND ***'
   ENDIF
ENDIF
ENDDO
```

```
*************************************
*                                   *
*               1.4                 *
*        FREDS FISH MARKET          *
*     CUSTOMER DISPLAY PROGRAM      *
*           CUSTDIS.PRG             *
*                                   *
*************************************


USE CUSTOMER INDEX CUSTOMER
STORE 'T' TO MORECUST
STORE '      ' TO CSN
CLEAR
DO WHILE MORECUST = 'T'
   @  1,20 SAY 'FREDS FRIENDLY FISH MARKET'
   @  3,20 SAY '     CUSTOMER DISPLAY       '
   @  7,18 SAY 'CUSTOMER NUMBER: ' GET CSN PICTURE '#####'
   READ
   @ 5,1
   IF CSN = '      '
      USE
      CLEAR
      RETURN
   ELSE
      FIND &CSN
      IF .NOT. EOF()
         SET DELIMITER OFF
         @  9,15 SAY 'COMPANY:        '   GET COMP
         @ 10,15 SAY 'LAST NAME:      '   GET LNAME
         @ 11,15 SAY 'FIRST NAME:     '   GET FNAME
         @ 13,15 SAY 'ADDRESS:        '   GET ADDR
         @ 14,15 SAY 'CITY:           '   GET CITY
         @ 16,15 SAY 'STATE:          '   GET ST
         @ 16,35 SAY 'ZIP: '              GET ZIP
         @ 18,15 SAY 'PHONE NUMBER: '     GET PHONE
         @ 20,15 SAY 'DISCOUNT:       '   GET DIS
         STORE ' ' TO RESP
         CLEAR GETS
         @ 5,20 SAY 'ENTER ANY KEY TO CONTINUE'   GET RESP
         READ
         SET DELIMITER ON
         STORE '      ' TO CSN
         CLEAR
      ELSE
         ? CHR(7)
```

```
        CLEAR
        @ 5,15 SAY '*** CUSTOMER NUMBER NOT FOUND ***'
      ENDIF
   ENDIF
ENDDO
```

```
*****************************************
*                                       *
*              1.5                      *
*         FREDS FISH MARKET             *
*    CUSTOMER MAILING LABEL PRINT       *
*           CUSTLBL.PRG                  *
*                                       *
*****************************************
USE CUSTOMER INDEX CUSTOMER
STORE 'T' TO MOREANS
STORE ' ' TO OPTION
PUBLIC A1,A2,A3,B1,B2,B3,C1,C2,C3,D1,D2,D3
DO WHILE MOREANS = 'T'
  CLEAR
  @  1,20 SAY 'FREDS FRIENDLY FISH MARKET'
  @  3,20 SAY ' CUSTOMER MAILING LABELS'
  @  7,18 SAY 'ENTER "A" FOR ALIGNMENT PRINT,'
  @  8,18 SAY '        "X" TO EXIT PRINT,'
  @  9,18 SAY '    OR <cr> TO BEGIN PRINT'
  @ 11,18 SAY '           ====> ' GET OPTION
  READ
  IF UPPER(OPTION) = 'X'
    USE
    RELEASE A1,A2,A3,B1,B2,B3,C1,C2,C3,D1,D2,D3
    CLEAR
    RETURN
  ENDIF
  IF UPPER(OPTION) = 'A'
    DO CUSTLBLA
  ENDIF
  IF UPPER(OPTION) # 'A' .AND. UPPER(OPTION) # 'X'
    USE CUSTOMER INDEX CUSTOMER
    STORE 0 TO LBLCNT
    DO WHILE .NOT. EOF()
      DO CUSTLBLF
      IF LBLCNT = 3
        SET PRINT ON
        ? A1,'        ',A2,'        ',A3
        ? B1,'    ',B2,'    ',B3
        ? C1,' ',C2,' ',C3
        ? D1,' ',D2,' ',D3
        ?
        STORE 0 TO LBLCNT
      ENDIF
      SKIP
    ENDDO
```

```
        IF LBLCNT = 1
           ? A1
           ? B1
           ? C1
           ? D1
           ?
        ENDIF
        IF LBLCNT = 2
           ? A1,'        ',A2
           ? B1,'     ',B2
           ? C1,' ',C2
           ? D1,' ',D2
           ?
        ENDIF
        SET PRINT OFF
     ENDIF
     STORE ' ' TO OPTION
ENDDO
```

```
********************************
*                              *
*       1.5.CUSTLBLA            *
*     FREDS FISH MARKET         *
*  CUSTOMER LABEL ALIGNMENT     *
*       CUSTLBLA.PRG            *
*                              *
********************************
SET DELIMITER OFF
STORE ' ' TO ANS
@ 7,13 SAY 'ALIGN PRINTER AND HIT ANY KEY TO CONTINUE' GET ANS
@ 8,1
@ 9,8  SAY 'THIS WILL PRINT THREE ROWS OF LABEL ALIGNMENT DATA'
@ 11,1
READ
SET PRINT ON
STORE 1 TO COUNT
DO WHILE COUNT <= 3
   STORE COUNT + 1 TO COUNT
   ? 'XXXXXXXXXXXXXXXXXXXXX          XXXXXXXXXXXXXXXXXXXXXXXXX'
   ? 'X. XXXXXXXXXXXXXXXXXXXXXXX      X. XXXXXXXXXXXXXXXXXXXXXXX'
   ? 'XXXXXXXXXXXXXXXXXXXXXXXXX       XXXXXXXXXXXXXXXXXXXXXXXXX'
   ? 'XXXXXXXXXXXXXXX, XX XXXXX       XXXXXXXXXXXXXXXX, XX XX'
   ? ' '
ENDDO
SET PRINT OFF
RETURN
```

```
****************************************
*                                      *
*          1.5.CUSTLBLF                *
*        FREDS FISH MARKET             *
*  CUSTOMER MAILING LABEL FORMAT       *
*          CUSTLBLF.PRG                 *
*                                      *
****************************************
STORE LBLCNT + 1 TO LBLCNT
IF LBLCNT = 1
   STORE COMP TO A1
   STORE SUBSTR(FNAME,1,1)-'. '+LNAME TO B1
   STORE ADDR TO C1
   STORE CITY+'  '+ST+' '+SUBSTR(ZIP,1,5) TO D1
ENDIF
IF LBLCNT = 2
   STORE COMP TO A2
   STORE SUBSTR(FNAME,1,1)-'. '+LNAME TO B2
   STORE ADDR TO C2
   STORE CITY+'  '+ST+' '+SUBSTR(ZIP,1,5) TO D2
ENDIF
IF LBLCNT = 3
   STORE COMP TO A3
   STORE SUBSTR(FNAME,1,1)-'. '+LNAME TO B3
   STORE ADDR TO C3
   STORE CITY+'  '+ST+' '+SUBSTR(ZIP,1,5) TO D3
ENDIF
RETURN
```

```
**********************************
*                                *
*              1.6               *
*        FREDS FISH MARKET       *
*     CUSTOMER DIRECTORY PRINT    *
*          CUSTDIR.PRG           *
*                                *
**********************************
USE CUSTOMER INDEX CUSTOMER
STORE 'T' TO MOREANS
STORE ' ' TO OPTION
DO WHILE MOREANS = 'T'
  CLEAR
  @  1,20 SAY 'FREDS FRIENDLY FISH MARKET'
  @  3,20 SAY ' CUSTOMER DIRECTORY PRINT '
  @  7,20 SAY 'ENTER "X" TO EXIT PRINT,'
  @  8,18 SAY '    OR <cr> TO BEGIN PRINT'
  @ 10,18 SAY '           ====> ' GET OPTION
  READ
  IF UPPER(OPTION) = 'X'
    USE
    STORE ' ' TO OPTION
    CLEAR
    RETURN
  ENDIF
  USE CUSTOMER INDEX CUSTOMER
  STORE 1 TO LINECNT
  SET DEVICE TO PRINT
  DO WHILE .NOT. EOF()
    IF LINECNT = 1 .OR. LINECNT = 56
      @ 1,30 SAY '   FREDS FISH MARKET'
      @ 2,30 SAY 'CUSTOMER DIRECTORY PRINT'
      STORE 4 TO LINECNT
    ENDIF
    STORE LINECNT + 4 TO LINECNT
    @ LINECNT,1 SAY 'Customer Number:'
    @ LINECNT,18 SAY CUSTN
    STORE LINECNT + 2 TO LINECNT
    @ LINECNT,1 SAY COMP
    STORE LINECNT + 1 TO LINECNT
    @ LINECNT,1 SAY TRIM(LNAME)+', '+FNAME
    STORE LINECNT + 1 TO LINECNT
    @ LINECNT,15 SAY ADDR
    STORE LINECNT + 1 TO LINECNT
    @ LINECNT,15 SAY TRIM(CITY)+', '+ST+' '+ZIP
    STORE LINECNT + 2 TO LINECNT
```

```
      @ LINECNT,15 SAY 'Phone: '+PHONE
      STORE LINECNT + 2 TO LINECNT
      @ LINECNT,15 SAY 'Discount: '
      @ LINECNT,25 SAY DIS
      @ LINECNT,27 SAY '%'
      SKIP
   ENDDO
   @ LINECNT+1,1 SAY ' '
   SET DEVICE TO SCREEN
   STORE ' ' TO OPTION
ENDDO
```

```
***************************************
*                                     *
*                 3                   *
*        FREDS FISH MARKET            *
*           ORDER MENU                *
*           ORDER.PRG                 *
*                                     *
***************************************
STORE 'F' TO ORDREXIT
STORE ' ' TO OPTION
DO WHILE ORDREXIT = 'F'
   CLEAR
   @  1,20 SAY 'FREDS FRIENDLY FISH MARKET'
   @  3,20 SAY '    ORDER SYSTEM MENU     '
   @  7,19 SAY '  ENTER SELECTION  ===>   ';
           GET OPTION
   @ 10,21 SAY ' 1 - ADD ORDERS            '
   @ 11,21 SAY ' 2 - CHANGE ORDERS         '
   @ 12,21 SAY ' 3 - REMOVE ORDERS         '
   @ 13,21 SAY ' 4 - DISPLAY ORDERS        '
   @ 15,21 SAY ' 5 - PRINT ORDER FORMS     '
   @ 16,21 SAY ' 6 - PRINT SHIPPING FORMS '
   @ 18,21 SAY ' R - RETURN TO MAIN MENU  '
   @ 19,21 SAY ' X - EXIT SYSTEM           '
   READ
   @ 5,20
   DO CASE
     CASE OPTION = '1'
       DO ORDRADD
     CASE OPTION = '2'
       DO ORDRCHG
     CASE OPTION = '3'
       DO ORDRREM
     CASE OPTION = '4'
       DO ORDRDIS
     CASE OPTION = '5'
       DO ORDRFMS
     CASE OPTION = '6'
       DO ORDRSHP
     CASE UPPER(OPTION) = 'R'
       CLEAR
       RETURN
     CASE UPPER(OPTION) = 'X'
       QUIT
     OTHERWISE
```

```
        ? CHR(7)
        @ 5,20 SAY '*** INVALID ENTRY -TRY AGAIN ***'
    ENDCASE
    STORE ' ' TO OPTION
ENDDO
```

```
**************************************
*                                    *
*          3.1.ORDRADIT              *
*        FREDS FISH MARKET           *
*  ORDER ITEM ADDITIONS PROGRAM      *
*          ORDRADIT.PRG              *
*                                    *
**************************************
SELECT A
USE ORDERITM INDEX ORDERITM
SELECT B
USE ITEM INDEX ITEM
STORE .T. TO MOREORDI
CLEAR
@  1,20 SAY 'FREDS FRIENDLY FISH MARKET'
@  3,20 SAY 'ORDER ITEM ADDITIONS MENU'
@  7,20 SAY 'ORDER NUMBER:    '
@  7,37 SAY ORN
@  9,20 SAY 'COMPANY:'
@  9,37 SAY COMP
@ 10,20 SAY 'LAST NAME:'
@ 10,37 SAY LNAME
@ 11,20 SAY 'FIRST NAME:'
@ 11,37 SAY FNAME
@ 13,15 SAY '#'
@ 13,20 SAY 'QUANTITY'
@ 13,35 SAY 'ITEM NUMBER'
STORE 15 TO LINECNT
STORE 1 TO CNT
STORE '   ' TO QT
STORE '     ' TO ITN
DO WHILE MOREORDI = 'T'
   @ LINECNT,14 SAY CNT PICTURE '99'
   @ LINECNT,22 GET QT PICTURE '###'
   @ LINECNT,38 GET ITN PICTURE '#####'
   READ
   @ 5,1
   IF QT = '   '
       RETURN
     ELSE
       SELECT B
       FIND &ITN
       IF .NOT. EOF()
           STORE B->PRICE TO PRI
           SELECT A
           APPEND BLANK
```

267

```
            REPLACE ORDRN WITH VAL(ORN),QTY WITH VAL(QT) ;
               ITEMN WITH VAL(ITN),PRICE WITH PRI
            @ 5,20 SAY '  *** ORDER ADDED  *** '
            STORE '    ' TO QT
            STORE '      ' TO ITN
            STORE CNT + 1 TO CNT
            STORE LINECNT + 1 TO LINECNT
            IF LINECNT = 25
               STORE 15 TO LINECNT
               STORE 15 TO ERASER
               DO WHILE ERASER < 25
                  @ ERASER,1
                  STORE ERASER + 1 TO ERASER
               ENDDO
            ENDIF
         ELSE
            ? CHR(7)
            @ 5,15 SAY '*** ITEM NUMBER NOT ON FILE ***'
      ENDIF
   ENDIF
ENDDO
```

```
**************************************
*                                    *
*              3.2                   *
*        FREDS FISH MARKET           *
*     ORDER CHANGES PROGRAM          *
*          ORDRCHG.PRG               *
*                                    *
**************************************
CLEAR
USE ORDER INDEX ORDER
STORE .T. TO MOREORDR
STORE '      ' TO ORN
STORE '          ' TO DTO
DO WHILE MOREORDR = 'T'
   @  1,20 SAY 'FREDS FRIENDLY FISH MARKET'
   @  2,20 SAY '   ORDER CHANGES MENU   '
   @  7,15 SAY 'ORDER NUMBER:      ' GET ORN     PICTURE '#####'
   READ
   @ 5,1
   IF ORN = '      '
      STORE 'F' TO MOREORDR
    ELSE
      SELECT A
      FIND &ORN
      IF .NOT. EOF()
          @  9,15 SAY 'CUSTOMER NUMBER: '
          @  9,32 SAY CUSTN
    STORE DATE TO DATE
          SELECT B
          USE CUSTOMER INDEX CUSTOMER
          STORE STR(CUSTN,5) TO CSN
          FIND &CSN
          @ 11,15 SAY 'COMPANY: '
          @ 11,32 SAY COMP
          @ 12,15 SAY 'LAST NAME:'
          @ 12,32 SAY LNAME
          @ 13,15 SAY 'FIRST NAME: '
          @ 13,32 SAY FNAME
          @ 15,15 SAY 'DATE ORDERED: '
          @ 15,32 SAY DATE
          STORE COMP TO COMP
          STORE LNAME TO LNAME
          STORE FNAME TO FNAME
          SELECT A
          STORE ' ' TO ANS
          @ 4,20 SAY 'CHANGE ITEMS? ===> ' GET ANS
```

```
              @ 5,15 SAY 'ENTER <cr> TO CONTINUE, X TO EXIT'
              READ
              IF UPPER(ANS) # 'X'
                 DO ORDRCHIT
              ENDIF
              CLEAR
              @ 5,20 SAY '*** ORDER CHANGED *** '
              SELECT A
              USE ORDER INDEX ORDER
              STORE '        ' TO ORN
              STORE '          ' TO DTO
           ELSE
              ? CHR(7)
              CLEAR
              @ 5,15 SAY '*** ORDER NUMBER NOT FOUND ***'
         ENDIF
    ENDIF
ENDDO
SELECT B
USE ORDERITM INDEX ORDERITM
PACK
USE
SELECT A
USE
STORE ' ' TO OPTION
RETURN
```

```
************************************
*                                  *
*          3.2.ORDRCHIT            *
*       FREDS FISH MARKET          *
*  ORDER ITEM CHANGES PROGRAM      *
*         ORDRCHIT.PRG             *
*                                  *
************************************
SELECT A
USE ORDERITM INDEX ORDERITM
SELECT B
USE ITEM INDEX ITEM
STORE .T. TO MOREORDI
CLEAR
@ 1,20  SAY 'FREDS FRIENDLY FISH MARKET'
@ 2,20  SAY ' ORDER ITEM CHANGES MENU'
@ 7,20  SAY 'ORDER NUMBER:        '
@ 7,37  SAY ORN
@ 9,20  SAY 'COMPANY:'
@ 9,37  SAY COMP
@ 10,20 SAY 'LAST NAME:'
@ 10,37 SAY LNAME
@ 11,20 SAY 'FIRST NAME:'
@ 11,37 SAY FNAME
@ 13,18 SAY '#'
@ 13,23 SAY 'QUANTITY'
@ 13,38 SAY 'ITEM NUMBER'
STORE 1 TO CNT
STORE '        ' TO QT
STORE '        ' TO ITN
STORE 10 TO SCRLCNT
DO WHILE MOREORDI = 'T'
  STORE 15 TO LINECNT
  SELECT A
  FIND &ORN
  STORE 1 TO LOOPCNT
```

```
DO WHILE LOOPCNT <= SCRLCNT-10 .AND. VAL(ORN)=A->ORDRN .AND. .NOT. EOF()
   IF .NOT. DELETE()
      STORE LOOPCNT+1 TO LOOPCNT
   ENDIF
   SKIP
ENDDO
DO WHILE LOOPCNT <= SCRLCNT .AND. VAL(ORN)=A->ORDRN .AND. ..NOT. EOF()
   IF .NOT. DELETED()
      @ LINECNT,17 SAY LOOPCNT PICTURE '99'
      @ LINECNT,25 SAY QTY PICTURE '999'
      @ LINECNT,41 SAY ITEMN PICTURE '99999'
      STORE LOOPCNT+1 TO LOOPCNT
      STORE LINECNT+1 TO LINECNT
   ENDIF
   SKIP
ENDDO
DO WHILE LINECNT < 25
   @ LINECNT,17 SAY LOOPCNT PICTURE '99'
   @ LINECNT,25
   STORE LOOPCNT+1 TO LOOPCNT
   STORE LINECNT+1 TO LINECNT
ENDDO
STORE ' ' TO SEL
@ 4,1
@ 5,1
@ 4,20 SAY 'ENTER SELECTION ===> ' GET SEL
@ 5,20 SAY 'C/CHANGE,S/SCROLL,X/EXIT'
@ 6,1
READ
DO CASE
   CASE UPPER(SEL) = 'X'
      RETURN
   CASE UPPER(SEL) = 'C'
      STORE ' ' TO RN
      STORE 'T' TO MORERN
      DO WHILE MORERN = 'T'
```

```
@ 4,1
@ 5,1
@ 4,20 SAY 'RECORD NUMBER ==> ' GET RN
@ 5,16 SAY 'ENTER RECORD NUMBER TO BE CHANGED'
READ
@ 6,1
IF RN # ' '
    IF VAL(RN) <= SCRLCNT .AND. VAL(RN) > SCRLCNT-10
        STORE 1 TO LOOPCNT
        FIND &ORN
        DO WHILE LOOPCNT < VAL(RN) .AND. VAL(ORN)=A->ORDRN
            IF .NOT. DELETE()
                STORE LOOPCNT+1 TO LOOPCNT
            ENDIF
            SKIP
        ENDDO
        IF DELETE()
            SKIP
        ENDIF
        IF VAL(ORN) # A->ORDRN .OR. EOF()
            STORE ' ' TO QT
            STORE ' ' TO ITN
            STORE 'T' TO ISW
            DO WHILE ISW = 'T'
                @ 4,1
                @ 4,14 SAY 'QUANTITY: ' GET QT PICTURE '###'
                @ 4,34 SAY 'ITEM NUMBER: ' GET ITN PICTURE '#####'
                @ 5,1
                READ
                @ 6,1
                IF QT = ' '
                    STORE 'F' TO ISW
                ELSE
                    SELECT B
                    FIND &ITN
                    IF .NOT. EOF()
```

```
            STORE B->PRICE TO PRI
            SELECT A
            APPEND BLANK
            REPLACE ORDRN WITH VAL(ORN),QTY WITH VAL(QT) ;
              ITEMN WITH VAL(ITN),PRICE WITH PRI
            @ 6,20 SAY '    *** ITEM ADDED *** '
            STORE 'F' TO ISW
            STORE 'F' TO MORERN
          ELSE
            SELECT A
            ? CHR(7)
            @ 6,15 SAY '*** ITEM NUMBER NOT ON FILE ***'
          ENDIF
        ENDIF
      ENDDO
    ELSE
      STORE STR(QTY,3) TO QT
      STORE STR(ITEMN,5) TO ITN
      STORE 'T' TO ISW
      DO WHILE ISW = 'T'
        @ 4,1
        @ 4,14 SAY 'QUANTITY: ' GET QT PICTURE '999'
        @ 4,34 SAY 'ITEM NUMBER: ' GET ITN PICTURE '99999'
        @ 5,1
        READ
        @ 6,1
        IF VAL(QT) = 0
          DELETE
          @ 6,20 SAY '    *** ITEM DELETED *** '
          STORE 'F' TO ISW
          STORE 'F' TO MORERN
        ELSE
          SELECT B
          FIND &ITN
          IF .NOT. EOF()
            STORE PRICE TO PRI
```

```
SELECT A
REPLACE ORDRN WITH VAL(ORN),QTY WITH VAL(QT);
    ITEMN WITH VAL(ITN),PRICE WITH PRI
    @ 6,20 SAY ' *** ITEM CHANGED *** '
    STORE 'F' TO ISW
    STORE 'F' TO MORERN
ELSE
    ? CHR(7)
    @ 6,20 SAY '*** ITEM NUMBER NOT ON FILE ***'
ENDIF
    ENDIF
    ENDDO
ENDIF
ELSE
    ? CHR(7)
    @ 6,15 SAY '*** RECORD NUMBER NOT ON SCREEN ***'
ENDIF
ELSE
    STORE 'F' TO MORERN
ENDIF
ENDDO
CASE UPPER(SEL) = 'S'
    STORE SCRLCNT+10 TO SCRLCNT
ENDCASE
ENDDO
RETURN
```

```
*************************************
*                                   *
*            3.3                    *
*       FREDS FISH MARKET           *
*     ORDER REMOVAL PROGRAM         *
*         ORDRREM.PRG               *
*                                   *
*************************************
CLEAR
USE ORDER INDEX ORDER
STORE .T. TO MOREORDR
STORE ' ' TO ORN
DO WHILE MOREORDR = 'T'
  @ 1,20 SAY 'FREDS FRIENDLY FISH MARKET'
  @ 2,20 SAY '  ORDER REMOVAL MENU '
  @ 6,15 SAY 'ORDER NUMBER: '      GET ORN      PICTURE '#####'
  READ
  @ 4,1
  IF ORN = '     '
     STORE 'F' TO MOREORDR
  ELSE
     FIND &ORN
     SELECT A
     IF .NOT. EOF() .AND. .NOT. DELETE()
        SELECT B
        USE CUSTOMER INDEX CUSTOMER
        STORE STR(CUSTN,5) TO CSN
        FIND &CSN
        @ 8,15 SAY 'COMPANY:  '
        @ 8,32 SAY COMP
        @ 9,15 SAY 'LAST NAME:'
        @ 9,32 SAY LNAME
        @ 10,15 SAY 'FIRST NAME: '
        @ 10,32 SAY FNAME
        SELECT A
        @ 12,15 SAY 'DATE ORDERED: '
```

```
@ 12,32 SAY DATE
@ 14,18 SAY '#'
@ 14,23 SAY 'QUANTITY'
@ 14,38 SAY 'ITEM NUMBER'
STORE 1 TO LOOPCNT
STORE 15 TO LINECNT
SELECT B
USE ORDERITM INDEX ORDERITM
FIND &ORN
DO WHILE LOOPCNT <= 10 .AND. VAL(ORN)=B->ORDRN .AND. .NOT. EOF()
    IF .NOT. DELETE()
        @ LINECNT,17 SAY LOOPCNT PICTURE '99'
        @ LINECNT,25 SAY QTY PICTURE '999'
        @ LINECNT,41 SAY ITEMN PICTURE '99999'
        STORE LOOPCNT+1 TO LOOPCNT
        STORE LINECNT+1 TO LINECNT
    ENDIF
    SKIP
ENDDO
SELECT A
STORE ' ' TO ANS
@ 4,1
@ 4,17 SAY 'ENTER D TO CONFIRM DELETE ==> ' GET ANS
READ
IF UPPER(ANS) = 'D'
    DELETE
    SELECT B
    USE ORDERITM INDEX ORDERITM
    DELETE ALL FOR VAL(ORN) = B->ORDRN
    SELECT A
    CLEAR
    @ 4,21 SAY '*** ORDER DELETED *** '
ELSE
    CLEAR
    @ 4,19 SAY '*** ORDER NOT DELETED *** '
ENDIF
```

```
      STORE '     ' TO ORN
   ELSE
      ? CHR(7)
      CLEAR
      @ 4,17 SAY '*** ORDER NUMBER NOT FOUND ***'
   ENDIF
 ENDIF
ENDDO
SELECT B
USE ORDERITM INDEX ORDERITM
PACK
USE
SELECT A
PACK
USE
STORE ' ' TO OPTION
RETURN
```

```
********************************************
*                                          *
*                  3.4                     *
*          FREDS FISH MARKET               *
*       ORDER DISPLAY PROGRAM              *
*           ORDRDIS.PRG                     *
*                                          *
********************************************
CLEAR
USE ORDER INDEX ORDER
STORE .T. TO MOREORDR
STORE ' ' TO ORN
DO WHILE MOREORDR = 'T'
  @ 1,20 SAY 'FREDS FRIENDLY FISH MARKET'
  @ 2,20 SAY ' ORDER DISPLAY MENU '
  @ 6,15 SAY 'ORDER NUMBER: ' GET ORN      PICTURE '#####'
  READ
  @ 4,1 '         '
  IF ORN = '         '
    STORE 'F' TO MOREORDR
  ELSE
    SELECT A
    FIND &ORN
    IF .NOT. EOF() .AND. .NOT. DELETE()
      SELECT B
      USE CUSTOMER INDEX CUSTOMER
      STORE STR(CUSTN,5) TO CSN
      FIND &CSN
      @ 8,15 SAY 'COMPANY: '
      @ 8,32 SAY COMP
      @ 9,15 SAY 'LAST NAME:'
      @ 9,32 SAY LNAME
      @ 10,15 SAY 'FIRST NAME: '
      @ 10,32 SAY FNAME
      SELECT A
      @ 12,15 SAY 'DATE ORDERED: '
```

279

```
@ 12,32 SAY DATE
@ 14,18 SAY '#'
@ 14,23 SAY 'QUANTITY'
@ 14,38 SAY 'ITEM NUMBER'
STORE 1 TO LOOPCNT
STORE 15 TO LINECNT
SELECT B
USE ORDERITM INDEX ORDERITM
FIND &ORN
DO WHILE VAL(ORN)=B->ORDRN .AND. .NOT. EOF() .AND. VAL(ORN)=B->ORDRN .AND. .NOT. EOF()
   IF .NOT. DELETE()
      @ LINECNT,17 SAY LOOPCNT PICTURE '99'
      @ LINECNT,25 SAY QTY PICTURE '999'
      @ LINECNT,41 SAY ITEMN PICTURE '99999'
      STORE LOOPCNT+1 TO LOOPCNT
      STORE LINECNT+1 TO LINECNT
   ENDIF
   SKIP
ENDDO
IF LINECNT < 24
   DO WHILE LINECNT <= 24
      @ LINECNT,1
      STORE LINECNT + 1 TO LINECNT
   ENDDO
ENDIF
SELECT A
SET DELIMITER OFF
STORE ' ' TO ANS
@ 4,1
@ 4,21 SAY 'ENTER <cr> TO CONTINUE' GET ANS
READ
SET DELIMITER ON
STORE 15 TO LINECNT
ENDDO
CLEAR
```

280

```
        STORE '       ' TO ORN
      ELSE
        ? CHR(7)
        CLEAR
        @ 4,17 SAY '*** ORDER NUMBER NOT FOUND ***'
      ENDIF
    ENDIF
  ENDDO
SELECT B
USE
SELECT A
USE
STORE ' ' TO OPTION
RETURN
```

```
************************************
*                                  *
*         FREDS FISH MARKET        *
*    ORDER FORMS PRINT PROGRAM     *
*         ORDRFMS.PRG              *
*                                  *
************************************
             3.5
CLEAR
USE ORDER INDEX ORDER
STORE .T. TO MOREORDR
STORE '  ' TO ORN
DO WHILE MOREORDR = 'T'
   @ 1,20 SAY 'FREDS FRIENDLY FISH MARKET'
   @ 2,18 SAY '  ORDER FORMS PRINT MENU  '
   @ 6,15 SAY 'ORDER NUMBER:    ' GET ORN        PICTURE '#####'
   READ
   @ 4,1
   IF ORN = '  '
      STORE 'F' TO MOREORDR
   ELSE
      SELECT A
      FIND &ORN
      IF .NOT. EOF() .AND. .NOT. DELETE()
         SET DELIMITER OFF
         STORE ' ' TO ANS
         @ 4,1
         @ 4,23 SAY 'ENTER <cr> TO PRINT' GET ANS
         READ
         SET DELIMITER ON
         SET DEVICE TO PRINT
         SELECT B
         USE CUSTOMER INDEX CUSTOMER
         STORE STR(CUSTN,5) TO CSN
         FIND &CSN
         @ 1,25 SAY 'FREDS FRIENDLY FISH MARKET'
```

```
@ 3,25 SAY '   CUSTOMER ORDER FORM
@ 6,15 SAY 'Order Number: '
@ 6,29 SAY ORN PICTURE '99999'
@ 8,15 SAY COMP
@ 9,15 SAY TRIM(FNAME)+' '+LNAME
SELECT A
@ 11,15 SAY 'Date Ordered: '
@ 11,29 SAY DATE
@ 14,15 SAY 'ITEM #'
@ 14,26 SAY 'QUANTITY'
@ 14,38 SAY 'ITEM NUMBER'
@ 14,58 SAY 'DESCRIPTION'
STORE 1 TO LOOPCNT
STORE 17 TO LINECNT
SELECT B
USE ORDERITM INDEX ORDERITM
SELECT A
USE ITEM INDEX ITEM
SELECT B
FIND &ORN
DO WHILE VAL(ORN)=B->ORDRN .AND. .NOT. EOF()
   IF .NOT. DELETE()
      @ LINECNT,17 SAY LOOPCNT PICTURE '99'
      @ LINECNT,27 SAY B->QTY PICTURE '999'
      @ LINECNT,39 SAY B->ITEMN PICTURE '99999'
      STORE STR(B->ITEMN,5) TO ITN
      SELECT A
      FIND &ITN
      @ LINECNT,55 SAY DESC
      STORE LOOPCNT+1 TO LOOPCNT
      STORE LINECNT+1 TO LINECNT
   ENDIF
   SELECT B
   SKIP
ENDDO
@ LINECNT+1,1 SAY '    '
```

283

```
        SELECT A
        USE ORDER INDEX ORDER
        SET DEVICE TO SCREEN
        CLEAR
        STORE '    ' TO ORN
      ELSE
        ? CHR(7)
        CLEAR
        @ 4,17 SAY '*** ORDER NUMBER NOT FOUND ***'
      ENDIF
    ENDIF
  ENDDO
  SELECT B
  USE
  SELECT A
  USE
  STORE '  ' TO OPTION
  RETURN
```

Appendix C

dBASE III Database
Commands Used in this Book

DATABASE STRUCTURE COMMANDS

```
CREATE
USE
MODIFY STRUCTURE
SELECT
```

DATABASE RECORD COMMANDS

```
APPEND
COPY
EDIT
DELETE
PACK
RECALL
```

DATABASE SEARCH COMMANDS

```
LOCATE
FIND
SKIP
```

DATABASE DISPLAY COMMANDS

```
DISPLAY
LIST
CREATE REPORT
REPORT FORM
```

DATABASE MANIPULATION COMMANDS

```
JOIN
SORT
INDEX
```

Appendix D

dBase III Programming
Commands Used in this Book

HOUSEKEEPING COMMANDS

```
SET BELL OFF
SET CONFIRM OFF
SET DEFAULT TO drive
SET DELETED ON
SET DELIMITER TO '   '
SET DELIMITER ON
SET DEVICE TO SCREEN/PRINTER
SET ECHO OFF
SET TALK OFF
SET EXACT ON
```

INPUT COMMANDS

```
@ line,column GET PICTURE
READ
CLEAR GETS
```

OUTPUT COMMANDS

```
SET PRINT ON
```

```
SET PRINT OFF
?
SET DEVICE TO PRINT
EJECT
SET DEVICE TO SCREEN
CLEAR
@ line,column SAY PICTURE
```

**CHARACTER, STRING,
AND NUMERIC COMMANDS**

```
STR
VAL
TRIM
SUBSTR
INT
UPPER
ROUND
```

CONNECTORS

```
.AND.
.OR.
.NOT.
```

LOGICAL CONSTRUCTS

STORE

IF
 THEN
 ELSE
ENDIF

DOWHILE
ENDDO

LOOP

SKIP

DO
RETURN

QUIT

DO CASE
 CASE
 OTHERWISE
ENDCASE

DATA MANAGEMENT COMMANDS

APPEND BLANK
REPLACE
FIND
EOF()
DELETE
DELETED()
PACK
PUBLIC
RELEASE

Index

Index

Edited by Marilyn L. Johnson

Programming with dBASE III

If you are intrigued with the possibilities of the programs included in *Programming with dBASE III* (TAB Book No. 1976), you should definitely consider having the ready-to-use disk containing the dBASE III routines. This software is guaranteed free of manufacturer's defects. (If you have any problems, return the disk within 30 days, and we'll send you a new one.) Not only will you save the time and effort of typing the programs, the disk eliminates the possibility of errors that can prevent the programs from functioning. Interested?

Available on disk for IBM PC with dBASE III and 256K at $24.95 for each disk plus $1.00 each shipping and handling.

I'm interested. Send me:

_____ disk for IBM PC with dBASE III and 256K (6626S)
_____ TAB BOOKS catalog
_____ Check/Money Order enclosed for $24.95
plus $1.00 shipping and handling for each disk ordered.

_____ VISA _____ MasterCard

Account No. _____ Expires _____

Name _____

Address _____

City _____ State _____ State _____

Signature _____

Mail To: **TAB BOOKS INC.**
Blue Ridge Summit, PA 17214

(Pa. add 6% sales tax. Orders outside U.S. must be prepaid with international money orders in U.S. dollars.)

TAB 1976

OTHER POPULAR TAB BOOKS OF INTEREST

TAB TAB BOOKS Inc.

Blue Ridge Summit, Pa. 17214

Send for FREE TAB Catalog describing over 750 current titles in print.